ActiveX Sourcebook

Build an ActiveX-Based Web Site

Ted Coombs

Jason Coombs

Donald Brewer

WILEY COMPUTER PUBLISHING

John Wiley & Sons, Inc.

New York • Chichester • Brisbane • Toronto • Singapore • Weinheim

Publisher: Katherine Schowalter
Editor: Philip Sutherland
Managing Editor: Micheline Frederick
Text Design & Composition: Benchmark Productions, Inc.

Designations used by companies to distinguish their products are often claimed as trademarks. In all instances where John Wiley & Sons, Inc., is aware of a claim, the product names appear in initial capital or ALL CAPITAL LETTERS. Readers, however, should contact the appropriate companies for more complete information regarding trademarks and registration.

This text is printed on acid-free paper.

This publication is designed to provide accurate and authoritative information in regard to the subject matter covered. It is sold with the understanding that the publisher is not engaged in rendering legal, accounting, or other professional service. If legal advice or other expert assistance is required, the services of a competent professional person should be sought.

Library of Congress Cataloging-in-Publication Data:

ISBN 0-471-16714-2
Printed in the United States of America
10 9 8 7 6 5 4 3 2 1

CONTENTS

1

ON BEING

HYPERACTIVE

This book shows you how to activate your World Wide Web site, your intranet, or your Windows applications with Microsoft's ActiveX technology. Whether you're a Web publisher, a Web application developer, or a Windows software developer, this book will help you unlock the power of Microsoft's ActiveX technology. If you're a Web publisher, you'll be amazed at how quickly compelling Web content can be created and how little maintenance an ActiveX Web site requires compared to conventional HTML. If you're an application programmer, you'll learn how to build sophisticated applications using ActiveX controls, scripts, and Active Documents. Most importantly, this book shows you how the Microsoft technology for Internet software and multimedia content directly incorporates into the Windows operating system all of the best ideas and technology from the World Wide Web, then goes several steps beyond it.

Luckily, you won't have to start from scratch developing all new applications to take advantage of ActiveX. Microsoft lets you leverage the applications and content you've already developed by fully supporting all existing Web technologies and other Internet standards including HTML and CGI. This book will show you how the Microsoft Web browser, Internet Explorer, rivals Netscape's Navigator feature-for-feature when it comes to support for existing Web technology and Internet standards. But unlike other Internet application and content development platforms, ActiveX doesn't limit your abilities to just those features that the Internet standards committees decide are worthwhile. And ActiveX doesn't attempt to gain a strangle-hold on the Web by continually introducing new HTML tags while at the same time creating the only Web browser that can view those tags. Instead, ActiveX opens up the Internet to real software and interactive multimedia content development that is restricted only by your imagination.

Further, ActiveX provides a simple migration path for your existing Windows software by introducing an ActiveX SDK, as well as new Win32 API functions designed to give Windows programs full access to the features and functionality of Internet software. In the longer term, all of your Windows software should be extended to include the ability to host ActiveX controls, Active Documents, and to be hosted within other applications through a series of interfaces known collectively as a *container*. Visual Basic 5.0 promises to deliver the ability to rapidly create your own ActiveX controls; an ability that will forever change the face of the Web as even productivity-oriented software developers will be able to build and deploy ActiveX components.

At the center of the ActiveX platform is the concept of safe, automatic code download and installation. Just like a Java applet, an ActiveX component can be deployed automatically to end users when you embed it in a Web page. Unlike Java applets, however, ActiveX components aren't crippled by a slow run-time engine or absurd security concerns which assume that even respected, well-known software vendors are going to try to infect user's computers with damaging viruses. ActiveX includes support for Java because there are times that Java is an ideal solution for developing active content, but the potential of the ActiveX architecture goes beyond the potential of Java for creating active applications and real interactive and multimedia Internet content.

Overview of This Book

Throughout this book, we mix hands-on instruction with conceptual explanations and sprinkle in technical detail and real-world samples to give you a broad understanding of ActiveX while simultaneously providing you with the skills required to activate your Web site or Windows software. Each of the chapters in this book covers a distinct group of tools or techniques that collectively represent Microsoft's ActiveX development architecture. In Chapter 2 you'll find a thorough overview of ActiveX including an introduction to the special features of the ActiveX Internet client platform based upon Internet Explorer. Understanding the technical structure of ActiveX will become increasingly important as you begin to consider the creation of your own ActiveX controls and Java applets as a way to deploy your own sophisticated interactive Web applications.

Chapter 2 also presents a very brief overview of the ActiveX SDK that can serve as a reference to the overwhelming quantity of documentation provided by Microsoft. In order to make use of the ActiveX SDK in software development, you must have knowledge of a programming language like C++ or a Windows software development tool like PowerBuilder that gives you the ability to use the ActiveX SDK and Windows API. Due to the complexity involved in programming with the ActiveX SDK we have limited our coverage of it in this book. However, even if you aren't a C++ programmer, the SDK overview in Chapter 2 should give you a valuable glimpse into the future of network software.

Another major consideration that is explained in Chapter 2 involves creating Web applications and content that are compatible with other browsers and operating systems other than Windows. You need to think through the issue of compatibility before you launch into the creation of a full-scale active Web site because the choices you make will have long-term ramifications for the visitors of your site. For the most part we recommend that you fully embrace active Web technology and insist that your visitors upgrade to an active Web browser in order to view the important content and use the real applications provided by your Web site.

Chapter 3 covers FrontPage, which is a development tool for creating, deploying, and maintaining Web pages quickly with the help of HTML wizards and prefabricated HTML layout templates. FrontPage includes an Editor, for creating and editing pages, an Explorer, for monitoring and managing Web sites, a Personal Web Server similar to the Internet Information Server and a few additional utilities for administering your Web site. FrontPage is a great test and development environment that you can use to design and implement your Web site prior to moving the site to your production Web server. Chapter 3 also covers the Internet Information Server version 2.0 so that you will be able to move your Web site from the Personal Web Server development environment to a full-blown Web site without problem.

Chapter 4 covers Visual Basic Scripting Edition, the scripting language used within Web pages to glue components together and provide common features like history navigation. Internet Explorer 3.0 supports both JavaScript and Visual Basic Script, so you have a choice between the two scripting languages as a way to embed snippets of application logic right in your HTML pages. One of the benefits of Visual Basic Script is that other Windows applications will also make use of it as a standard way to include scripting ability for all programs. On the other hand, the drawback to VB Script is that Internet Explorer is currently the only Web browser that supports it.

This is an issue of compatibility with other browsers that you'll need to keep an eye on as you build and deploy your active content.

Chapter 5 takes you on an exploration of ActiveX where you learn about the technique for incorporating ActiveX controls into your Web pages. You also learn about the ActiveX controls that are built-in to Internet Explorer 3.0 including the password, radio, list, button, checkbox, combo, text, chart, marquee, and pop-up menu controls. With built-in controls you can provide high-quality active content with the confidence that your end users can see the content without having to wait for new ActiveX controls to download.

Chapter 6 features the Microsoft dbWeb utility. With dbWeb you are able to construct a simple Web interface to a database. The Web interface generated by dbWeb is full of valuable features including a query-by-example utility, selectable query response format allowing free-form, tabular, or custom layout, and even data entry and data manipulation tools that provide the user with the ability to add, edit, or delete information from the database. Every screen generated by dbWeb uses conventional HTML to provide maximum compatibility with Web browsers other than Internet Explorer.

Chapter 7 explains the ActiveX multimedia technologies like the Active Movie format and PowerPoint animation technology. With ActiveX multimedia you can incorporate streaming audio and video as well as interactive presentations into your Web pages. Java and third-party ActiveX controls also play an important role in ActiveX multimedia, and Chapter 7 shows you how to make use of these multimedia features on your Web site.

Chapter 8 covers the ActiveX conferencing system around which a sophisticated conferencing software package called NetMeeting is built. Chapter 8 shows you how NetMeeting works and why network conferencing is important enough for Microsoft to have designed a brand-new software development kit that enables programmers to write conferencing software.

With the ActiveX conferencing tools, it won't be long before we see conferencing features included in just about every software package for Microsoft Windows.

Chapter 9 introduces the Internet Server Application Programming Interface (ISAPI). ISAPI is a way to build CGI-style programs to generate dynamic HTML or execute server-side programs without the technical problems associated with CGI. In addition to providing super-charged CGI-like ability, ISAPI enables a new class of server application called a filter. Filters are programs that execute every single time the server is accessed over the network that can make decisions about which documents to deliver to a client or even whether or not to allow the client access to the server. Because ISAPI programming requires knowledge of C++, we limit our coverage of ISAPI in Chapter 9 to an overview only.

Chapter 10 shows you how to build Visual Basic applications using the ActiveX Internet controls. Each of the controls is covered in depth including the FTP client, for connecting to FTP servers for file transfer; HTTP control, which provides a simple way to retrieve data from Web servers; HTML control, for embedding Web pages in your application; POP control, for retrieving e-mail from a mail server; SMTP control, for sending e-mail; and NNTP control, for accessing Internet newsgroups. In addition, there are two other controls that give you full access to the power of WinSock in your Visual Basic program. WinSock is the network programming interface for Microsoft Windows and is the technology upon which Internet Explorer, Netscape Navigator, and all other Internet software is built. Through the WinSock controls, creating new network applications that don't rely on existing Internet technology is easy. Think of it as being able to extend the abilities of the Internet itself.

Overview of ActiveX

ActiveX has something to offer to everyone from end users to the programmers working at Microsoft. There is a great number of new abilities introduced in ActiveX, and it will take you a while to learn about them all. The most important thing to bear in mind as you explore ActiveX is that for every new feature you learn about, there are almost certainly three or four ways to approach the subject. For the C++ programmer there are operating system extensions and new software development technologies, for the Visual Basic programmer there are new ActiveX controls and Active Documents that can be embedded into your applications, for the Webmaster there are ways to support new features on your Web site, and for the power-user there are new software tools with an unprecedented support for programmability through technologies like Visual Basic Script. You are the best filter available when it comes to sorting through the wealth of ActiveX; if you discover a new ability that only seems to be accessible to C++ programmers, keep looking for a tool that implements that ability in a way that you find to be accessible, there's probably one out there already either as part of ActiveX or as a third-party ActiveX add-on. Also be sure to visit the Microsoft home page often to keep up with new developments (see Figure 1.1).

Inserting ActiveX Controls into Your Web Page

The ActiveX Control Pad is a new Microsoft application that lets you easily insert an ActiveX control into a Web page and set its parameters by dropping it into the ActiveX Control Pad text editor (see Figure 1.2). For the non-programmer, the scripting Wizard will help you through writing VBScript or JavaScript (ActiveX scripting). The HTML layout control gives you a way to position your ActiveX controls on your Web page.

When you begin working with ActiveX controls on the Web, it is very important to keep in mind that your end users are asked to trust that the ActiveX controls on your Web page won't do any harm to their computer. There are a number of security mechanisms designed to give the end users every opportunity to decide for themselves whether or not to trust your Web site, including a way for the user to find out who it was that wrote the code

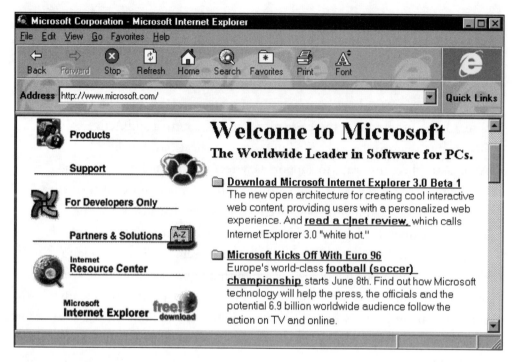

■■■■■ **Figure 1.1** Explore this Web site for all the hottest ActiveX information and software.

for a particular ActiveX control. Be sensitive to the concerns of end users and take extra precautions to only deploy content on your Web site that uses ActiveX controls designed by you or by a well-known software company. Always inspect your ActiveX controls with your virus checker before putting them on the Web.

ActiveX Scripting

The ActiveX system is made up of many different components, including "wrapped code" such as the applications in the Microsoft Office suite, ActiveX controls, and most importantly the pieces that act as the glue to hold the components together: ActiveX scripts.

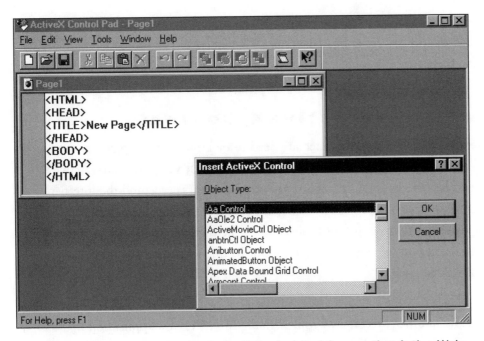

Figure 1.2 Use the ActiveX Control Pad for creating Active Web pages.

Internet Explorer has incorporated scripting engines that allow real programs to be embedded into a Web page. Internet Explorer includes scripting engines for both JavaScript and Visual Basic Script (VB Script). Although JavaScript is a part of ActiveX, it was covered in our *Netscape LiveWire Source Sourcebook* and is not covered in this text. The HTML <SCRIPT> tag lets you specify which scripting language is being used in that particular tag. You can mix and match scripting languages to take advantage of the power found in different languages.

VB Script (Visual Basic Scripting Edition) is important because it's 100% compatible with Visual Basic. The idea of using a scripting language is to integrate components, therefore using a language that is being inserted into most of Microsoft's applications makes sense.

Scripts attached to an object's event can be used to customize the object's behavior. For example, in a Web page you can modify an object's labels, change the object's color, or even change its position on the screen by using scripts inserted into the HTML of the Web page.

Producing ActiveX Content

Never again does your Internet site need to be limited to a conglomeration of static Web pages. Using all of the technologies at your disposal—ActiveX controls, Active Scripting, the Internet Information Server, and the Internet Database Connectivity—your Web sites can be interactive, exciting places to visit. Visual development tools can now help you construct these compelling sites on the Internet without your having to write a single line of HTML.

Your desktop applications, once foreign territory to the Internet, have now met the Internet welcome wagon. *ActiveX is the desktop application's passport to the Internet.* For example, PowerPoint presentations, seen at every seminar and meeting in the world, can now be viewed via the World Wide Web through the creation of fully animated PowerPoint presentations. Desktop integration doesn't stop with PowerPoint, just about any major Windows application can be used to develop and deploy Internet content.

Beyond desktop applications, ActiveX multimedia features make it possible to distribute full-motion video and CD-quality sound via the Internet; provided that your end users have very high-speed Internet connections. You could just about start your own television network or Internet movie studio with ActiveX. The ActiveX multimedia components provide you with almost everything you need to create exciting multimedia content. RealAudio, a program allowing you to play audio while it's downloading, is now built in to Internet Explorer as an ActiveX control. You can provide real-time audio to viewers of your Web site. You'll need some extra software from RealAudio to be able to create the RealAudio content. Still, everyone who uses the Internet Explorer can listen to your RealAudio content. You can see for yourself how RealAudio works by using the Internet Explorer to view some Internet sites that provide RealAudio content, such as National Public Radio (*http://www.npr.org*).

ActiveMovie lets viewers watch your video productions and ActiveVRML can launch viewers into virtual worlds. Why would anyone want to read a static Web page when they could be watching movies or navigating through virtual reality Web pages? If you're more of an animator than a movie producer, or the creator of virtual worlds, you'll enjoy using PowerPoint to create fun animations. The free PowerPoint Viewer allows everyone to view your creations.

Conferencing with ActiveX

Microsoft's NetMeeting enables groups of people to work together over the Internet through the use of ActiveX conferencing. The NetMeeting application is shown in Figure 1.3. Using the NetMeeting software, you can:

- Share programs
- Transfer files
- Talk with one another using Internet phone software
- Chat with one another using text
- Share visual ideas on a shared electronic whiteboard

New ActiveX conferencing software will no doubt emerge soon. Eventually, interacting with other people in real-time through applications like NetMeeting will be commonplace activity on the Internet.

Building ActiveX Controls

Visual Basic 5 will give you the ability to create your own ActiveX controls easily. ActiveX controls were previously known as OCX controls, and every

Figure 1.3 NetMeeting lets you work remotely over the Internet.

OCX control is an ActiveX control. By creating your own custom ActiveX controls, you can create complete Web applications that do anything you need them to rather than struggling to fit your Web application into the confines of HTML, CGI, and a single-page-at-a-time user interface. Figure 1.4 shows a picture of Visual Basic 4.

Chapter 2 provides a much more complete overview of ActiveX technology, including an explanation of how Web applications will be constructed in the near future through the creation of ActiveX controls. You can already see the potential of the ActiveX architecture in the kinds of applications that have been created for multimedia content, Internet conferencing, and active application development. As application developers, experienced Webmasters, and authors of the *Netscape LiveWire Sourcebook* we can personally say that we are very excited about ActiveX. Real programming power has finally been introduced into the World Wide Web, and the Web has finally been incorporated into an operating system.

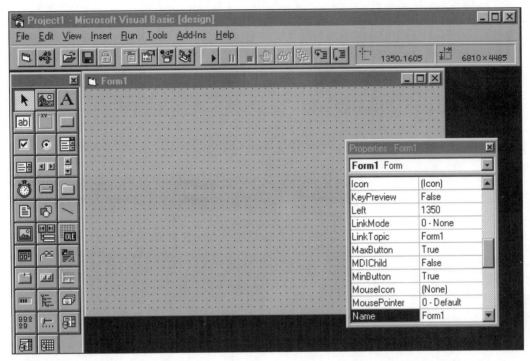

▮▮▮▮▮ **Figure 1.4** Learn Visual Basic in order to build custom ActiveX controls.

These are exciting times on the Internet. ActiveX will help to fuel the next stage of Internet growth, which, prior to learning about ActiveX and writing this book, we weren't even certain would occur due to the severe technical flaws of conventional Web technology. Now we're positive that the Internet will grow into the backbone of electronic commerce and digital communications for the next century.

2

THE ACTIVE INTERNET MODEL

Businesses have struggled for years to overcome problems associated with incompatible hardware and software in constructing and operating large-scale computer networks. Prior to the creation of the World Wide Web, however, the focus was on software engineering technology and very little attention was given to content development. The content was, after all, already built in to the software and databases that formed the core of a company's information system.

Work in progress *was* content in a business setting. Provided that a company's database servers and application software didn't malfunction, content got created and was used in a timely manner to create more work. Content created for the sole benefit of others was called the publishing industry. Those were the good old days.

Incompatible hardware and software was a manageable problem in a typical business, provided that good decisions were made by experienced computer professionals. This same problem on the Web, however, is intractable. When it comes to creating sophisticated Web applications, no single decision can be made that results in universal access to applications and content.

The only guarantee that you have as a Web developer, whether you're building content or applications, is that everyone can see your HTML 1.0 Web pages and access your CGI scripts. You're reading this today because HTML and CGI are inadequate technology upon which to build the future of interactive media and you are directly affected by the decisions that are made by Microsoft in this area. This chapter explains the ActiveX architecture and the reasoning behind it, while the rest of the book focuses on giving you hands-on experience with ActiveX.

The first point that needs to be made about ActiveX is that it is not a panacea to interactive content incompatibility. When developing with ActiveX technology, you must consider carefully your strategy for content deployment and evaluate the pros and cons of the options available to you. Sometimes this approach can lead to very tough decisions concerning the relative value of supporting old technology versus the amount of time and money required to do so. Fortunately, Microsoft recognizes the need of many content and application developers to reach the largest possible audience on the Web and therefore ActiveX includes two distinct categories of technology:

- Tools for building conventional inactive content with HTML and dynamic HTML
- Tools for active content and application development based on ActiveX and DCOM

If you are concerned about providing content and applications that will be accessible by the widest possible audience on the Web, then you must limit your development efforts to the conventional, inactive model. Figure 2.1 depicts the three architectural models supported by ActiveX. The inactive model is conventional Web technology involving an HTTP server program that supplies static or dynamic HTML pages to an HTTP client. Binary files, including executable programs and files that contain multimedia content, can be provided to the HTTP client in the inactive model; but viewing the content or executing the programs is anything but simple for the end user. Most significant in the inactive model is that the average Web user is unable or unwilling to resolve the technical problems associated with

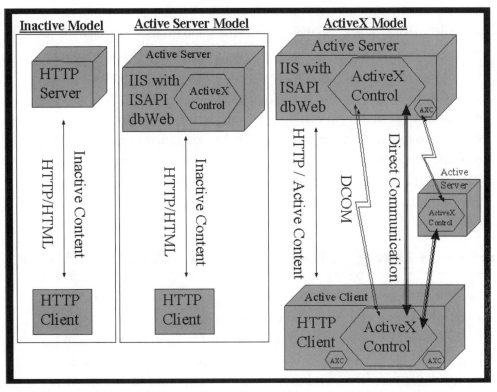

Figure 2.1 ActiveX supports three architectural models for maximum flexibility.

extending the ability of their client programs to support new features on the client side. Thus all of the intelligence must be built on the server side.

Through the active server model, Microsoft has given more powerful tools to developers who need to continue to provide inactive content to the widest possible audience. Although still limited to HTML and dynamic HTML for content, developers can begin the transition to ActiveX technology by building ActiveX controls and COM objects on the server side. In addition, the server side can be easily extended to provide HTML-based database access and more powerful CGI-style programs with ISAPI.

The primary drawback of an inactive Web architecture is that while it is not impossible to deliver new abilities and new features to Web users, it is impractical. Even before the Web emerged, innovative companies were building quality network software including applications that would run over the Internet. When the Web became the standard user interface for the Internet, a content boom ensued that forced real network software to take a back seat. Now, however, Web content developers have exhausted the potential of the inactive model, and most have realized that there is little difference between delivering innovative interactive Web content and conventional software development. To build the next generation of interactive content, developers must be given the ability to write software that is accessible to end users and end users must be protected from hostile software. This is the ActiveX model.

Activating the World Wide Web

Content development with ActiveX is as much about the applications that you deploy to end users as it is about the media types that the users view. Inactive Web technology has been characterized as "nothing more than interactive color fax machines"—which is an accurate assessment. The ActiveX model is real network computing brought to the Web. Note that Microsoft is not the only company responsible for the development of active Web technology. Sun Microsystems is responsible for pioneering two critical aspects of active Web architecture: Java and the Common Object Request Broker Architecture (CORBA).

Java is especially important in the ActiveX model because with Java you can create platform-independent software components, even ActiveX controls. Anyone on the Web will be able to use the network applications provided by your Web site regardless of the computing platform in use. Of course, this assumes that the user has a Web browser that supports active Web technology. And here is the most important question: Will every Web user upgrade their browser, or will the Web be doomed to remain interactive color fax machine technology that isn't even as useful as DOS was for developing new software?

Consider the fact that HTML 3.0 is faced with precisely the same problem. With HTML 3.0, new features have been added that make HTML almost useful as a content development tool. The only drawback is that in order to view HTML 3.0 content, end users must get a new Web browser. And, because every new Web browser that supports HTML 3.0 also supports active Web technology in the form of ActiveX controls and/or Java applets, the only real decision that you need to make once you've decided to move beyond HTML 1.0 and CGI is whether to continue using HTML at all to develop and deploy content on your Web site.

Consider also the fact that component software technology like ActiveX controls and Java applets are going to play an important role in the future of computing, no matter what else happens on the Web. The same cannot be said for HTML 3.0. Investing your time and money in developing quality active content and new software components clearly makes more sense than investing in HTML. The same observation can be made concerning server-side technology like CGI scripts or ISAPI DLLs. Why invest time and money building upon inadequate technology of the past, when you can activate the Web?

Finally, consider the millions of users who access the Web through online services such as CompuServe or America Online. They are all being given a new Web browser that supports active Web technology. Sooner or later, HTML and CGI will fade away. You can help make it happen sooner by building active Web content that is only accessible from an active Web browser like Netscape Navigator 3 or Internet Explorer 3. Inform visitors who continue to use old Web browsers that the real content of your site can only be accessed through an active Web browser and give them step-by-step instructions for upgrading their browser.

To make this strategy simpler for you to implement, SCIENCE.ORG provides free software tools and Web-based instruction that will guide your users through every detail of upgrading their browser. Contact the following URL to learn more about incorporating this free SCIENCE.ORG resource into your Web site:

```
http://internet.science.org/upgrade/webmaster/
```

Using the SCIENCE.ORG browser upgrade resource lets you concentrate on building active content and applications for your Web site without worrying about providing end user support to people with inactive browsers. Figure 2.2 gives an overview of the technical function of the browser upgrade resource.

The decision to activate the Web isn't an easy one. There are compelling reasons for sticking with inactive Web technology. Think about all of the Web-aware applications that will no longer function once content is active rather than HTML-based. For instance, every Web search engine that finds and indexes content using a "spider" or other automated utility will no longer be able to index the full text of your site; none of the many programs created with built-in support for HTML-based Web browsing will be usable for accessing your active content, either. To summarize, you either embrace active technology completely, or you must create and manage duplicate Web sites with different versions for each possible category of Web user.

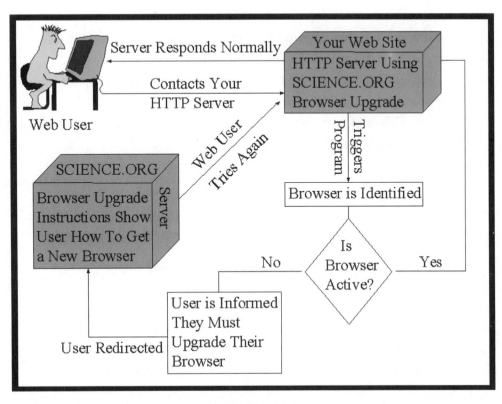

Figure 2.2 Use the SCIENCE.ORG browser upgrade resource on your active Web site.

Building and Deploying Active Web Applications

ActiveX enables the creation and deployment of serious network applications as well as sophisticated interactive content. ActiveX applications come in two styles: components called *ActiveX controls* and complete application modules called *Active Documents*, which are also known as *DocObjects*. Every ActiveX application requires a container object in which to execute. Internet Explorer 3.0, the Microsoft Office Binder, and the new Windows shell are examples of ActiveX container objects. Other containers will appear in the future, especially when a large number of ActiveX applications begin to appear on the Web.

Your Web application development strategy, therefore, is not a lot different than the strategy that you'll begin to use in all of your software development for the Windows platform. The major difference in developing ActiveX applications for the Web is that you must create platform-independent software in order for every Web user to have access to your Web applications. There are four options available to you for the creation of platform-independent software:

- Java applets
- Platform-specific compiled application objects
- HTML 3.0 with ActiveScripts
- Rapid application development tools for the Web

Java applets are an appealing option, and one that will become even more appealing once the execution performance of applets is improved. Java applets are delivered to client computers in the form of platform-independent byte code. The byte code is then executed within the Java Virtual Machine; the run-time engine that maps Java byte code instructions into platform-specific instructions. With Java applets, you write software once and it will run anywhere without modification. Java is the ideal solution for developing client-side ActiveX Web application logic.

The alternative to building Java applets is to write and compile a different version of your client-side program for each computing platform that you decide to support. The three most important platforms today are Windows (Microsoft), Macintosh (Apple), and Solaris (Sun Microsystems). If you are concerned about providing universal access to your Web applications, then this option should not be your first choice. Even though your ability to produce sophisticated Web applications is not limited in the way that it is with HTML, creating and maintaining multiple versions of your application is far from ideal.

The third option for application development is to use HTML 3.0 along with ActiveScripts. JavaScript is one of the languages that can be used to create ActiveScripts within HTML pages. JavaScript is supported by both Internet Explorer 3.0 and Netscape Navigator 3.0, which provides a platform-independent option for creating simple application logic. To learn about JavaScript, read the *Netscape LiveWire Sourcebook*. ActiveScripts also include support for Visual Basic Script, which is quickly being implemented on other computing platforms, including Macintosh and UNIX.

The fourth and final option for Web application development is to use a third-party rapid Web application development tool. Many such tools will probably emerge in the future, now that active Web technology is replacing inactive technology. Any third-party Web application development tool that you use will provide a run-time module in the form of an ActiveX control, just like active content development tools do. Some of the active content development tools, in fact, offer powerful application development features. For example, Macromedia Director is both a multimedia content-authoring package and a programming tool with which you can create sophisticated user interfaces for your Web applications. Macromedia Director requires an ActiveX control in order to view Director productions on the Web.

Internet Explorer 3.0 and the Active Client Architecture

Internet Explorer 3.0 plays a very important role in ActiveX Web technology. Internet Explorer is the first Web browser designed to fully support the ActiveX architecture. It is also the first significant Web application created entirely with the ActiveX SDK: the Windows application development technology for the Internet. The main application, *IEXPLORE.EXE,* is an ActiveX container application in which both Active Documents and ActiveX controls can reside. On top of the Internet Explorer container is an

HTML ActiveX control, kept in the file *MSHTML.DLL,* that enables Internet Explorer to display Web pages.

Also included in Internet Explorer is ActiveScript technology and all of the scripting engine and scripting hook services required to facilitate scripting in the ActiveX SDK. Although outside the scope of this book, it is interesting to note the existence of the ActiveX SDK and the fact that ActiveX is more than just a Web technology. ActiveX is in fact a direct extension to the Microsoft Windows operating system to support Internet software development. Microsoft is using ActiveX to write programs such as the Internet Explorer, which should give you some idea of the true power behind ActiveX compared to inactive Web technology.

Most experienced developers have navigated the Internet, but now it's time to explore. You can begin your journey by first downloading and installing Internet Explorer 3.0 from Microsoft's Web site. If you haven't done so already, visit the Internet Explorer home page on the Microsoft Web site:

```
http://www.microsoft.com/ie/
```

Figure 2.3 shows the Internet Explorer version 3.0 displaying a typical Web page. Other Web browsers provide features such as a history list and a data cache but don't offer those features to other programs on the computer. Instead of building technology and designating it for exclusive use in the company's Web browser, Microsoft built a generic SDK that anyone can use to write software. From that SDK has come the Internet Explorer. The Favorites list and network data cache feature are two of the Internet Explorer features that are available for use in other programs as a result of Microsoft's approach to Internet computing.

To the end user, Internet Explorer is basically the same as any other Web browser. The following table shows an alphabetical list of HTML tags supported by Internet Explorer 3.0. As you can see, the list is comprehensive.

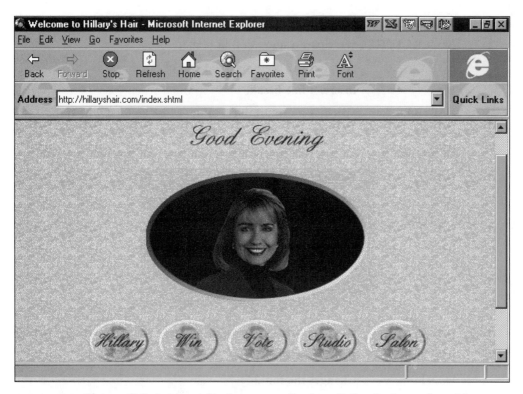

Figure 2.3 Internet Explorer can display all the features found in existing Web pages.

Tag	Description
A	Stands for anchor and specifies a hyperlink.
ADDRESS	Renders text as italics.
AREA	Specifies the shape of a hot spot in a client-side image map.
B	Renders text in boldface.
BASE	Specifies a document's URL.
BASEFONT	Sets base font value.
BGSOUND	Adds background sounds or soundtracks.
BIG	Enlarges the font size.

Tag	Description
BLOCKQUOTE	Sets apart a quotation in text.
BODY	Specifies the beginning and end of document body.
BR	Inserts a line break.
CAPTION	Specifies a caption for a table. Must be used within the TABLE tag.
CENTER	Causes subsequent text and images to be centered.
CITE	Renders text in italics.
CODE	Specifies a code sample.
COMMENT	Indicates a comment.
DD	Specifies a definition in a definition list.
DFN	Renders text in italics.
DIR	Denotes a directory list.
DL	Denotes a definition list.
DT	Specifies a term in a definition list.
EM	Renders text in italics.
FONT	Changes the font.
FORM	Denotes a form.
FRAME	Creates permanent panes for displaying information.
FRAMESET	The main container for a frame.
Hn	Renders text in heading style.
HR	Draws a horizontal rule.
HTML	Denotes the file is an HTML document.
I	Renders text in italics.
IMG	Embeds .AVI (Audio Video Interleave) video clips and images.
INPUT	Specifies a form control.
ISINDEX	Indicates the presence of a searchable index.
KBD	Renders text in fixed-width and boldface type.
LI	Denotes one item of a list.

Tag	Description
LISTING	Renders text in fixed-width type.
MAP	Specifies a collection of hot spots for a client-side image map.
MARQUEE	This new tag enables you to create a scrolling text marquee.
MENU	Denotes a list of items.
META	Internet Explorer supports client pull using the META tag.
NOBR	Turns off line breaking.
NOFRAMES	Content viewable by browsers that do not support frames.
OBJECT	Inserts an OLE control.
OL	Draws lines of text as an ordered list.
OPTION	Denotes one choice in a list box.
P	Denotes a paragraph.
PLAINTEXT	Renders text in fixed-width type without processing tags.
PRE	Renders text in fixed-width type.
S	Renders text in strikethrough type.
SAMP	Specifies a code sample.
SELECT	Denotes a list box or drop-down list.
SMALL	Decreases the font size.
STRIKE	Renders text in strikethrough type.
STRONG	Renders text in boldface.
SUB	Renders text in subscript.
SUP	Renders text in superscript.
TABLE	Internet Explorer 3.0 fully supports HTML 3.0 tables.
TITLE	Specifies a title for the document.
TT	Renders text in fixed-width type.
U	Renders text underlined.
UL	Draws lines of text as a bulleted list.

Tag	Description
VAR	Renders text as a small fixed-width font.
WBR	Inserts a soft linebreak in a block of NOBR text.
XMP	Renders text in fixed-width type.

There are two important features that are worth noting about Internet Explorer because they affect you as a Web developer:

- Password-protected rating controls allow the user to prevent access to Web sites containing nudity, sex, or violence.
- Trust verification settings let the user decide how safe they want the browser to be about downloading and executing code in the form of ActiveX controls.

███████ TIP

Developers who are switching from using Netscape to Internet Explorer can convert their bookmarks file into a Favorites file. Contact the following URL and download the MS Bookmark Conversion utility:

http://www.windows95.com/apps/url.html

███████

Internet Explorer's rating control lets supervisors or parents designate limitations on the content that can be viewed in a particular client. Internet Explorer's rating control is based on the PICS (Platform for Internet Content Selection, developed by MIT) technology used to define and create ratings systems.

There are several categories that can be controlled. Each category has five levels of control that can be set allowing you to vary the allowable content:

- *Language.*   Inoffensive slang, mild expletives, moderate expletives, obscene gestures, explicit or crude language
- *Violence.*   No violence, fighting, killing, killing with blood and gore, wanton and gratuitous violence
- *Nudity.*   None, revealing attire, partial nudity, frontal nudity, provocative display of frontal nudity
- *Sex.*   None, passionate kissing, clothed sexual touching, nonexplicit sexual touching, and explicit sexual activity

Here is the simple procedure to set the viewing ratings control of your Internet Explorer:

1. Select **View|Options.**
2. Choose the **Ratings** folder.
3. Click on **Set Ratings**.
4. Enter your administration password.

The Internet Ratings window opens, as shown in Figure 2.4.

As you can guess, not every Web developer includes ratings information about their Web pages. The Microsoft Internet Explorer ratings control therefore lets the user prevent the viewing of unrated Web pages. Select the **General** folder in the Internet Ratings window, and deselect the check box labeled Users can see unrated sites, thereby preventing anyone using Internet Explorer to view unrated Web pages. At times, a user may want to override the default ratings controls. In the Internet Ratings window, select the **Advanced** folder and check the box labeled User can type in supervisor password to see restricted sites. Now when a user is visiting an unrated site, a window opens requiring the entry of the supervisor password before the Web page is loaded.

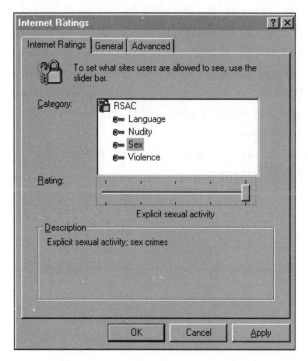

■■■■■■■ **Figure 2.4** Choose the desired ratings category, and select the level of rating control.

If you plan to provide your Web pages on the Internet, you will soon have to have your pages rated. You can either obtain a rating from an independent bureau or generate one yourself. The main independent bureau for rating Web pages is the Recreational Software Advisory Council (RSAC), which can be found at the following URL:

```
http://www.rsac.org/
```

You can contact this organization and register your Web pages or Web sites in a few minutes. After you fill out the questionnaire, RSAC gives you a rating for placement in your Web page. The ratings for a Web page are designated with the <META> tag. Here is an example of the <META> tag for a rated Web page.

```
<META http-equiv="PICS-Label" content='(PICS-1.0 "http://www.rsac.org/
ratingsv01.html" l gen true comment "RSACi North America Server" by
"donb@science.org" for "http://www.science.org" on "1996.04.16T08:15-0500"
exp "1997.01.01T08:15-0500" r (n 0 s 0 v 0 l 0))'>
```

For those Web developers who will grumble about rating their Web pages, remember that self-regulation is better than regulation by Uncle Sam.

There are pitfalls on the active Web. ActiveX controls bring a new age of interactivity to Web pages, but they do that by enabling the download of code that isn't already resident on the client computer system. Allowing code to be downloaded from the Web has obvious security implications. Like your mother used to say, "You don't know where that code has been." For example, code could be downloaded that was created with deliberate malicious intentions, such as deleting vital files on your computer system, or the code could have become infected with a virus.

Recognizing these potential security problems, the Internet Explorer lets you control the code that is downloaded. You can designate the desired code security of Internet Explorer by selecting the **View|Options** command. Choose the **Security** folder (shown in Figure 2.5) and click on the **Programs** button in the Safe Content section. The window shown in Figure 2.6 opens.

When you select **Expert,** Internet Explorer opens a warning window before downloading code, such as an ActiveX control, and lets you choose whether to download the code. The code security system built into Internet Explorer lets you know who produced the code, and if it has been tampered with before you download it to your computer. Figure 2.7 shows the window that appears when an ActiveX control is encountered that does not contain a registered signature. In the future, all software vendors will need to obtain digital signatures for their software components if they are to be used on the Internet.

When Internet Explorer encounters code on the Web that does have a digital signature and whose credentials seem to be in order, a window like the one shown in Figure 2.8 opens. With such a clear and prominent

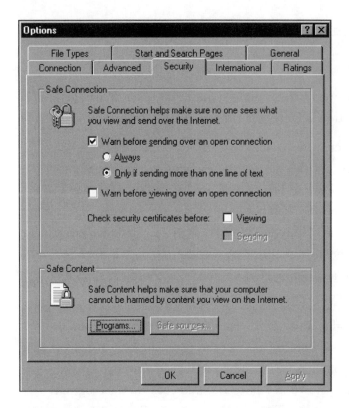

Figure 2.5 Modify security options for connections and content.

identification screen, the user can make an in-formed decision about whether to execute the code. Behind the scenes, the ActiveX architecture ensures that the information contained in the code's digital signature is in fact valid, and that the credentials are not forged in an attempt to mislead the end user about the origin of the code.

Advanced software download security settings, including those shown in Figure 2.9, can also be set by the user. In addition to concern over downloaded software components, there is also reason to be concerned about the content that some components download. It's possible for a program you download to continue downloading additional programs of which you are

Figure 2.6 Choose the level of security that you want for your system.

totally unaware. The concern over malicious content is similar to the concern over malicious Java applets, because Java applets are only limited in

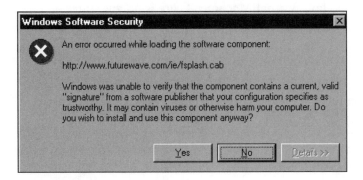

Figure 2.7 The Internet Explorer warning regarding anonymous and potentially dangerous code.

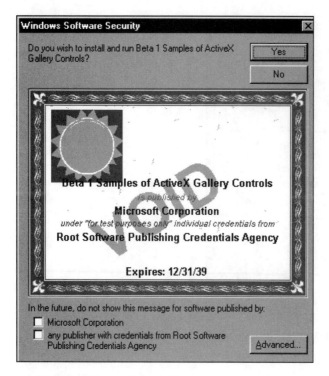

Figure 2.8 Authentic credentials are displayed for the user to inspect.

their ability to do damage to the files of a client computer based on the restrictions imposed by the Java Virtual Machine. There is no guarantee that an ActiveX control will impose those same restrictions on its content.

To address the concern over malicious content separately from the concern over malicious code, Internet Explorer displays the window shown in Figure 2.10 whenever content is encountered that can't be verified as trustworthy. The trust model provided by ActiveX is actually more sophisticated than the trust model provided by a software store. When you go into a store and buy software, you trust that the vendor of that software hasn't included viruses or designed the software so that it will damage your computer or its files. Nothing except trust prevents the software vendor from writing malicious code and selling it to you through a computer store.

▰▰▰▰▰▰ **Figure 2.9** Different ways that downloaded software can be handled by Internet Explorer.

When you think about it, the important files on your computer stand a better chance of being destroyed by a hardware failure, an accident, or a malicious former employee than by software that you buy. With the trust model

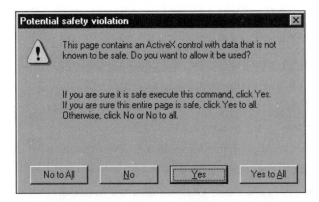

▰▰▰▰▰▰ **Figure 2.10** Separate scrutiny of content by Internet Explorer.

built into ActiveX, end users are given even more reason to trust known software vendors who provide quality products and good customer service. With everyone thinking regularly about trust on the Internet, a good reputation becomes critical to the success of your Web-based business, even if you only produce content and don't build new software.

The end result of this new active client architecture is simplicity itself. When Internet Explorer is used to view active content, any application components that are required to view the content are automatically downloaded and installed if they're not already present on the client. The code is executed by Internet Explorer as needed, resulting in a truly seamless on-demand integration of new software extensions into the client. Figure 2.11 shows one of Microsoft's ActiveX controls executing within Internet Explorer to extend its abilities in a unique way.

Simplicity, security, and the full power of software development are now available on the Internet. The World Wide Web is gradually being integrated directly into the operating system. From Java-based operating systems to ActiveX, there is a movement underway to unleash the potential of the Internet by completely rethinking and reengineering software technology from the ground up. ActiveX, in more ways than this book is able to reveal, is an important part of Microsoft's strategy to do just that.

Distributed Component Object Model and the Active Application Architecture

Active application development is the future of the Internet. Content is pretty, and pretty is important; but only through the development of innovative software applications will the Internet be able to mature into a powerful computing environment for use by the general public. However, like most things on the Internet today, it's not that simple. If the development of innovative software were the only issue, then there would be no need for a fundamental change in technology: HTML and CGI, along with network

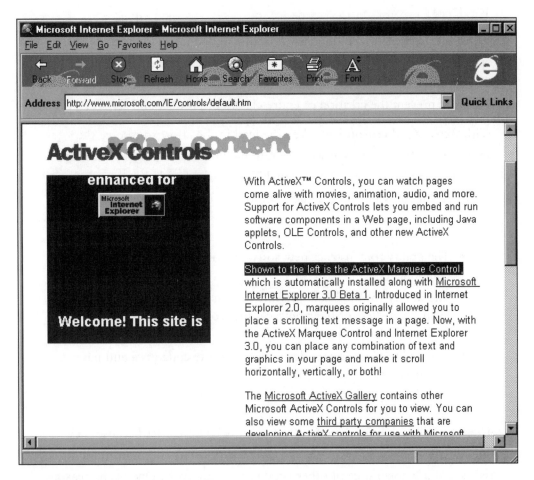

Figure 2.11 An active client leads to a happy Webmaster.

software like PointCast (*http://www.pointcast.com/*), transferRNA (*http://www.science.org/tRNA/*), RealAudio (*http://www.realaudio.com/*) and conventional e-mail, Internet news, IRC, and FTP, would be sufficient to foster the next generation of interactive communication.

A radically new architecture is emerging for Internet software to address the limitations of traditional software development technology. Software developers have been aware of certain technical flaws in the way that software is designed and built for a long time. For the most part, these flaws were not significant barriers to creating new products or services. However, as developers try to apply old approaches to software development to the Internet, they find that the flaws which were once an annoyance are now major problems that prevent the creation of entire classes of product and service.

With ActiveX, Microsoft has taken the lead in the effort to resolve the architectural flaws in top down programming that have plagued the software industry for so long. Three capabilities have already been recognized as key factors in whatever technical solution is ultimately created:

- The ability to construct new software easily using reliable software components
- The ability for modular software objects to work together seamlessly, regardless of their physical location on the network or the operating system on which each runs
- The ability for software developers to write code once and have it run anywhere

These three capabilities directly affect every Web developer because they directly affect every software developer. Microsoft has addressed these three issues and a whole range of others in designing ActiveX. One of the reasons that the company's response has been so quick and a long-term solution has been achieved is that ActiveX is based on technology that Microsoft has been working on for years. ActiveX is more than just an Internet technology: it is a general improvement in the way that software works.

Distributed Component Object Model (DCOM) is Microsoft's object communication standard that enables software on one computer to work seamlessly with software on another computer. Instead of relying on CGI scripts to enable Web clients to interact with application logic stored on a Web server, developers who build DCOM applications can create any logic required in the client object and enable the client object to communicate with server objects in any way necessary. The potential of DCOM on the Web is huge.

DCOM may not be terribly significant now, as few products have been designed to take advantage of it; but its importance will grow in the future. Microsoft is recommending that all Windows software be designed to utilize ActiveX technology. ActiveX isn't a specialized feature of Windows that only applies on the Internet. Applications in the future will be Active Documents and those Active Documents will host ActiveX controls. Active Documents and any hosted ActiveX controls will in turn be hosted by containers like Internet Explorer or the Windows shell. Figure 2.12 shows how Microsoft Office for Windows 95 is already designed to support Active Document technology, with each of the Office applications centered around the ActiveX model. Internet Explorer is able to host the entire Microsoft Word program in the form of an Active Document.

The next version of Microsoft Office will host ActiveX controls as well. This means that any ActiveX control that you build today will be able to plug in later to applications such as Microsoft Word. As DCOM objects begin to pop up that offer valuable services to other objects or to other applications over the network, you'll see ActiveX controls, which are also DCOM objects, talking to other objects right in a Word document.

HTML 3.0 doesn't hold a candle to ActiveX when it comes to long-term software value. At the same time, however, ActiveX gives your HTML 3.0 and JavaScript-based Web applications the long-term value that they would otherwise lack. Thanks to the Microsoft HTML ActiveX control (used even in Internet Explorer), you will be able to plug your HTML-based Web applications and content into any container of ActiveX controls. Whether you choose HTML and CGI as your Web application development strategy or exclusively support ActiveX technology, you can rest assured that the

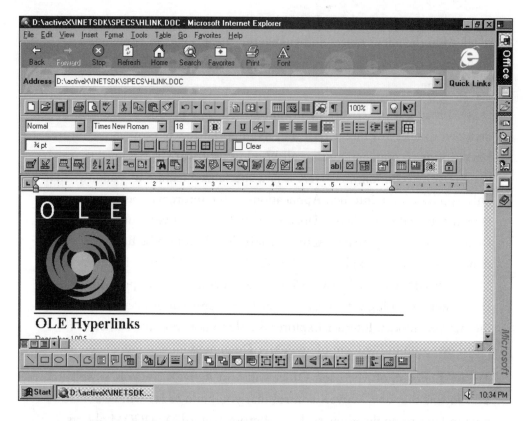

Figure 2.12 Microsoft Office for Windows 95 supports the ActiveX architecture.

applications you build today will be useful in the construction of new Windows and Internet applications tomorrow. ActiveX gives you an unprecedented level of guarantee that your investments in software will retain their value over time.

Focusing on Active Content Development

Active content means power and flexibility, but it also means portability. Active content is portable because almost every popular active content format, such as RealAudio, ShockWave, PowerPoint, or Acrobat, provides free cross-platform viewers that enable any Web user to access the content. When you focus on building and deploying active content, you get to use simple and powerful authoring tools that often include programming or scripting ability, and you get platform independence all at once.

Compared to all other options for application development, focusing on active content is by far the simplest approach to building Web applications. Watch for more powerful active content authoring tools based on Java and other technology, new and old alike. Many authoring tools, like Macromedia Director, even offer scripting or database access.

Activating Windows Software Development

The message for Windows software developers is to write Active Documents and ActiveX controls. If your Windows software is based on the ActiveX architecture, then you don't have to do any work in order to integrate with other applications like the Internet Explorer. You also don't need to change your program in order to use the abilities that other developers have also created: their software just plugs right in to your containers. Unless you're a very experienced programmer this section provides more details than you would want to know about developing ActiveX Windows software, with too little instruction for you to do anything with the details. Read through this material anyway, in order to take a quick glance at the technology that is now available to Windows programmers.

Active Documents support a standard set of COM interfaces. An Active Document container such as Internet Explorer supports the following COM interfaces: **I/OKnown, IOLeContainer, IOLeDocumentSite,** and **IHLinkFrame. IOLeDocumentSite** is the interface used by Active Documents as they integrate into the container. **IHLinkFrame** enables a Windows application to support hyperlinking to the Web and to other

Windows applications and Active Documents. Active Documents supports the following COM interfaces: **IOLeObject, IOLeDocument,** and **IOLeHLinkSite.** These are the interfaces that mesh with the ones supported by the container. An Active Document knows how to be contained, how to print, how to merge its application menu and toolbar with those of the container, and how to support hyperlinking to and from other locations.

Component Object Model (COM) is the way that objects are packaged in a language-, tool-, and platform-independent way. Your Windows software is able to query a COM object to determine what interfaces and services it supports without caring about what authoring tool it was built in or how it was distributed to you.

COM provides two things to Windows software. First, it's versionable, which means that software can actually ask a COM object what it does before deciding whether to use the abilities of the object. If a COM object doesn't support the right interfaces, the ones required by your program, then your program locates and uses a different object, one that supports the right interfaces. Second, COM is programmable. COM provides your software with a standard way to access the methods, properties, and events built in to other objects.

Then there's Distributed COM (DCOM), which is a way to distribute COM objects over the network seamlessly. The COM client architecture today works by enabling a client to make a **CoCreateInstance** call to create a COM object. In response to this call, Windows finds the object on the client and instantiates it. Windows gives a pointer to the object to the client in the form of an **IUnknown.** The client can then make use of the COM object through the IUnknown reference. In Distributed COM, the client works exactly the same. It still makes the **CoCreateInstance** call but DCOM, behind the scenes, sends that call out to a remote network server.

The IUnknown reference returned by DCOM actually references a remote object, but your client program needn't care about that. The DCOM client can use the services and call the interfaces of the remote object just as though the object were a local one. Microsoft has plans to distribute DCOM over HTTP to provide compatibility with firewalls and the Web without sacrificing any of the programming power that DCOM provides. Because DCOM works behind the scenes, the switch to HTTP-based DCOM won't change the way that your software works at all. DCOM is the solution for easy object programming over the Internet.

At the same time that Microsoft worked to build DCOM, Sun Microsystems has worked with many other computer companies in a partnership called the Object Management Group (OMG) to build the Common Object Request Broker Architecture (CORBA). CORBA is a more powerful distributed object computing architecture than is DCOM. CORBA and DCOM are somewhat compatible, however, which means that a DCOM object can easily be made to talk to a CORBA object. Instead of returning an IUnknown reference that points to a DCOM object, the DCOM engine can return an IUnknown that points to a CORBA object. The DCOM engine can handle the translation for you transparently so that any CORBA object on the network can be accessed from your Windows software. For more information about CORBA, contact the Object Management Group on the Web at *http://www.omg.org*.

Distributed object computing is the future of Windows software, and it is the future of Internet computing. By supporting ActiveX technology today in your Windows programs, you are preparing to participate in the distributed object revolution. Programmers on platforms other than Windows are already building CORBA objects. Eventually, your DCOM applications will work seamlessly with those CORBA objects over the network. Gradually, the incompatibilities of computing past will become a faded memory.

Components and Scripting

Microsoft has provided several ActiveX Internet controls that you can integrate into your applications. Shipped as full-fledged OCX components, which are compatible with ActiveX controls, any development tool that supports the use of OCX technology is already compatible with these

Internet controls. The ActiveX Internet controls include an HTML display object, HTTP, FTP, and WinSock communications objects, and a VRML object. For details on incorporating these Internet controls into your Visual Basic applications, see Chapter 5.

Along with ActiveX, Microsoft has introduced an innovative script engine technology that promises to add a dimension of programmability to every Windows application. First, any software developer can provide a custom scripting language and make it compatible with features of other scripting languages. You can even make the language available for use in any Windows application. This means that scripting on the Web is no longer limited to just JavaScript or Visual Basic Script. Second, every object can include scripting hooks that make it possible to access the methods, properties, or events of the object through scripting. Entire applications can be constructed using only components and scripting to tie the components together, and those applications will execute anywhere that you find the Windows operating system.

A superb example of components and scripting can be seen in the Internet Explorer itself. Internet Explorer supports the JavaScript object model that enables JavaScripts or Visual Basic Scripts to access the properties, methods, and events of the Web browser. We included detailed coverage of the JavaScript object model for active scripting in *Netscape LiveWire Sourcebook*. Internet Explorer goes beyond the JavaScript object model, providing full scripting access to the properties and methods exposed by ActiveX controls and other objects.

Internet Explorer hosts an ActiveX control called WebBrowser that provides the core functionality of the browser application. In addition to HTML-based scripting, Internet Explorer provides an OLE automation object called InternetExplorer that can be used from other programs through the OLE Automation interface to control the behavior of the Internet Explorer. Both objects can be used from within your own Windows software to add Web browsing capability to your programs. The following documentation details the properties, methods, and events supported by these two objects through their OLE automation interfaces.

WebBrowser Object

The WebBrowser object is an ActiveX control that is hosted by the Internet Explorer in order to provide Web-browsing capability to the user. By hosting the WebBrowser ActiveX control, you can add browsing capabilities to your own applications. The WebBrowser object has the following properties:

Application	FileName	Parent
AutoSize	ForeColor	Path
AutoSizePercentage	FullName	Top
BackColor	FullScreen	TopLevelContainer
Busy	Height	Type
Container	IncludeFiles	Value
Document	Left	Visible
ExcludeFiles	Location	Width

In addition, the WebBrowser object provides the following object methods:

Browse	GoHome	Quit
GoBack	GoSearch	Refresh
GoForward	Navigate	Stop

Visual Basic Script can easily access the properties and methods of WebBrowser. The events that occur in a WebBrowser can also be useful for scripting. The events are:

OnBeginNavigat	OnDownloadComplete	OnProgress
OnCommandStateChange	OnNavigate	OnQuit
OnDownloadBegin	OnNewWindow	OnStatusTextChange

InternetExplorer Object

The InternetExplorer object lets applications control the behavior of the Internet Explorer itself. The properties, methods, and events of the InternetExplorer OLE automation object are listed here.

Properties	Methods	Events
Application	GoBack	OnBeginNavigate
Busy	GoForward	OnCommandStateChange
Container	GoHome	OnDownloadBegin
Document	Navigate	OnDownloadComplete
FileName	Quit	OnNavigate
FullName	Refresh	OnNewWindow
FullScreen	Stop	OnProgress
Height		OnQuit
Left		OnStatusTextChange
Name		
Parent		
Path		
StatusBar		
StatusText		
ToolBar		
Top		

▰▰▰▰ Continued

Properties	Methods	Events
TopLevelContainer		
Type		
Visible		
Width		

▰▰▰▰

As you can see from the list of properties, methods, and events for the WebBrowser and InternetExplorer objects, they have a number of characteristics in common. More information is given in the following pages about each of the properties, methods, and events belonging to objects of type WebBrowser or InternetExplorer. The OLE Automation interface to these objects gives your Windows software a programmatic way to incorporate Web functionality in your programs. Soon, this same programmatic functionality will be available through Visual Basic Script as well, bringing the power of component scripting to the Web.

Application   Refers to the Application object that contains the WebBrowser control or the current instance of the Internet Explorer application.

```
WebBrowser.Application
```

```
InternetExplorer.Application
```

AutoSize   The long integer value that determines whether the web browser control is in autosize mode. True (nonzero) indicates autosize is turned on. False (zero) indicates off.

```
WebBrowser.AutoSize [= value]
```

AutoSizePercentage   Contains the autosize mode percentage as a long integer; used only if autosize mode is turned on.

```
WebBrowser.AutoSizePercentage [= value]
```

BackColor The background color of the WebBrowser control in the form of the Microsoft Windows red-green-blue (RGB) color scheme. The valid range for a normal RGB color is 0 to 16,777,215. Only solid colors are allowed; dithered color values will be replaced with the nearest solid color.

```
WebBrowser.BackColor [= color]
```

Browse Displays a dialog box that allows the user to select a new folder.

```
WebBrowser.Browse
```

Busy Contains a Boolean value specifying whether a download or other activity is in progress.

```
InternetExplorer.Busy
```

```
WebBrowser.Busy
```

Container Refers to the container object in which the WebBrowser or InternetExplorer object are contained.

```
WebBrowser.Container
```

```
InternetExplorer.Container
```

Document Refers to the active document object.

```
InternetExplorer.Document
```

```
WebBrowser.Document
```

ExcludeFiles Lists the filenames excluded.

```
WebBrowser.ExcludeFiles [= filenames]
```

FileName Contains the name of the file that the WebBrowser control or the Internet Explorer application is currently displaying.

```
InternetExplorer.FileName
```

```
WebBrowser.FileName
```

ForeColor The foreground color of the WebBrowser control in the form of the Microsoft Windows red-green-blue (RGB) color scheme. The valid range for a normal RGB color is 0 to 16,777,215. Only solid colors are allowed; dithered color values will be replaced with the nearest solid color.

```
WebBrowser.ForeColor [= color]
```

FullName A string that evaluates to the full path of the executable file that contains the WebBrowser control or the Internet Explorer application.

```
InternetExplorer.FullName
WebBrowser.FullName
```

FullScreen A Boolean value indicating whether the object is in full screen or normal window mode. This property only applies if the object is hosted in a container.

```
InternetExplorer.FullScreen [= value]
```
```
WebBrowser.FullScreen [= value]
```

GoBack Goes to the previous item in the history list.

```
InternetExplorer.GoBack
WebBrowser.GoBack
```

GoForward Goes to the next item in the history list.

```
InternetExplorer.GoForward
```
```
WebBrowser.GoForward
```

GoHome Goes to the current home or start page.

```
InternetExplorer.GoHome
```
```
WebBrowser.GoHome
```

GoSearch Goes to the current search page.

```
InternetExplorer.GoSearch
```

`WebBrowser.GoSearch`

Height The vertical dimension, in pixels, of the frame window that contains the object.

`InternetExplorer.Height [= height]`

`WebBrowser.Height [= height]`

IncludeFiles The list of filenames to include.

`WebBrowser.IncludeFiles [= filenames]`

Left The distance between the internal left edge of the object and the left edge of its container. The Left property is measured in units matching the coordinate system of its container. The value for this property changes as the object is moved by the user or by code.

`InternetExplorer.Left [= distance]`

`WebBrowser.Left [= distance]`

Location The location for the WebBrowser to browse. For example, the location could be a site on the World Wide Web, a file on the local machine, or a directory on a network server.

`WebBrowser.Location [= value]`

Name A string containing the name of the object that contains the WebBrowser control.

`InternetExplorer.Name`

Navigate Navigates to a resource identified by a Uniform Resource Locator (URL). URL is specified as a string while Flags is a bit-mask combination of the following values:

Constant	Value	Meaning
navOpenInNewWindow	1	Open in a new window.
NavNoHistory	2	Exclude from the history list.

Constant	Value	Meaning
NavNoReadFromCache	4	Do not read from the cache.
NavNoWriteToCache	8	Do not write to the cache.

TargetFrameName is a string that specifies the name of the frame in which to display the contents of the resource specified in URL. PostData is data to be sent in an HTTP POST operation using the URL specified. Headers can be used to specify the HTTP headers to send. And Referrer can contain the URL of the referring document or Web page.

```
InternetExplorer.Navigate URL [Flags,] [TargetFrameName,] [PostData,]
[Headers,] [Referrer]
```

```
WebBrowser.Navigate URL [Flags,] [TargetFrameName,] [PostData,] [Headers,]
[Referrer]
```

OnBeginNavigate Occurs when the object is about to navigate to a new hyperlink. URL identifies the hyperlink to which the object is about to navigate. Flags is a bitmask combination of the following values:

Constant	Value	Meaning
navOpenInNewWindow	1	Open in a new window.
navNoHistory	2	Exclude from the history list.
navNoReadFromCache	4	Do not read from the cache.
NavNoWriteToCache	8	Do not write from the cache.

```
Private Sub InternetExplorer_OnBeginNavigate(ByVal URL As String, ByVal Flags
As Long, ByVal TargetFrameName As String, PostData As Variant, ByVal Headers
As String, ByVal Referrer As String, Cancel As Boolean)
```

```
Private Sub WebBrowser_OnBeginNavigate(ByVal URL As String, ByVal Flags As
Long, ByVal TargetFrameName As String, PostData As Variant, ByVal Headers As
String, ByVal Referrer As String, Cancel As Boolean)
```

TargetFrameName is a string that specifies the name of the frame in which to display the contents of the resource specified in URL. PostData is data to be sent in an HTTP POST operation using the URL specified. Headers can be used to specify the HTTP headers to send. And Referrer can contain the URL of the referring document or Web page. Cancel is a Boolean value that is True if the navigation operation was canceled.

OnCommandStateChange Occurs when the enabled state of a command changes. Command is a long integer specifying the identifier of the command that changed. Enable is a Boolean value that is True if the command is enabled.

```
Private Sub InternetExplorer_OnCommandStateChange (ByVal Command As Long,
ByVal Enable As Boolean)

Private Sub WebBrowser_OnCommandStateChange (ByVal Command As Long,
ByVal Enable As Boolean)
```

OnDownloadBegin Occurs when a new page is about to be downloaded.

```
Private Sub InternetExplorer_OnDownloadBegin ( )

Private Sub WebBrowser_OnDownloadBegin ( )
```

OnDownloadComplete Occurs when the current page has finished being downloaded.

```
Private Sub InternetExplorer_OnDownloadComplete ( )

Private Sub WebBrowser_OnDownloadComplete ( )
```

OnNavigate Occurs when the object navigates to a new hyperlink. URL is a string containing the URL of the hyperlink. Flags is a bitmask combination of the following values:

Constant	Value	Meaning
navOpenInNewWindow	1	Open in a new window.

Constant	Value	Meaning
navNoHistory	2	Exclude from the history list.
navNoReadFromCache	4	Do not read from the cache.
NavNoWriteToCache	8	Do not write from the cache.

```
Private Sub WebBrowser_OnNavigate(ByVal URL As String, ByVal Flags As Long,
ByVal TargetFrameName As String, PostData As Variant, ByVal Headers As String,
ByVal Referrer As String)

Private Sub InternetExplorer_OnNavigate(ByVal URL As String, ByVal Flags As
Long,

ByVal TargetFrameName As String, PostData As Variant, ByVal Headers As String,
ByVal Referrer As String)
```

TargetFrameName is a string that specifies the name of the frame in which to display the contents of the resource specified in URL. PostData is data to be sent in an HTTP POST operation using the URL specified. Headers can be used to specify the HTTP headers to send. And Referrer can contain the URL of the referring document or Web page. Cancel is a Boolean value that is True if the navigation operation was canceled.

OnNewWindow   Occurs when the WebBrowser control is about to create a new window for displaying information. URL is a string containing the URL of the hyperlink. Flags is a bitmask combination of the following values:

Constant	Value	Meaning
navOpenInNewWindow	1	Open in a new window.
navNoHistory	2	Exclude from the history list.
navNoReadFromCache	4	Do not read from the cache.
NavNoWriteToCache	8	Do not write from the cache.

```
Private InternetExplorer_OnNewWindow (ByVal URL As String, ByVal Flags As Long,
ByVal TargetFrameName As String, PostData As Variant, ByVal Headers As String,
ByVal Referrer As String)
```

```
Private WebBrowser_OnNewWindow (ByVal URL As String, ByVal Flags As Long,
ByVal TargetFrameName As String, PostData As Variant, ByVal Headers As String,
ByVal Referrer As String)
```

TargetFrameName is a string that specifies the name of the frame in which to display the contents of the resource specified in URL. PostData is data to be sent in an HTTP POST operation using the URL specified. Headers can be used to specify the HTTP headers to send. And Referrer can contain the URL of the referring document or Web page. Cancel is a Boolean value that is True if the navigation operation was canceled.

OnProgress Occurs when the progress of a download operation is updated. Progress is a long integer that specifies the number of bytes downloaded so far. ProgressMax is a long integer that specifies the total number of bytes that will be downloaded. ProgressMax is zero if the total number of bytes is unknown.

```
Private Sub InternetExplorer_OnProgress(ByVal Progress As Long, ByVal
ProgressMax As Long)
```

```
Private Sub WebBrowser_OnProgress(ByVal Progress As Long, ByVal ProgressMax As
Long)
```

OnQuit Occurs when the Internet Explorer application is ready to quit. Cancel is True if the last quit attempt was canceled.

```
Private Sub InternetExplorer_OnQuit(Cancel As Boolean)
```

```
Private Sub WebBrowser_OnQuit(Cancel As Boolean)
```

OnStatusTextChange Occurs when the status bar text changes. bstrText is the new status bar text.

```
Private Sub InternetExplorer_OnStatusTextChange(ByVal bstrText As String)
```

```
Private Sub WebBrowser_OnStatusTextChange(ByVal bstrText As String)
```

Parent Refers to the object container of the referenced hyperlink.

```
InternetExplorer.Parent
```

```
WebBrowser.Parent
```

Path The string of the full path to the resource that the WebBrowser control or Internet Explorer is currently displaying.

```
InternetExplorer.Path
```

```
WebBrowser.Path
```

Quit Closes the WebBrowser control or quits the Internet Explorer application.

```
WebBrowser.Quit
```

```
InternetExplorer.Quit
```

Refresh Reloads the file that the WebBrowser control is currently displaying. Level can be one of the following values:

Constant	Meaning
refreshAll	Refresh entirely.
RefreshDontSendNoCache	Do not send the HTTP header pragma:nocache. This header tells the server not to return a cached copy, but to make sure the information is as fresh as possible. This header causes problems for some servers.

```
WebBrowser.Refresh [Level]
```

```
InternetExplorer.Refresh [Level]
```

StatusBar A Boolean value that determines whether the status bar is visible.

```
InternetExplorer.StatusBar [= value]
```

StatusText The text displayed in the status bar.

```
InternetExplorer.StatusText [= value]
```

Stop Stops opening a file.

```
WebBrowser.Stop
```

```
InternetExplorer.Stop
```

ToolBar A Boolean value that determines whether the toolbar is visible.

```
InternetExplorer.ToolBar [= value]
```

Top The distance between the internal top edge of the WebBrowser control and the top edge of its container. The Top property is measured in units matching the coordinate system of its container. The value for this property changes as the object is moved by the user or by code.

```
InternetExplorer.Top [= value]
```

```
WebBrowser.Top [= value]
```

TopLevelContainer A Boolean value indicating whether the current object is the top-level container of the WebBrowser control.

```
InternetExplorer.TopLevelContainer
```

```
WebBrowser.TopLevelContainer
```

Type A string that specifies the type of the current contained object.

```
InternetExplorer.Type
```

```
WebBrowser.Type
```

Value A string that contains the friendly name of the location of the current window.

```
WebBrowser.Value
```

Visible A Boolean value indicating whether the browser is visible or hidden.

```
InternetExplorer.Visible [= value]
```

```
WebBrowser.Visible [= value]
```

Width The horizontal dimension, in pixels, of the frame window that contains the WebBrowser control.

```
InternetExplorer.Width [= width]
```

```
WebBrowser.Width [= width]
```

Between the WebBrowser object, the InternetExplorer OLE automation object, and the Microsoft HTML control, the Web has been fully integrated into Microsoft Windows as a system service. This directly benefits your application development approach for Windows, because you don't have to rewrite services that everyone is going to have. You can just use the system service.

Windows System Services

Microsoft provides thousands of pages of good documentation on every detail of OLE, OLEscript, OLE hyperlinking, simple hyperlink navigation API, WinInet API, COM, DCOM, Windows trust verification (WinVerifyTrust) API, URL Monikers, Internet Component Download, URL Open Stream (UOS) functions, persistent URL cache functions, and the rest of the ActiveX SDK. Hidden in this mass of documentation is a wealth of power for Windows application development. This section summarizes some of the ActiveX SDK features about which you may want to learn more.

Simple Hyperlink Navigation API

The OLE hyperlinking specification defines a complete hyperlinking architecture for Microsoft Windows software and application content that includes system-wide history and favorites as well as other advanced features. The complete OLE hyperlinking functionality is overkill for many applications that just need to support a subset of hyperlinking functionality like that found on the Web. To address this situation, Microsoft has introduced a simple hyperlink navigation API. The function declarations for the simple hyperlink navigation API are shown below.

```
typedef enum tagHLNF {

        HLNF_INTERNALJUMP,

        HLNF_OPENINNEWWINDOW

        } HLNF;

HRESULT HlinkSimpleNavigateToString ([in] LPCWSTR szTarget, [in] LPCWSTR
szLocation, [in] LPCWSTR szTargetFrameName, [in] IUnknown* punk, [in]
IBindCtx* pbc, [in] IBindStatusCallback* pbsc, [in] DWORD grfHLNF,
[in] DWORD dwReserved);

HRESULT HlinkSimpleNavigateToMoniker ([in] IMoniker* pmkTarget, [in]
LPCWSTR szLocation, [in] LPCWSTR szTargetFrameName, [in] IUnknown*
punk, [in] IBindCtx* pbc, [in] IBindStatusCallback* pbsc, [in] DWORD
grfHLNF, [in] DWORD dwReserved);

HRESULT HlinkNavigateString ([in] IUnknown* punk, [in] LPCWSTR
szTarget);

HRESULT HlinkNavigateMoniker ([in] IUnknown* punk, [in] IMoniker*
pmkTarget);

HRESULT HlinkGoBack([in] IUnknown* punk);

HRESULT HlinkGoForward([in] IUnknown* punk);
```

WinVerifyTrust API

The Windows trust verification API centers around a single function: WinVerifyTrust.

The format of the WinVerifyTrust function is as follows:

```
HRESULT

WINAPI

WinVerifyTrust(

        HWND        hwnd,

        DWORD       dwTrustProvider,

        DWORD       dwActionID,

        LPVOID      ActionData,

        );
```

Internet Component Download

To enable software components to be retrieved, verified, and installed automatically from remote code repositories on the Internet, Microsoft has introduced a system service known as Internet Component Download.

The Internet Component Download service is used by Internet Explorer to enable the automatic download and execution of ActiveX controls and other components. Your applications can use this same service to provide a similar seamless Internet component retrieval. Component download services enable network applications to extend themselves dynamically and always operate with the newest version of critical application logic.

The Internet Component Download service is exposed to applications via a single API function, **CoGetClassObjectFromURL**. This system function is called by an application that wishes to download, verify, and install code. The function is used in Internet Explorer. The implementation uses URL Moniker to asynchronously download code, and it uses the WinVerifyTrust service to verify validity and authenticity of the code. **The CoGetClassObjectFromURL** API function is defined as follows:

```
STDAPI CoGetClassObjectFromURL ( [in] REFCLSID rclsid, [in] LPCWSTR szCodeURL,
[in] DWORD dwFileVersionMS, [in] DWORD dwFileVersionLS, [in] LPCWSTR
szContentTYPE, [in] LPBINDCTX pBindCtx, [in] DWORD dwClsContext, [in] LPVOID
pvReserved, [in] REFIID riid, [out] VOID **ppv );
```

To distribute a component through component download, you must prepare your component in a certain way and create an .INF setup script. Future releases will support "hooks" that allow custom setup handlers to interact with the component download and installation process. For example, the use of Win32 SetupX .INF files for installation would be a better approach to installation and setup. However, such scripts would need to be signed and authenticated, something that is not part of the current architecture for .INF installation scripts.

URL Open Stream Functions

The new URL Open Stream (UOS) functions introduced in the ActiveX SDK provide a very simple way for applications to deal with network data. Rather than working at the protocol level when sending or receiving data over the network, an application that uses UOS functions treats the data as a normal stream. Unlike other more complex interface negotiations, UOS functions require the programmer to have knowledge of no more than two COM interfaces: IStream and IBindStatusCallback.

To call a UOS function, you first implement an IBindStatusCallback interface and then call the UOS function. Certain UOS functions such as **URLOpenStream** and **URLOpenPullStream** require the calling entity to be on a thread that has a message loop. The UOS functions are declared as follows:

```
URLOpenStream(

LPUNKNOWN pCaller,

LPCWSTR szURL,

DWORD dwResv,

LPBINDSTATUSCALLBACK lpfnCB);


URLOpenBlockingStream(

LPUNKNOWN pCaller,

LPCWSTR szURL,

LPSTREAM *ppStream,

DWORD dwResv,

LPBINDSTATUSCALLBACK lpfnCB);


URLDownloadToFile(
```

```
    LPUNKNOWN pCaller,

    LPCWSTR szURL,

    LPCTSTR szFileName,

    DWORD dwResv,

    LPBINDSTATUSCALLBACK lpfnCB);


    URLOpenPullStream(

    LPUNKNOWN pCaller,

    LPCWSTR szURL,

    DWORD dwResv,
    LPBINDSTATUSCALLBACK lpfnCB);


    URLOpenHttpStream(
    LPUOSHTTPINFO * lphttpInfo );
```

WinInet Win32 Internet Functions

The Microsoft Win32 Internet functions provide Windows applications
with a higher-level interface to Internet functionality, including the Gopher,
FTP, and HTTP protocols. Initially, the Win32 Internet functions are distributed as WININET.DLL, but they will eventually be included standard in
all Microsoft operating systems. The WinInet functions are summarized in
the following table:

WinInet Function	Description
InternetOpen	Initializes the application's use of the Win32 Internet functions.
InternetOpenUrl	Begins retrieving an FTP, Gopher, or HTTP URL.
InternetReadFile	Reads URL data.
InternetSetFilePointer	Sets the position for the next read in a file.

WinInet Function	Description
InternetCloseHandle	Stops reading data from the URL. Can also com-plete the application's use of the Win32 Internet functions.
InternetSetStatusCallback	Sets a callback function that is called with status information.
InternetQueryOption	Queries the setting of an Internet option.
InternetSetOption	Sets an Internet option.
InternetCrackUrl	Parses a URL string into components.
InternetCreateUrl	Creates a URL string from components.
InternetCanonicalizeUrl	Converts a URL to a canonical form.
InternetCombineUrl	Combines base and relative URLs.
InternetErrorDlg	Displays predefined dialog boxes for common Internet error conditions.
InternetConfirmZoneCrossing	Checks for changes between secure and non-secure URLs.
InternetTimeFromSystemTime	Formats a date and time according to the specified RFC format.
InternetConnect	Opens an FTP, Gopher, or HTTP session with a server.
FtpFindFirstFile	Starts file enumeration in the current directory.
InternetFindNextFile	Continues file enumeration.
FtpGetFile	Retrieves an entire file from the server.
FtpPutFile	Writes an entire file to the server.
FtpDeleteFile	Deletes a file on the server.
FtpRenameFile	Renames a file on the server.
FtpOpenFile	Initiates access to a file on the server for either reading or writing.
InternetQueryDataAvailable	Queries the amount of data available.
InternetWriteFile	Writes data to an open file.

WinInet Function	Description
InternetCloseHandle	Ends a read or write operation to or from a remote file. Can also close an FTP, Gopher, or HTTP session.
FtpCreateDirectory	Creates a new directory on the server.
FtpRemoveDirectory	Deletes a directory on the server.
FtpSetCurrentDirectory	Changes the client's current directory on the server.
FtpGetCurrentDirectory	Returns the client's current directory on the server.
InternetGetLastResponseInfo	Retrieves the text of the server's response to the FTP command.
GopherFindFirstFile	Starts enumerating a Gopher directory listing.
GopherOpenFile	Starts retrieving a Gopher object.
GopherCreateLocator	Forms a Gopher locator for use in other Gopher function calls.
GopherGetAttribute	Retrieves attribute information on the Gopher object.
AuthenticateUser	Called on receipt of an HTTP "Access Denied" to verify a challenge.
PreAuthenticateUser	This function determines what authentication header may be needed, and returns it.
UnloadAuthenticateUser	Indicates the completion of an HTTP session.
HttpOpenRequest	Opens an HTTP request handle.
HttpAddRequestHeaders	Adds HTTP request headers to the HTTP request handle.
HttpSendRequest	Sends the specified request to the HTTP server.
HttpQueryInfo	Queries information about an HTTP request.

WinInet Function	Description
InternetGetCookie	Returns cookies for the specified URL and all its parent URLs.
InternetSetCookie	Sets a cookie on the specified URL.
CommitUrlCacheEntry	Caches data in the specified file in the cache storage and associates it with the given URL.
CreateUrlCacheEntry	Allocates requested cache storage and creates a local filename for saving the cache entry corresponding to the source name.
GetUrlCacheEntryInfo	Retrieves information about a cache entry.
ReadUrlCacheEntryStream	Reads the cached data from a stream that has been opened using the function **RetrieveUrlCacheEntryStream**.
RetrieveUrlCacheEntryFile	Retrieves a cache entry from the cache in the form of a file.
RetrieveUrlCacheEntryStream	Provides the most efficient and implementation independent way of accessing the cache data.
SetUrlCacheEntryInfo	Sets the specified members of the INTERNET_CACHE_ENTRY_INFO structure.
UnlockUrlCacheEntryFile	Unlocks the cache entry that was locked while the file was retrieved for use from the cache.
UnlockUrlCacheEntryStream	Closes the stream that has been retrieved using the **RetrieveUrlCacheEntryStream** function.
DeleteUrlCacheEntry	Removes the file associated with the source name from the cache, if the file exists.

WinInet Function	Description
FindCloseUrlCache	Closes the specified enumeration handle.
FindFirstUrlCacheEntry	Begins the enumeration of the cache.
FindNextUrlCacheEntry	Retrieves the next entry in the cache.

WebPost API

The WebPost Software Development Kit (SDK) allows authoring tools to easily send files to a Web site in order to publish those files. WebPost API functions allow applications to connect to the Internet Service Provider (ISP), determine the protocol needed to copy the files, and deliver the files to the server for publishing.

The WebPost dynamic-link library (DLL) can post Web pages to some of the po-pular types of Internet servers, including the National Center for Supercomputing Applications' (NCSA's) and Microsoft's Internet Information Server (IIS). To post to other types of Internet servers, the WebPost API uses the WebPost Service Provider Interface (SPI) to communicate with DLLs that "know how" to post Web pages to those servers. The WebPost API includes the following functions:

WebPost API Function	Description
WpDeleteSite	Deletes a friendly site name that has been configured.
WpListSites	Retrieves a list of the friendly site names that the user has configured.
WpPost	Posts a file name to the URL at a given site. If the URL and site name are set to NULL, the function starts a wizard that asks the user to choose or set up a URL and site.

WebPost API Function	Description
WpBindToSite	Returns a COM object to the WebPost service provider that supports the given site name or URL.
WpPostFile	An OLE automation-enabled and very similar to WpPost. The major difference is that **WpPostFile** can only post one file or directory at a time.

The WebPost SDK also includes a Service Provider Interface (SPI) that is used by developers who create custom interfaces for sending files to other Web servers. The WebPost SPI functions are as follows:

WebPost SPI Function	Description
AddWizardPages	Allows the provider DLLs to plug pages into the wizard invoked by the WpPost function.
Commit	Ensures that all the files posted to this server with the **PostFiles** function are actually written to the Internet server.
DeleteFile	Deletes the given file from the destination site.
FindClose	Closes the specified search handle.
FindFirstFile	Searches a directory for a file whose name matches the specified file name on the destination site identified.
FindNextFile	Continues a file search from a previous call to the **FindFirstFile** function.
GetError	Retrieves additional information about an error.
GetParam	Retrieves the configuration parameters for this site.

WebPost SPI Function	Description
GetSiteInfo	Retrieves the site information for the current object.
NetworkConnect	Connects to the Internet. Initiates modem dial if necessary.
NetworkDisconnect	Disconnects from the Internet (hang-up if a dial-up connection was used).
PostFiles	Posts files to the specified URL on the destination site identified by this object.
ServerLogin	Logs the user on to the Internet server. The given user name and password are for the Internet server.
ServerLogout	Logs the user out of the Internet server.
SetParam	Sets a configuration parameter for a given site.

Internet Ratings API

The Internet Ratings API provides Win32-based applications with an easy way to support PICS-based Internet ratings. Through the Ratings API, application software can provide full Internet ratings features to the end-user in a way that is compatible with the standard for content rating on the Internet. The following table summarizes the PICS Internet Ratings API functions:

Ratings API Function	Description
RatingObtainQuery	Obtains ratings from certain locations and compares them.
RatingObtainCancel	Cancels a call to RatingObtainQuery.
RatingCheckUserAccess	Takes in a PICS rating, parses it, and compares it against what a specified user can see.
RatingAccessDeniedDialog	Displays a system dialog informing the user that access has been denied.

Ratings API Function	Description
RatingFreeDetails	Frees a pointer to denial information.
RatingGetSupervisorOverride	Requests override by a supervisor user.
RatingIsUserSupervisor	Returns Boolean value for whether a given user is a supervisor (Nashville only).
RatingEnabledQuery	Specifies whether ratings are on or off.

This chapter explains the new ActiveX architecture for building active Web applications and creating next-generation Windows software. The ActiveX SDK is a huge extension to the Windows operating system, one that provides Internet application developers with unparalleled functionality for creating active applications. With all this new functionality now available, and with a good deal of it provided only for backwards compatibility with older Web technology, it's important to take the time to develop a good strategy for application and content development before jumping in to a large project.

3

WEB SITE DEVELOPMENT AND PUBLISHING

The proper tools are an absolute necessity for creating impressive Internet applications and cutting-edge content on your Web site. Today, the requirements of sophisticated Web developers range from HTML creation and editing to link management and administration of complex Web sites. Microsoft's FrontPage software is the answer to these needs. FrontPage is a client/server tool that will become one of your main Web site development and maintenance resources. It not only gives you administrative capabilities, but even provides a Personal Web Server that you can use to serve, or just test, your own Web pages.

Today's Web developer is faced with many choices for HTML authoring, Web site management, and content deployment tools. Microsoft's FrontPage is challenged by products offered by Netscape as part of their LiveWire tool suite, and by products created by other independent software vendors who are also building sophisticated Web site developer tools. As you'll discover throughout this book and in your work with ActiveX technology, the line between the Web developer and the seasoned application programmer is blurring. At the same time, the line between the Internet and the operating system is also blurring; as technology like ActiveX begins to replace the static content of the old World Wide Web with a new Internet landscape full of serious business, productivity, entertainment, and communications software. Choosing the right tool for creating Web applications is an important endeavor. As Internet development becomes more complex, the time it takes to create and maintain your applications is increasing at an amazing rate.

Like the Netscape LiveWire tool suite, Microsoft FrontPage consists of several programs that work together as a cohesive Web page authoring and deployment environment. FrontPage includes the following software tools:

- *FrontPage Editor.* Use the editor to easily create and edit your Web pages with its point-and-click toolbar capabilities and WYSIWYG (What-You-See-Is-What-You-Get) user interface. FrontPage Editor is similar in scope and function to the Netscape Navigator Gold editor environment.

- *FrontPage Explorer.* Monitor and fix any problem hyperlinks that exist on your Web site, while also allowing collaborative administration and authoring. Netscape's site manager product performs some of the same functions as the FrontPage Explorer.

- *FrontPage Personal Web Server.* Within minutes of installing the FrontPage software, you can provide your own Web pages on an intranet or the Internet. The Personal Web Server is a valuable development tool for testing your Web pages on a personal server before posting them on your primary server.

- *FrontPage Server Administrator.* The Administrator program lets you modify the network characteristics of your server system.

- *FrontPage TCP/IP Test.* Test and monitor the TCP/IP characteristics of your system using the TCP/IP Test program.

Use FrontPage to simplify the creation and administration of your traditional Web sites based on HTML and static content. Then, invest the time that you saved by using FrontPage to develop exciting active content and real Internet applications. In no time at all, your HTML-based Web site will fade into the background and your ActiveX-based Internet presence will merge with the other network computing resources used by your audience to create a truly compelling Internet experience.

FrontPage Editor

The days of manually writing HTML code are over. No longer do you have to use your reliable Notepad accessory for creating Web content. FrontPage Editor is one of the best tools currently available for creating and editing HTML-based Web content. FrontPage Editor not only incorporates the most current HTML extensions in WYSIWYG buttons and menu commands, but it also lets you integrate predesigned functions. Now in seconds, you can modify text, insert images, or change hyperlinks. Here is a list of just some of the capabilities of FrontPage Editor:

- Edit the color and size of text with simple point-and-click capability
- Enter form fields such as radiobuttons and drop-down menu boxes using the toolbar
- Insert and edit tables
- Create and edit hyperlinks with a simple point-and-click of the mouse
- Use templates to instantly create personalized Web pages
- Insert WebBots with preconfigured capabilities

When you are editing Web pages, you can load them either from your local system or from any location on the Internet. Of course, to edit a Web page from an Internet location, you must be connected to the Internet. Figure 3.1 shows an example of a Web page loaded in the FrontPage Editor window.

Anyone who has used other HTML editors or even basic Windows-type word processors will be able to quickly create content with FrontPage Editor. Most of the buttons on the toolbar clearly define their function, and anyone familiar with HTML can immediately begin using the link, table, and text editor features. Those who have worked with visual development tools such as Visual Basic or PowerBuilder will also recognize the FrontPage Editor's visual layout method for adding forms to Web pages.

FrontPage Editor does have several very useful and non-obvious features. These include predefined Web page templates, point-and-click image

■■■■■ **Figure 3.1** Use the WYSIWYG toolbar to quickly edit your Web pages.

hotspot editing, and the addition of WebBots for the simple creation of search engines and other powerful Web site extensions.

Templates

There is no point to developing something that people have developed many times before. This philosophy has led to the template feature built in to FrontPage Editor. You can create simple Web pages in minutes using some of the predesigned templates available in FrontPage Editor. Simply choose the **File|New** menu command. The window that appears is illustrated in Figure 3.2.

There are over 25 different templates that you can choose from to generate Web pages. Here are some examples of the different templates available:

- Table of Contents
- Survey Form

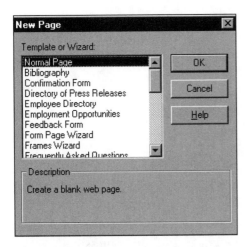

▮▮▮▮▮▮ **Figure 3.2** Select the desired template, or select Normal Page to begin with a blank Web page.

- Frequently Asked Questions
- Press Release
- Employee Directory

When you choose a template, the Web page that is created already contains the required content and style. All you have to do is customize the content for your particular needs, inserting specifics such as page title, and custom information. For those developers who need to create an entire Web site in a very short amount of time, the FrontPage template capability is an ideal solution. When you want to start with a "clean slate," choose the Normal template. The new Web page that is created will not have any predesigned content, giving you the freedom to create whatever you want.

Image HotSpots

You've seen it on numerous Web sites. Different areas of an image on a Web page link to different locations. These different active image areas are often referred to as "hotspots" or as a "clickable image map." FrontPage Editor has several features for adding hotspots to the images on Web pages. After you insert an image into your Web page, select the image. At that point, the hotspot buttons become active. Click on one of the hotspot shapes:

- Rectangle
- Circular
- Polygon

Draw the shape of your hotspot right on the image. No more guessing coordinates. After you've drawn the shape of the hotspot on the image, the Create Link window opens, allowing you to specify the type of link and location URL. Once you've created a hotspot, the link should be displayed in the bottom-left corner of the FrontPage Editor window when you pass your mouse pointer over the hotspot. When you have incorporated several hotspots within the same image, you may want to click on the **Highlight Hotspots** button. The image should disappear, revealing only the size and location of the hotspots you've created. You can appreciate this feature even more by realizing that you created the following HTML code within seconds. Let's see someone do that in Notepad!

```
BOT=ImageMap
   default="/misc/top.map"
   rectangle=" (175,34) (420, 92)  http://www.cnet.com"
   circle=" (45,22) 22  http://www.science.org"
   src="/images/home_igloo.jpg"
   alt="WELCOME TO DON's WORLD"
   align="bottom"
   border="0"
   width="468"
   height="107"
   ISMAP
```

Notice that there is no need to build a back-end CGI script in order to implement this clickable image map. In the past, a CGI script needed to be deployed on your Web site to process user selections from within hotspot-enabled images. With HotSpots, all of the intelligence is built into the HTML source code of your Web page.

WebBot

"Keep it simple, stupid" is a saying often heralded as the secret of successful products. It may sound condescending; but in the arena of Web development, this message rings loud and clear. No Web developer of any skill level wants to spend hours programming when the same objective can be achieved with a few mouse clicks. This realization may ultimately lead to the demise of HTML as Web developers turn to better technology such as ActiveX controls, which can be created using Visual Basic. Best of all, you can add new features not supported by the current version of the HTML standard and create custom Web page features—all without attending a single Internet standards committee meeting or asking your Web visitors to upgrade their browsers to be able to view your new HTML source code properly.

Microsoft recognizes the large install-base of existing HTML-based Web browsers and understands the need for many Web sites to continue to support HTML as long as people on the Internet are using HTML browsers. To this end, they have added powerful WebBot capability to FrontPage Editor to eliminate the need for laborious HTML programming. Using this utility, you can quickly add predesigned WebBot components that are built in to the FrontPage Editor. WebBots function in conjunction with server extensions for maximum compatibility with client-side HTML interpretation built in to older browsers. For example, with WebBots you can:

- Add a search tool to your Web site that allows users to search for keywords throughout all of the Web pages.
- Place an image in your Web pages that will appear on a particular date, and disappear at some other designated time without ever having to worry about it. Now your Web pages won't be filled with little "New" icons on products and press releases that are a year old.
- Insert scripting code, such as VBScript or JavaScript, or add actual HTML code for unsupported or new tags.

These capabilities and more can be added in seconds. Select the **Insert|Bot** menu command to display the WebBots that are available for insertion into your Web pages (Figure 3.3).

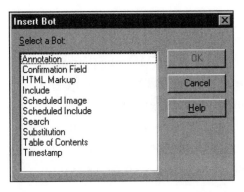

▰▰▰▰▰ **Figure 3.3** Add WebBots with preconfigured capabilities to your Web page.

As you edit Web pages, you can also quickly recognize existing WebBots. When your mouse pointer is over a WebBot, a robot-like image appears next to your pointer. Some of the more useful WebBots include HTML Markup, Annotation, Scheduled Image, and Search.

▰▰▰▰▰ **TIP**

When you save a Web page that contains a WebBot, it is saved in two versions: one with the WebBots expanded into the HTML, and the other with the WebBots in a source code form consisting of a list of name-value pairs. The expanded HTML version is stored in the main source directory, and it is the version that is retrieved and displayed by the browser. The source code form is placed in the _vti_shm_ directory on your server and is compiled by the FrontPage Server Extensions when the Web page is provided.

▰▰▰▰

HTML Markup

As you know, HTML is far from a static language. In fact, while you are reading this, companies are implementing new HTML tags that are a long time away from becoming standardized. The HTML Markup WebBot gives you a great deal of flexibility when designing your Web site. Use it to write the HTML code for tags that aren't yet implemented in the current version of FrontPage Editor. The HTML Markup tag also lets you include VBScript or JavaScript in the Web pages you create.

To use the HTML Markup WebBot, select the **Insert|Bot** menu command, and then select HTML Markup. In the window that appears, write the HTML code, as you would in Notepad or whatever HTML editor you previously used. Figure 3.4 shows the HTML Markup window containing the HTML code needed to place an ActiveX control on a Web page.

The HTML Markup WebBots that are placed in the FrontPage Editor window appear as yellow squares with the symbols <?> on them.

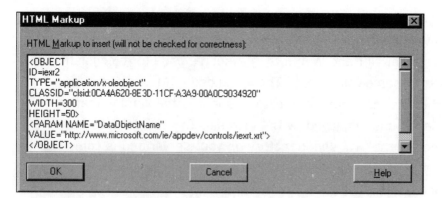

■■■■■■■ **Figure 3.4** Enter the entire HTML source code from the beginning to the end tag.

Annotation

The Annotation WebBot feature is useful for producing text that will appear only when the user is editing the Web page, but not when the Web page is displayed in a browser environment. You can see an example of the Annotation WebBot whenever you create a Web page using one of the predesigned templates. The Annotation text tells you what you need to change to customize the Web page for your own application.

Scheduled Image

The Scheduled Image WebBot is a handy way to highlight a new product or feature on your Web page while ensuring the image is removed at a specified time in the future. Activate the Scheduled Image Bot properties window shown in Figure 3.5 by selecting the **Insert|Bot** menu command.

Add the desired image file, and preset the period of time the image should be visible. Then worry no longer that your company's year-old product is still labeled as "released today" on one of your Web pages. The scheduled image automatically disappears from your Web site when the expiration date arrives. Aren't you looking forward to the day when Microsoft offers a

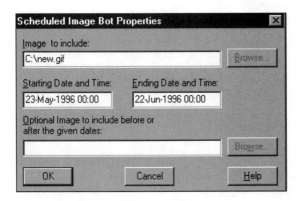

■■■■■■■ **Figure 3.5** Select the image and the dates that you want the image visible on the Web page.

similar feature in kitchen appliances that will link your refrigerator to your trash compactor so that spoiled food items can be disposed of automatically?

Search

As Web sites continue to grow in size, helping visitors to the site quickly find what they want is increasingly important. The Search WebBot lets you place this search capability on your Web site within seconds. Users can then type in a keyword in which they are interested, and click **Search Site**. The search form looks through all the Web pages that constitute the particular *WEB*. When you are using the FrontPage software, mainly FrontPage Explorer, a conventional Web site that consists of at least one Web page is referred to as a WEB. The results are then displayed below the search form. To place the Search WebBot on your site, select the **Insert|Bot** menu command and then choose Search. The window shown in Figure 3.6 opens.

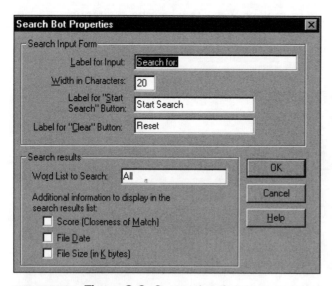

■■■■■■ **Figure 3.6** Customize the appearance and operational characteristics of the Search WebBot.

Modify the Search Bot Properties window to change the labels on the text fields and buttons. You can even customize what information will be displayed as the results of a search. Once you have finished customizing the Search WebBot, it will be added automatically to your Web page. Here is a sample of the HTML code that is generated when you insert a Search WebBot into one of your Web pages.

```
<form action="../_vti_bin/shtml.exe/_private/style.htm"
 method="POST">
<input type="hidden" name="VTI-GROUP" value="0">
<p><b>Search for: </b><input type="text" name="search"
size="20" value></p>
<p><input type="submit" value="Start Search"><input
 type="reset" value="Reset"></p>
</form>
```

When a user accesses the Search form, they enter search key words. Results of the query are then displayed, as shown in Figure 3.7.

The Search WebBot is a virtual necessity to a Web site of any significant size. Users will thank you a million times over for taking a few seconds to add this simple utility. If providing content that is compatible with HTML browsers is important to you, then WebBots have a lot to offer to speed up the creation of your Web pages. However, it's important to note that Microsoft has converted a number of the features supplied by WebBots into ActiveX controls. Whenever possible, switch from HTML authoring to ActiveX authoring to break free from the constraints of old, static Web technology.

FrontPage Explorer

You click a hyperlink on a Web page, and you are magically transported to . . . nowhere. Yes, once again you have hit on a broken hyperlink.

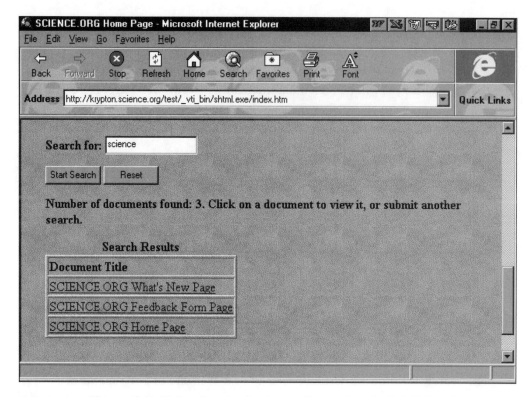

Figure 3.7 Enter the desired search word and click **Start Search** to begin a query.

Hyperlinks have proven to be a useful and powerful capability that has brought about information interconnection on the Internet; but in an environment that is growing and changing daily, hyperlinks can prove to be a series of dead ends. FrontPage Explorer gives you a simple way to check the hyperlink integrity of your WEB. This utility checks to make certain that none of the hyperlinks on your Web pages end up being dead ends. In addition to the ability to monitor hyperlink integrity, FrontPage Explorer has numerous other capabilities that allow you to manage and edit your WEB, including:

- Visually inspecting the hyperlink integrity of your WEB
- Modifying a broken file link in one Web page, with FrontPage then updating the other pages
- Collaborative WEB development and management

A few of the FrontPage Explorer features require the installation of server extensions. Think of your Web server not as a static server program, but as a software agent that works on your behalf to communicate with the rest of the network. With this perspective, it seems natural that your communications agent should grow in its abilities, not only enhancing its ability to communicate with others but also acquiring new methods of interacting with you and your company.

Be on the lookout for server extensions that will add new dimensions to your Internet presence. Server extensions can make the Internet publishing experience more interactive not only for your audience but for you as well as you develop a working relationship with your intelligent information server. With the right server extensions, we may see a day when the information server-turned-Chairman-of-the-Board monitors all servers for a particular industry and makes decisions for you about your Web site or the kind of products your company should produce.

Server Extensions

Before you can use FrontPage Explorer to administer your Web site, you need to install the server extensions with your current HTTP server. You must have the HTTP server and the FrontPage software installed before you can install the server extensions. FrontPage already has the server extensions for the Personal Web Server along with the following server extensions built in:

- Netscape Communications Server v1.12 for Windows NT

- Netscape Commerce Server for Windows NT
- O'Reilly WebSite 1.1 for Windows 95 and Windows NT

You can also download server extensions that are available for several other HTTP servers, including:

- Windows NT Server
- Solaris 2.4
- HP/UX 9.03
- IRIX 5.3
- SunOS 4.1.3

Download the server extensions for your particular operating system from: *http://www.microsoft.com/frontpage/*

After installing the server extensions, you are ready to use the full capabilities of the FrontPage Explorer to administer the WEBs on your HTTP server.

■■■■■■■ **TIP**

You can still use FrontPage to post an entire WEB or individual Web pages to a HTTP server that doesn't have the server extensions installed. Download the Publishing Wizard provided by Microsoft from this URL:

`http://www.microsoft.com/frontpage`

The Publishing Wizard checks the Web pages you edit and create with FrontPage to ensure that they will work on an HTTP server that doesn't have the server extensions installed.

■■■■■

Hyperlink Integrity

Many current Web sites have hundreds of different hyperlinks to both *internal* and *external* locations. An internal hyperlink would be to a Web page found at the same IP address as the Web page referencing it, while an external hyperlink is to a Web page located on a computer system with a different IP address. The management of large WEBs is made simple with FrontPage Explorer's visual link integrity display. Load a WEB, and click on the **Link View** button. Figure 3.8 shows FrontPage Explorer with the Link View option activated.

In the example shown in Figure 3.8, you can see how the visual environment displays broken local links as a broken page, such as the

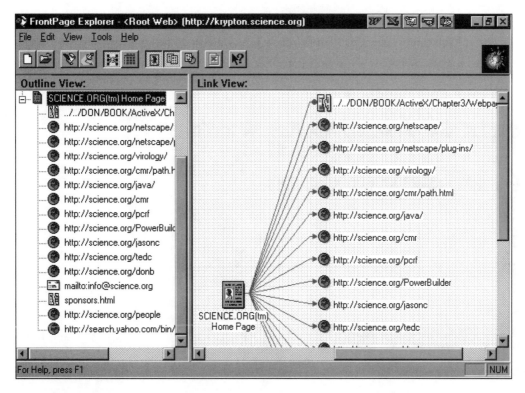

Figure 3.8 FrontPage Explorer allows you to visually inspect the hyperlinks on your Web site.

sponsors.html document, while remote links are represented by a world icon.

FrontPage Explorer also has several buttons on its toolbar that allow you to view different hyperlink information on a particular WEB, including:

- Summary view
- Image links
- Repeated links
- Links inside the page

With FrontPage, you can easily verify both the internal and external links on a Web page. Select the **Tools|Verify** Links menu command, and the Verify Links window shown in Figure 3.9 opens.

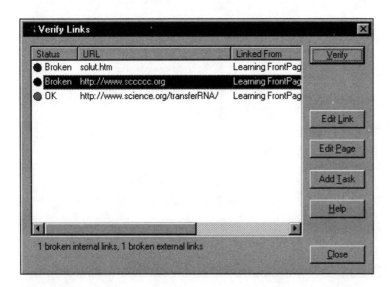

Figure 3.9 Click on the **Verify** button to check the external links.

In the Verify Links window, broken internal links will be shown first. Any internal links that are good will not be displayed in this window. When you click on the **Verify** button, FrontPage Explorer tests the external links. Before an external link is tested, it appears with a yellow dot. After it has been tested, the external link either appears with a red dot and is labeled Broken, or it has a green dot and is labeled OK.

When you do find a Web page with a broken link, you need only seconds to fix it. Highlight the link you want to fix, and click on the Edit Link button. In the window that opens, you can enter the correct link information. Because the same link may appear throughout a WEB, you also have the option to have this link modified in all your other Web pages. This feature can save you many hours of frustrated testing, and will save the viewers of your Web page from hitting broken links.

Collaborative WEB Management

As WEBs grow larger, and larger, the need to have more than one person working on the same site becomes more essential. The FrontPage Explorer is designed to easily allow several people to administer and manage a WEB. Permissions can be designated for several different types of individuals when you select the Tools|Permissions menu command, which opens the Web Permissions window. Here are the three types of users for which permissions can be set:

- Administrators
- Authors
- End users

When you want to designate the permissions for different administrators and authors for a specific WEB, you must first select the **User unique permissions for this web** radiobutton found in the Settings folder. Then click the **Apply** button, and you are ready to assign new permissions.

Another important feature necessary for collaboration is the To Do List. You can specify tasks and the individuals that should do them using the **To Do List.** Click on the **Show To Do List** button in the FrontPage Explorer toolbar to access this useful collaboration feature (see Figure 3.10).

When you add a task to the To Do List, you can specify a description of what needs to be done, by whom, and at what level of priority. When a task is completed, you can delete the task or mark it completed. The To Do List is a useful tool for organizing the management of your Web site.

FrontPage Personal Web Server

The release of the FrontPage Personal Web Server gives an important glimpse into the future of the Internet. Now anyone with a personal computer can provide their own active Internet content. At the same time we are seeing many Internet service providers such as AT&T and Netcom offer unlimited Internet access for only $19.95/month. Now people can leave their computer connected to the Internet all of the time.

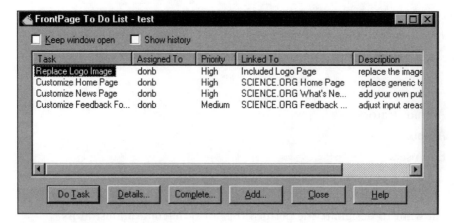

■■■■■■■ **Figure 3.10** Add or remove tasks as they are completed.

Developments such as Internet servers for personal computers combined with unlimited, and ever-increasing, bandwidth to the home will soon bring about the next generation of the Internet and all the opportunities associated with it.

Using the FrontPage Personal Web Server, you are on your way to providing Web pages right from your own desktop computer running Windows 95. Once you have FrontPage installed, simply run the Personal Web Server program. When you start the Personal Web server the window shown in Figure 3.11 opens.

That's all you need to do. Now you are providing content on the Web. Assuming that you have already set up your TCP/IP connection on your intranet or the Internet, the Personal Server Program simply uses this pre-existing information to correctly set up your new server capability. People can

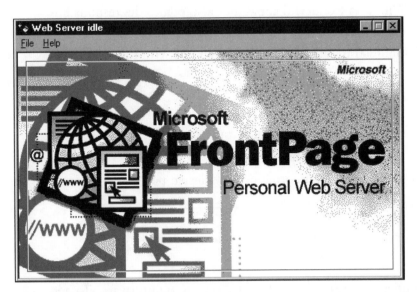

■■■■■ **Figure 3.11** Publish Web pages right from the desktop using Personal Web Server.

now contact you using the domain name of your computer or your IP address. Contact your own Personal Web Server using a Web browser from the same machine by typing your domain name or your IP address. After you successfully contact the Personal Web Server, you will see that the only Web page you are currently providing is the *default.html* file that comes with the program. Add other Web pages you want to publish through the Web to the folder:

```
C:\FrontPage Webs\Content
```

In addition to using the Personal Web Server to provide information on the Internet or corporate intranets, you can also use it to test your Web pages before publishing them through your primary Corporate Web server.

FrontPage Server Administrator

For some users of FrontPage, this may be the first time that you are running a server. With this wonderful capability also comes the responsibility of administration. The Server Administrator is available for you to monitor and administrate your FrontPage programs with the following capabilities:

- Designating users that have administration privileges
- Installing new server extensions
- Enabling or disabling authoring on the selected port

Running the Server Administrator launches the window shown in Figure 3.12.

The administrative features of FrontPage are very straightforward. To add, remove, or edit users to the list of administrators, click on the **Security**

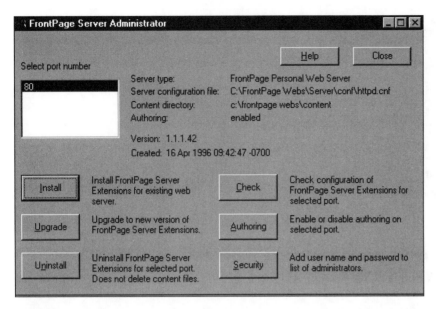

Figure 3.12 Click any one of the buttons in this window to access administration features.

button. The ability to install, upgrade, or uninstall server extensions is another administrative feature included as well. If you get lost, simply click the **Help** button.

FrontPage TCP/IP Test

Believe it or not, sometimes things don't always work correctly. When you installed FrontPage, the program should have determined the configured TCP/IP network characteristics of your system. FrontPage provides the TCP/IP test to quickly display these network characteristics and test to make sure they're correct. (See Figure 3.13.)

The FrontPage TCP/IP Test utility is a useful tool for other situations as well. Any time that you need information about the TCP/IP networking configuration on any Windows-based PC, you can run this utility.

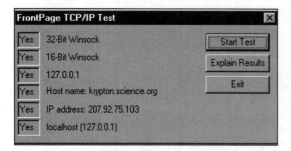

■■■■■■■ **Figure 3.13** Click on **Start Test** to quickly check your TCP/IP connection.

Internet Information Server (IIS)

The Microsoft Internet Information Server provides a high-performance and feature-rich server architecture with an integrated HTTP, FTP, and Gopher server. Through the addition of ISAPI modules (discussed in Chapter 9 of this book) and by virtue of the ActiveX and distributed COM computing technologies themselves, the Internet Information Server can be extended in a variety of ways. The next few sections introduce this important server component of the ActiveX Internet platform.

Installing IIS is a straightforward process with few pitfalls. After you have successfully installed IIS and rebooted the computer, the three servers launch automatically as part of Windows NT system services. To simplify management and detailed configuration of IIS, a software tool called the Internet Service Manager is provided by Microsoft.

As you can see in Figure 3.14, the Internet Service Manager window contains VCR buttons useful for starting, stopping, or pausing the selected service. To modify the service properties at a more detailed level for one of the services, double-click on the computer name for the service of

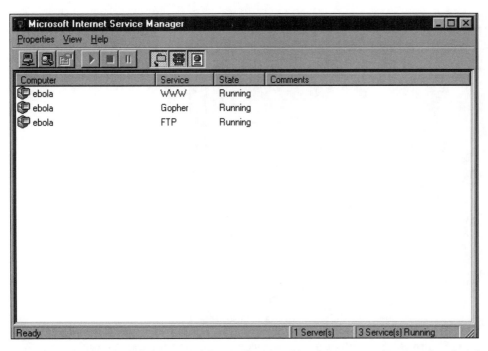

Figure 3.14 Use Internet Service Manager to set properties for the Information Server.

interest. Another window opens, like the one shown in Figure 3.15, that corresponds to a WWW service, in which the detailed service properties can be configured for the selected service.

Using the WWW Service Properties window, you can select settings such as maximum simultaneous connections, anonymous access preferences, and timeout interval. In addition, through the **Directories, Logging,** and **Advanced** tabs, other elements of server operation can be configured. Figure 3.16 shows the **Directories** tab on the Properties window. The **Directories** tab provides access to a range of configuration options, including the set up of *virtual servers* and registration of file and directory aliases for Web sites.

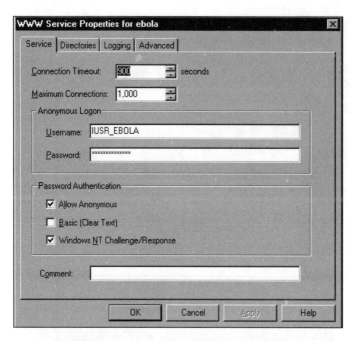

Figure 3.15 Configure Web service properties for the WWW Server.

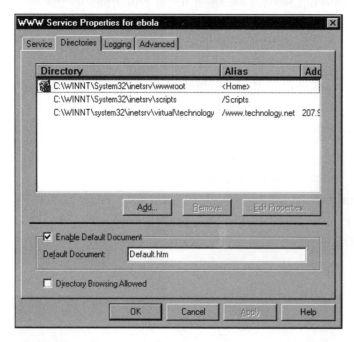

Figure 3.16 Add, edit, or remove directories for your Web server.

Creating virtual servers and configuring them through the **Directories** tab is explained later in this chapter. To add an entry to the Directory list, click on the **Add** button and fill out the form that appears on screen. Figure 3.17 shows the **Logging** tab for setting logging characteristics of IIS. Note that if you wish to log directly to a database, you can do so by clicking on the **Log to SQL/ODBC Database** radiobutton and supplying data source name, table name, user ID, and password. Consult the IIS documentation for more detailed instruction on logging onto database tables through ODBC.

The **Advanced** tab, shown in Figure 3.18, lets you configure security and usage settings. By default, IIS can deny access to every computer on the network except any you have specifically allowed. Restricting access to specific computers is a useful security feature for corporate intranets in which extra security is desired. The default mode, which grants access to all computers on

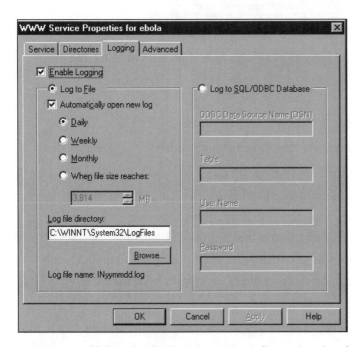

▬▬▬ **Figure 3.17** Enable and configure logging for all information services using the **Logging** tab.

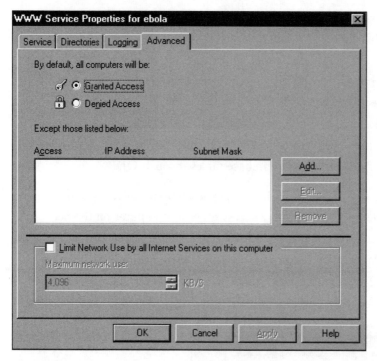

Figure 3.18 Control access restrictions and usage limits for the information server.

the network, should be acceptable for most intranet configurations, especially if the NT Server machine is behind a firewall.

Another useful feature of IIS advanced settings is the Limit Network Use threshold. By checking this box and selecting a threshold data rate from the drop-down list box, you can establish a maximum load level for the server that is based on the amount of network bandwidth being consumed. This feature acts like a governor on your site to keep it from becoming overloaded (every Webmaster's dream).

To configure Gopher service properties, return to the Internet Service Manager main window and select a Gopher server from the list. Either double-click on the server or choose from the Properties menu to access the window shown in Figure 3.19. The Gopher Service Properties window is similar to the one for WWW service properties, allowing you to set up timeout interval and maximum simultaneous connections. Verify that the Anonymous Logon user account is one with limited privileges on the system and enter a valid e-mail address for the service administrator.

To administer directory settings for the Gopher server, choose the **Directories** tab shown in Figure 3.20. Add, remove, or edit properties using this tab. Most often, the Gopher server will be configured to use the same directories as the FTP server. This is because Gopher's primary usefulness is to provide a simple and anonymous interface to the files in an FTP site. The default configuration suggested when you install IIS is to have a separate directory for FTP than you do for Gopher. Change the

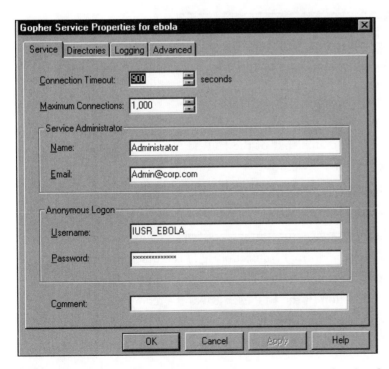

■■■■■■ **Figure 3.19** Change service properties for the Gopher server.

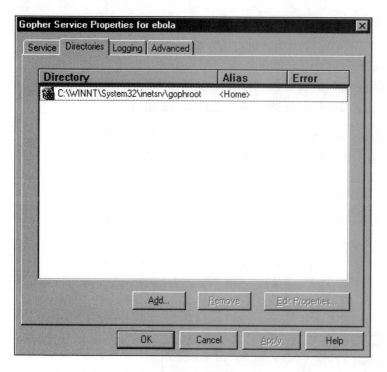

Figure 3.20 Select Gopher directories in the Gopher Properties window.

Gopher root directory to match that of the FTP server root directory using the Gopher Service Properties window.

FTP service properties are configured using the window shown in Figure 3.21. Again you see options for timeout interval and maximum simultaneous connections. For the FTP service, timeout interval is especially important. Unlike HTTP, for which the normal connection style is a quick file transfer followed by closing of the connection, FTP connections remain active until the user closes the connection. If the FTP user leaves the computer during a file transfer, the connection could remain open indefinitely. The Connection Timeout setting helps to avoid this problem by automatically shutting down

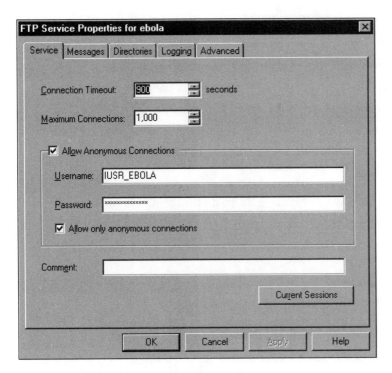

Figure 3.21 Prepare your FTP server for use by setting its service properties.

an FTP connection if the user doesn't issue a command for an extended period of time. To see all of the active FTP connections displayed, click on the **Current Sessions** button.

Notice also in Figure 3.21 that you can easily disable anonymous FTP access. Disabling anonymous FTP access is really a good idea. Instead of using your FTP server to provide files, use your Gopher server (with a different root directory than the FTP server) or configure the WWW service to allow directory navigation and provide files anonymously through the Web. Other configurations are possible, but consider reserving FTP for authorized users only.

Special directories can be added to the root directory of your FTP service to automatically alter the root directory as it is displayed to certain FTP users. User root directories must be physical subdirectories created in the FTP root directory. Any subdirectory that matches a username will be used as that user's root directory when they log in to the FTP server. This includes the Anonymous subdirectory, which can be used to display a different root directory for anonymous FTP users than for normal, or other, FTP users.

Use the **Messages** tab shown in Figure 3.22 to add informative messages that an FTP user will see as they access your FTP site. Welcome and Exit messages can be entered in the **Messages** tab as well as an error message

■■■■■■■■ **Figure 3.22** Add messages to provide FTP users with further instruction.

displayed when the maximum number of simultaneous connections is exceeded. In addition to these messages, a feature known as Directory Annotation can be enabled that will supply an FTP user with a different informative message for each directory on your FTP site. To enable Directory Annotation, do the following:

1. Create a file called *~ftpsvc~.ckm* in any directory for which you want to provide annotation.
2. Use the Windows NT explorer to make each *~ftpsvc~.ckm* file hidden.
3. Modify the Windows NT registry to add the following entry with a value of 1:

```
HKEY_LOCAL_MACHINE\SYSTEM\CurrentControlSet\Services\
MSFTPSVC\Parameters\AnnotateDirectories
```

The AnnotateDirectories entry is not added automatically to the NT registry. You'll have to add this entry manually and set it equal to 1 in order to activate Directory Annotation for your FTP server.

Use the FTP Service Properties window's **Directories** tab, shown in Figure 3.23, to configure directory information for the FTP server. You cannot create user subdirectories using the **Directories** tab; user subdirectories must be physical directories on the computer's hard drive.

If you make a change to the NT registry in the process of configuring IIS, you may need to restart the server in order for those changes to take effect. For complete instructions on administering IIS, see the online help provided with the product. The IIS online help can be terse at times, but most of its features are well documented.

One more software tool is provided with IIS that is important for configuring and administering security. The Key Manager, shown in Figure 3.24, lets

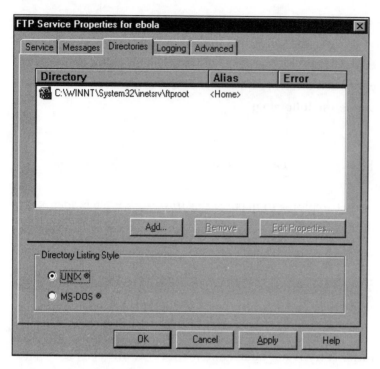

you generate and maintain Public Key/Private Key pairs for use in secure data communications.

In order to use the secure features of IIS, you must first generate and register a new key. Select the **Key|Create New Key** command to open the window shown in Figure 3.25. This window is used to generate a new key and a corresponding key request file that should be supplied to a Certificate Authority (CA) in order to register your server's public key. Note that this is not the same as a key escrow agent: the Certificate Request file does not contain your server's private key. When you register a server's public key with a Certificate Authority, it becomes an official, registered key that can be verified as authentic and belonging to your server.

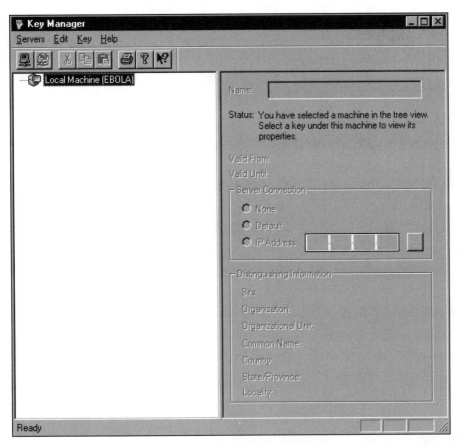

▬▬▬▬ **Figure 3.24** Administer Public Key/Private Key pairs with the IIS Key Manager.

In the field labeled Common Name, it is extremely important that you enter the fully qualified domain name of the Windows NT Server on which IIS is being run. The certificate supplied to you by a Certificate Authority incorporates reference to the domain name of the server for which the certificate is registered. This makes it possible for Web clients to quickly authenticate the secure server by comparing the domain name that appears in the current URL with the domain name embedded in the security certificate.

Create New Key and Certificate Request

Key Name: `New Key`	OK
Password: [ ] Bits: `1024` ▼	Cancel
	Help

Distinguishing Information

Organization: `Your Company`

Organizational Unit: `Your Unit`

Common Name: `Your Net Address`

Country: `US`

State/Province: `Your State`

Locality: `Your Locality`

Request File: `C:\New Key.req`   Browse...

■■■■■■ **Figure 3.25** Generate a new key pair for the Internet Information Server.

If a discrepancy exists, then the Web client is able to conclude that someone may be impersonating the organization whose certificate it received. One drawback to this arrangement is that a given certificate is good only for a single server. If you move your server to a new computer and give it a new domain name (say, www2.technology.net) then you must generate a new key pair and register once again with a CA to receive a new certificate.

After your new key and request file have been generated, instructions like those shown in Figure 3.26 appear on your screen. Follow these instructions to register your key and install the certificate supplied by your CA.

Figure 3.27 shows how the Key Manager displays keys for the selected server. Note that after you install the certificate supplied by your CA

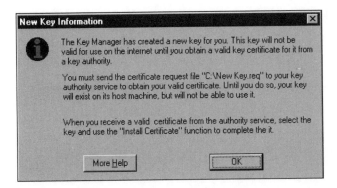

Figure 3.26 Follow the instructions displayed in New Key Information.

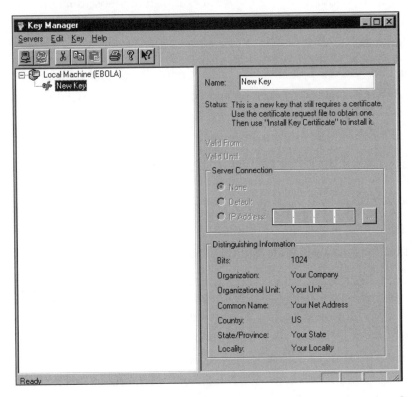

Figure 3.27 Keys are displayed for the Information Server.

(Certificate Authority), the key becomes active. Until then, the key is disabled and it appears with a red mark through it in the Key Manager window.

Now that your Internet Information Server is fully configured, there are several advanced features that you may wish to use immediately. Windows NT Server has the ability to assign multiple IP addresses to a single network adapter. This makes it possible for IIS to support a feature known as *virtual hosting*. When IIS is set up in virtual server mode, it can appear to host many Web sites rather than just one. For instance, your server might host a Web site for www.virtualcorporation.com as well as one for www.technology.net and one for www.research.org. Through virtual hosting, users see only the resources offered by the organization whose domain they contact. This creates the appearance that the organization has its own server on the Internet.

Setting up virtual hosting is simple. First, open the Control Panel and choose the Network applet. Select the **Protocols** tab and double-click on the TCP/IP Protocol line to access properties of the protocol. In the **IP Address** tab, click on the **Advanced** button to access the Advanced IP Addressing window shown in Figure 3.28. The Advanced window lets you configure up to five IP addresses for a single adapter. Click on the **Add** button to add new IP addresses to the list.

Enter the new IP address in the pop-up window that opens (see Figure 3.29) and enter a subnet mask as well. Note that the IP address you enter here must match the one configured on the DNS server that manages the domain for which you want to create a virtual server. Most often, the fully qualified domain name (FQDN) for the domain's Web server will include a WWW host name such as www.technology.net. Verify that the IP address entered is the one that corresponds to the WWW host and is not in use by another computer on the network. If you aren't the person who administers DNS for the domain in question, then you'll have to ask the DNS manager to do this for you and tell you what IP address to use for the virtual server.

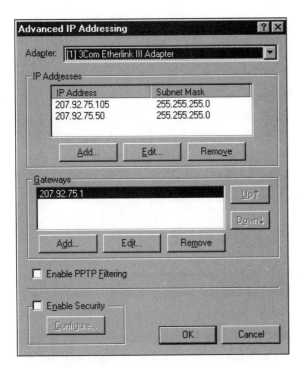

▬▬▬▬▬ **Figure 3.28** Keys are displayed for the Information Server.

To configure more than five IP addresses for a single adapter, you must edit the registry entry by hand using **Regedit**. Look for a registry entry like the following:

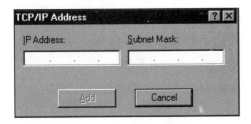

▬▬▬▬▬ **Figure 3.29** Enter an IP address for the virtual server and then click on the **Add** button.

HKEY_LOCAL_MACHINE\SYSTEM\CurrentControlSet\Services\<adapter>\Parameters\Tcpip

Enter each IP address to assign to the adapter separated by a space and enter each subnet mask in the same order as the IP addresses, also separated by spaces. After adding IP addresses to your TCP/IP configuration, you must reboot the computer so that the additional IP addresses will be configured properly. NT Server might not prompt you to do so, but without rebooting the additional IP addresses will not be bound to the selected network adapter. After rebooting, it's a good idea to attempt to ping the IP addresses you've added to make sure that they're alive and available on the network.

To configure IIS to support a virtual server, use the Internet Service Manager to modify WWW service properties. Select the **Directories** tab and click on the **Add** button to open the Directory Properties window shown in Figure 3.30. Enter the virtual server's fully qualified domain name in the Virtual Directory alias field and check the Virtual Server check box. Enter the virtual server's IP address and choose a directory in which to store files for the new Web site to complete the virtual server configuration.

Make sure that you put a *default.htm* file in the virtual server's directory before trying to connect to the server. When everything is configured correctly, your Internet Information Server will host multiple Web sites simultaneously. The only cost is the consumption of one of your unused IP addresses. Figure 3.31 shows the new www.technology.net home page being hosted by IIS as a virtual server.

Adding entries to the MIME types list of your Web server is a common requirement these days as new MIME content types emerge almost daily. In order to provide content such as multimedia presentations or new binary data formats to browsers that rely on MIME type identification, your Web server must have an entry for the MIME type and file extension used by the

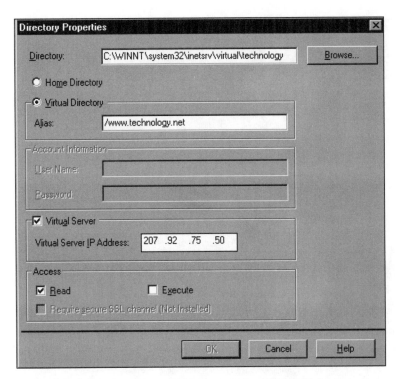

▰▰▰▰▰▰▰ **Figure 3.30** Finish configuring IIS as a virtual server by entering virtual directory properties.

data type. To update the MIME type list for IIS, use the Windows NT Registry to access the following setting:

```
HKEY_LOCAL_MACHINE\SYSTEM\CurrentControlSet\Services\InetInfo\Parameters\MimeMap
```

Figure 3.32 shows this registry entry being accessed in Regedit. The format for MimeMap entries is:

```
<mime type>,<filename extension>,,<gopher type>
```

One of the samples shown in Figure 3.32 is a MIME type entry for the standard HTML file format. It looks like this:

```
text/html,htm,,h
```

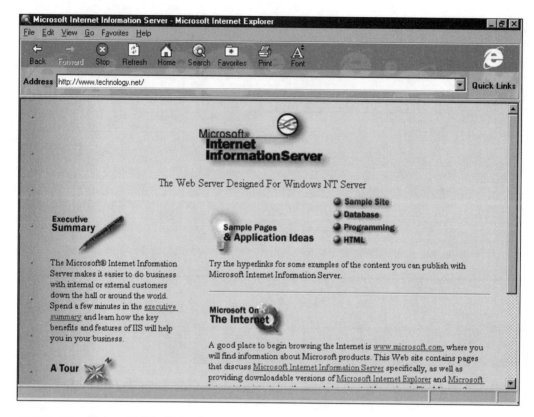

Figure 3.31 Virtual servers are a necessity if you need to host multiple Web sites.

Notice the double comma preceding the Gopher type identifier. This MIME type entry specifies that any file whose file extension is equal to *.htm* should be considered a text/html MIME type. This entry allows IIS to accurately identify the type of data being sent to a Web browser and increases the likelihood that the end user's Web browser will be able to handle the content gracefully.

The Internet Information Server is the core enabling tool for publishing in Microsoft's ActiveX Internet platform. IIS supports encryption standards

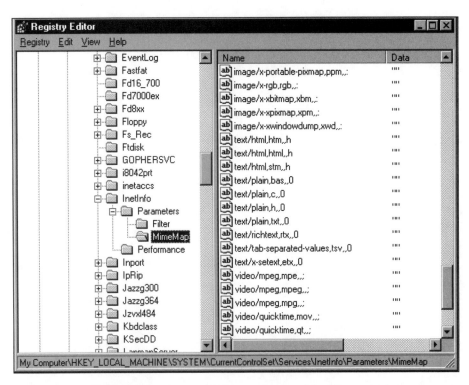

Figure 3.32 Every MIME type served by IIS must have an entry in the MimeMap registry.

like SSL and PCT to enable Internet commerce and features the performance and abilities of a high-end HTTP server. In addition, IIS presents an integrated set of SDKs meant to incorporate Internet publishing directly into the operating system. Later chapters in this book cover database integration with IIS, writing programs that use ISAPI, and making the most of operating system API additions that make it easier to provide resources on the Net.

4

ACTIVEX SCRIPTING

If you've ever put together airplane models, you know that you wouldn't get very far, or have very much fun, without the glue. Creating Web pages with ActiveX controls is much the same, only the glue is a scripting language that you use to glue the controls together in the same Web page.

Scripting languages are mini-programming languages designed to run in your Web browser. Quite often, scripting languages are based on full programming languages. If you've been involved with creating Web pages, you may have heard of JavaScript (for more information, check out the *Netscape LiveWire Sourcebook*), a scripting language based on the new programming language called Java. Microsoft created its own scripting language to help you bring your Web page to life, Visual Basic Script. Visual Basic Script (VBScript) is based on Microsoft's popular Visual Basic programming language. A scripting language, either JavaScript or VBScript, in combination with ActiveX controls is generically called ActiveX scripting.

Because this book addresses Microsoft technologies, this chapter focuses on VBScript.

Visual Basic Script is pretty easy to learn, even if you've never programmed. This book doesn't pretend to teach you to program. There are many good books on programming to help you get started if this chapter seems foreign to you. If you're programming for the first time, try the examples in this chapter. It should become really clear how everything works. Learning VBScript is a great introduction to learning other complete programming languages.

VBScript at Work

VBScript is added to the HTML of your Web page to enhance its abilities to use special HTML tags. With VBScript embedded in the HTML of your Web page, you can write programs that extend the functionality of your pages by:

- Writing scripts that check values entered into a form
- Processing form values before they are sent to the Web server
- Dynamically creating new Web pages
- Writing full client-side business applications, games, and utilities

Creating Powerful Forms

Forms in a Web page are great for accepting input from *users*. "User" is a term often used by programmers to refer to anyone using their programs. HTML forms have a shortcoming, they can't verify information entered by a user. VBScript overcomes this shortcoming by letting you write programs to process information entered by the user before it's sent to the server. In fact, in many cases, all the processing can be done directly in the browser without having to send any information to the server. In this way, VBScript can be a replacement for CGI programs.

Client-Server Applications

Creating Web applications normally involves a *client* side, which is a form or program running in a Web browser, as well as a *server*-side. The server is the computer running the Web server program that the client browser contacts to access Web pages. When there is a form submission sent to a Web server, three possible things can happen.

1. The server starts a CGI program and makes the form submission data available to the program. The CGI program processes the information and sends a response to the browser.

2. Server side JavaScript programs process the form submission information and send a response to the browser. (Not available using Internet Explorer.)

3. Nothing. If the server is not set up to handle form submissions, no data will be processed. This is an important point: many people think that creating a form in HTML is sufficient to create a Web application. In a traditional client-server application, there must be a program on the server to process information and return a reply to the client.

Before the invention of Web scripting languages, the only possibility was to use CGI programs to process information. The next development was the ability to write scripts and embed processing in the HTML page. Using VBScript, the Internet Explorer Web browser can process information without sending form information to the server.

Dynamic Web Pages

Web applications normally revolve around information. There are special Web applications that control devices such as electronic signs, robot arms, and a growing number of other things becoming connected to the Internet. But the majority of the applications are concerned with sending and receiving information. Once the user has entered information in a form and clicked a button to send the information, a response is expected. This response is sent in the form of a Web page created by the program that processed the form information.

When a program creates a Web page "on-the-fly," it's creating the page dynamically. This is different from loading a Web page that was created and stored in a file. No matter what kind of application you create using the World Wide Web, your program will need to send HTML back to the browser dynamically. This chapter introduces the process of creating Web pages dynamically using VBScript.

Supported Web Browsers

People who view your Web page using Internet Explorer will experience your Web page enhancements. VBScript won't work, however, if your Web page is viewed using Netscape Navigator, NCSA Mosaic, or any browser other than Internet Explorer. For now, the competition for the "standard scripting language" is high. Microsoft's browser supports both popular scripting languages, JavaScript and VBScript. Other browsers may eventually support both scripting languages; but for now, you'll have to live with this restriction.

The Guts of VBScript

Writing Web applications using VBScript requires that you know how to embed VBScript into your Web page, and you know how to write programs using VBScript. Adding VBScript into your Web page is easy as you'll see in the next section. Learning all the elements of the VBScript language can take some time. If you're already a Visual Basic programmer you'll see how easy writing VBScript Web applications really is.

Embedding VBScript into a Web Page

Before discussing VBScript, you should know how to include VBScript in your HTML. The HTML <SCRIPT></SCRIPT> tag is used to embed script within HTML of a Web page. As mentioned earlier, there is more than one scripting language, so the <SCRIPT> tag lets you identify which scripting language you're using:

```
<SCRIPT LANGUAGE="VBS">
```

Not all browsers are created equal. In other words, not all browsers can process embedded script. To be able to have your Web page appear in Web browsers that can't handle script, you can embed the script within comment marks:

```
<!-- script goes here -->
```

Web pages have three possible sections: a <HEAD>, <BODY>, and <FORM>. When a Web page loads, any HTML found between the <HEAD> and </HEAD> tags is loaded first. This is a great place to place VBScript that you would like to have accessible from other parts of the Web page. In programming terminology, script or program code that is available to all parts of an application is said to have *global scope*. VBScript that is included in the <HEAD> section of a Web page has global scope. VBScript that is included in either the <BODY> or <FORM> sections of a Web page is said to have *local scope*.

VBScript Variables

In VBScript, a good place to start is learning about *variables* and *data types*. Information in computer programs is stored in temporary storage places called variables. Variables are storage places in your computer's memory where you put temporary information. Each of these storage places is given a name, sometimes called the *variable name*. If you store the number 16 in a variable named *Age*, whenever you use the variable *Age* in your program, it's the same as using the number 16. For example, *Age* + 3 = 19.

Creating variables, storing information in them, and naming them is extremely simple. There are two ways to create a variable. One way is to declare the variable using the *Dim* statement, as shown in Figure 4.1.

You can declare more than one variable at the same time by separating them with commas, as shown in Figure 4.2.

■■■■■■■ **Figure 4.1** Create variables using the *Dim* statement.

```
<SCRIPT LANGUAGE="VBS">
<!--
Dim MyAge
-->
</SCRIPT>
```

■■■■■

■■■■■■■ **Figure 4.2** Create more than one variable with a single *Dim* statement.

```
<SCRIPT LANGUAGE="VBS">
<!--
Dim MyAge, MyName
-->
</SCRIPT>
```

■■■■■

The other way to declare a variable is easier but considered sloppy programming because of the chance for error. Set a variable name equal to a value and you have thereby created the variable and stored the value. Figure 4.3 shows some examples.

In the first example, a variable named *MyAge* was created with a numeric value of 16. In the second, the variable *MyName* was created and contains the character string "Joe Bob Barker".

There are a few rules to follow when creating variables.

- You have to start the variable name with a letter of the alphabet. A variable name can't start with a number or a nonalphabetic character.
- Variable names can be up to 256 characters in length. This will allow you to have really long variable names, such as *percent_rainfall_in_the_eastern_mississippi_river_valley_in_the_spring*.
- Periods have a special significance in VBScript. Don't use periods as part of a variable name.

As you can see, there aren't many rules to remember. VBScript gives you quite a bit of flexibility when creating variables.

▬▬▬▬ **Figure 4.3** Create variables by simply storing a value into a variable.

```
<SCRIPT LANGUAGE="VBS">
        <!--
        MyAge = 16
        MyName = "Joe Bob Barker"
        -->
</SCRIPT>
```

▬▬▬▬

Variable Data Types

In most programming languages, variables have a *data type*. The type determines what kind of information can be stored in the variable. For the two sample variables created previously, no attention was paid to data type. This is because VBScript has only one data type, called a variant. As a result, you can store anything you want in a VBScript variable.

Once information is stored in a variable, VBScript determines what type of information has been stored and classifies it as a *variant subtype*. Even though VBScript figures out the appropriate subtype, you will need a good idea of what type VBScript chose. In order to work with this information after it's stored in a variant, you have to know the subtype. For example, consider the two sample variables *MyAge* and *MyName*. One is an integer and the other is a string. If you try to add these two variables together (*MyAge* + *MyName*), you see an error message. If integer *MyAge* were made into a string, *MyAge* = " age 16" then you could add *My Age* and *My Name* together, as shown in Figure 4.4.

In this example, *MyInfo* would equal "Joe Bob Barker age 16". Table 4.1 lists the different subtypes that can be stored in a variable.

In some ways, having a single data type, variant, that automatically classifies its data into subtypes is easier than programming in other languages, in which you must declare a variable as a specific type before you use it. Variants can be tricky, however, because you should know what subtype your data has been classified as before you use it.

■■■■■ **Figure 4.4** Values stored in variables can be used in your VBScript.

```
MyAge = " age 16"
MyName = "Joe Bob Barker"
MyInfo = MyName & MyAge
```

■■■■■■ **Table 4.1** VBScript Variant Subtypes

Type	VarType Return Value	Description
*Array	8192	An array is designated as other possible subtypes, for example, an array of strings.
Boolean	11	True and False values.
Byte	17	An integer value from 0 to 255.
Currency	6	A two-decimal-precision number representing currency.
Date(Time)	7	A number representing a date beginning New Years day 100 and continuing to the last day of 1999. What happens next?
Double	5	Double-precision, floating-point number.
Empty	0	An empty value is stored in the variant. For numbers, this is 0 and for character strings this is an empty string. Empty is a valid amount.
Error	10	This value is a number representing an error.
Integer	2	A whole number between -32,768 and 32,767.
Long	3	A long can store an integer that is in the range of plus or minus 2 billion.
Null	1	Nothing stored in the variant. This is different from empty. Nothing is stored in this variant type.
Object	13	Non-ActiveX automation object.
Object	9	Contains an ActiveX automation object.
Single	4	A single-precision, floating point number.
String	8	A string of text characters. Maximum string length is 2 billion characters.

■■■■ **Table 4.1** Continued

Type	VarType Return Value	Description
*Variant	12	Used only to designate an array of variants.

Not an actual subtype.

■■■■

VBScript has a special function called **Vartype**(). This function returns an integer value representing the subtype of the variable passed as a parameter. If you aren't familiar with the concept of a function, it's similar to a miniprogram that can receive values as parameters, has a name, and returns values back when it is finished processing. The **Vartype**() function receives the variant type variable as a parameter. See Table 4.1 for the integer returned by **Vartype**().

Converting Variable Data Types

Just because VBScript chooses the subtype of your data stored in a variant variable doesn't mean you can't change it. You can change many variables from one subtype to another. Table 4.2 shows most of the functions in VBScript used for converting values into specific subtypes of a variant. Also useful is the **IsDate**() function, which determines whether the value you are going to convert to a Date subtype is valid. These functions give you complete control over how VBScript processes your data.

The Life and Times of VBScript Variables

Where you declare your variable in a VBScript program is important. Where a variable is declared determines its *scope*. A good way to think of scope is to think about your house or apartment. When you invite guests into the living room and ask them to have a seat, hopefully they'll choose seats in the living room. The scope of where a visitor can sit is limited to the living room. If the visitor happened to think the kitchen was a better place to sit, conversation with you in the living room may become difficult or impossible. A variable's scope can be either *script-level (global)*, which means that it can be accessed from any part of your VBScript program; or it's *procedure-level (local)*, which means that only the procedure or function in which it's declared can access the variable.

■■■■■■ **Table 4.2** Conversion Functions

Function	Description
Asc(*string*)	Returns the ASCII value of the first character of the *string*.
AscB(*string*)	Returns the first byte of the *string* when the *string* contains byte data.
CBool(*expression*)	Converts an *expression* that returns a numeric value to a Boolean subtype.
CByte(*expression*)	Converts an *expression* to a Byte subtype.
CDate(*date*)	Converts a *date/time* literal or number to a Date subtype.
CDbl(*expression*)	Converts an *expression* to a Double subtype.
Chr(*ASCII code*)	Converts an *ASCII code* to a Character.
CInt(*expression*)	Converts an *expression* to an Integer subtype.
CLng(*expression*)	Converts an *expression* to a Long subtype.
CSng(*expression*)	Converts an *expression* to a Single subtype.
CStr(*expression*)	Converts an *expression* to a String subtype.
Hex(*number*)	Returns a string containing the hexadecimal equivalent of *number*.
Oct(*number*)	Returns a string containing the octal equivalent of *number*.
Str(*number*)	Returns the string equivalent of *number*.

■■■■■ **Table 4.2** Continued

Function	Description
Val(*string*)	Returns the numeric value of numbers in the left portion of a *string*. Val() stops reading the *string* at the first unrecognized character.

■■■■■

Diamonds may be forever, but variables aren't. In a world limited by the dimensions of time and space, variables hang around for only so long and can take up only so much space. Script-level variables have a lifetime that begins when your script first creates the variable, to the time that your script stops running. A procedure-level variable exists only from the time it's created until the procedure ends.

Use script-level (global) variables sparingly. They use valuable and limited memory for the entire time a script is running. Another reason to use them sparingly is that they can be accidentally changed by parts of your program, thus causing bugs in your program.

Use global variables when you need a value to exist for the entire duration of the script. Don't use global variables for communicating values from one procedure to another. Use parameters instead.

Use procedure-level (local) variables whenever possible. They are destroyed when the procedure finishes, freeing up the memory they used. You can use the same variable name in different procedures when using local variables without confusing the values between procedures.

Using Arrays in VBScript

An *array* is a special type of variable that allows you to store multiple values in a single variable. Values stored in an array variable must be of the same type. You can't store a string and a number and a date all in the same array unless you use the functions listed in Table 4.2 to convert the values to the same type.

An array keeps track of each of its values with an index number beginning at 0. Think of an array as a variable with several numbered compartments. Refer to the value in each compartment by referring to the index number of the compartment. The correct name for an array compartment is an *element.* Therefore, an array element is one of the compartments within an array.

Before you can store values in an array, you must create it. You create arrays as you do normal variables. Use the **Dim** command, followed by the name of the array variable and the largest index number you want in the array, within parentheses. Remember that arrays begin numbering their elements at zero. So, if you need five elements, the highest index you'll need is 4 (see Figure 4.5).

▰▰▰▰▰ **Figure 4.5** Create arrays using the *Dim* statement.

```
<SCRIPT LANGUAGE="VBS">
<!--
        Dim colors(4)

-->
</SCRIPT>
```

▰▰▰▰▰

▰▰▰▰▰ **Figure 4.6** Store values in an array just as you do in variables (but with an index number).

```
<SCRIPT LANGUAGE="VBS">
<!--
        Dim colors(4)

        colors(0)="Black"
```

Continued...

■■■■■■■ **Figure 4.6** Continued

```
        colors(1)="Brown"
        colors(2)="Red"
        colors(3)="Green"
        colors(4)="Blue"
-->
</SCRIPT>
```

■■■■■

■■■■■■■ **Figure 4.7** Choose from values stored in an array to use in your VBScript.

```
<SCRIPT LANGUAGE="VBS">
<!--
        Dim favorite_color_sentence
        favorite_color_sentence="My favorite color is "

        Dim colors(4)

        colors(0)="Black"
        colors(1)="Brown"
        colors(2)="Red"
        colors(3)="Green"
        colors(4)="Blue"

        favorite_color_sentence=favorite_color_sentence & colors(4)
-->
</SCRIPT>
```

■■■■■

This example (Figure 4.5) creates an array called *colors*, with places to store five colors. In the next step (Figure 4.6) you can see how to store values into each of the array elements by referring to the element by its index number.

Putting information into an array is simple, as is referring to the values in the array. Following is a slightly more complex example of a script that uses arrays. The script performs these steps:

1. Create a string variable with part of a sentence stored in it.
2. Create the colors array.
3. Store values in the colors array.
4. Add one of the array elements to our string.

Another Dimension

The discussion so far has covered arrays that store information in a single dimension. Now, imagine that each array element is an array. This type of array, called a *two-dimensional array,* is easy to visualize. It is a series of rows and columns like a spreadsheet or a chessboard. You refer to elements of a two-dimensional array by using the index of the first element that contains another array (the row), and then the index of the element in the second array (the column).

To create a two-dimensional array, you must identify how many elements are in each array. Figure 4.8 shows a two-dimensional array in which the primary or first-dimension array has five elements and the array contained in each of these elements has four elements. (Remember that elements begin their index numbers at zero.)

To store information in the sample array, refer to each element using the index numbers of both arrays.

■■■■ **Figure 4.8** Create two-dimensional arrays by adding the
index of the second array dimension.

```
<SCRIPT LANGUAGE="VB">
        <!--
        Dim colors(4, 3)
        -->
</SCRIPT>
```

In Figure 4.9, only the first two rows of five columns have been filled in
with values. You can see that the first index number refers to the row and
the second index number refers to the column.

■■■■ **Figure 4.9** Enter values in a multidimensional array
referencing each dimension with an index number.

```
<SCRIPT LANGUAGE="VBS">
<!--
        Dim colors(4,3)

        colors(0,0)="Black"
        colors(0,1)="Brown"
        colors(0,2)="Red"
        colors(0,3)="Green"
        colors(0,4)="Blue"
        colors(1,0)="Dark Grey"
        colors(1,1)="Burnt Sienna"
        colors(1,2)="Vermillion"
```

```
        colors(1,3)="Cyan"
        colors(1,4)="Azure"
-->
</SCRIPT>
```

▰▰▰

You can increase the number of dimensions of an array. Just imagine that when creating a new dimension, you are storing an array in the previous array's elements. Create and reference the elements of each array, separated by commas: ARRAY(*index, index, index,...*).

Dynamic Arrays

A *dynamic array* is one in which the number of elements in the array changes while your script is executing. The ability to change the size of an array is important if you don't know before the script is run how many elements are required. For example, if you ask a user to enter the names of their aunts and uncles, the answer will be different for each person. A *static* array, which has a fixed size, is inappropriate in this situation because you could exceed the size of the array while the script is running (if a person listed many aunts and uncles).

You can create an empty dynamic array using either the **Dim** command or the **ReDim** command (see Figure 4.10).

Initially, both the arrays in this example are empty. You can't store values in an empty array. You must first change the dimensions of the array using the **ReDim** command (see Figure 4.11).

You can see that changing the size of a dynamic array is a simple task. Note this important point, however: Unless you include the keyword

■■■■■■ **Figure 4.10** Two ways to create dynamic arrays; using **Dim** or **ReDim.**

```
<SCRIPT LANGUAGE="VBS">
        <!--
        Dim DynamicArray_1()
        ReDim DynamicArray_2()
          -->
</SCRIPT>
```

■■■■■■

■■■■■■ **Figure 4.11** Changing the size of a dynamic array using the *ReDim* statement.

```
<SCRIPT LANGUAGE="VBS">
        <!--
        ReDim DynamicArray_1(10)
        -->
</SCRIPT>
```

■■■■■■

Preserve after the **ReDim** command, all of the information previously stored in the array will be wiped out. Use the *Preserve* keyword to preserve data already stored in the array.

Figure 4.12 started by creating an array that can contain three items. Sometime later in the program the array was resized while the first three favorite things were preserved. After resizing the array, there was room for eleven favorite items, and two more were added. You can fill in the rest of the array elements with your own favorite things.

▬▬▬ **Figure 4.12** Using the *Preserve* keyword to keep data when redimensioning.

```
<SCRIPT LANGUAGE="VBS">

    <!--

    ReDim FavoriteThings(2)

    FavoriteThings(0) = "Raindrops on Roses"

    FavoriteThings(1) = "Warm woolen mittens"

    FavoriteThings(2) = "Snowflakes that land on my nose
and eyelashes"


    ReDim Preserve FavoriteThings(10)

    FavoriteThings(3) = "4 Wheel Drive"

    FavoriteThings(4) = "Surfboard"

    -->

</SCRIPT>
```

▬▬▬

Keep in mind that if you shrink an array by resizing it, you'll lose the data in the elements that are lopped off. The data loss occurs even if you use the *Preserve* keyword.

Semper VBScript

Just like marines who are always faithful (semper fidelis) *constants* are special variables that never change their value. Constants in VBScript are actually regular variables. In other languages, they are a slightly different type of variable. You must learn how to use them and how to differentiate them from other variables.

A constant is a variable that represents a value that never changes. A good example of a constant used in math programs is *pi.* By creating a PI constant for use in math equations, you don't have to redefine the value every time you need it in an equation (see Figure 4.13).

Other examples of constants include a date constant, which you can use for major holidays, and text constants, which you could use to refer to machine and user names or company names.

Traditionally, constants are written in uppercase letters. Using this convention is not a requirement, but it is a great way to keep track of which variables are constants and which are script variables.

Controlling VBScript

Programming involves more than storing values into variables. Programming with VBScript requires that you use *expressions, operators,* and *control statements* that direct the "flow" of your script. These are the elements of a program that use the variables you've learned to create in the first part of this chapter.

■■■■■ **Figure 4.13** Create constants as you would a variable.

```
<SCRIPT LANGUAGE="VBS">
    <!--
    PI = 3.141592654
    -->
</SCRIPT>
```

■■■■

Expressions

An expression is a program statement that evaluates to a single value. For example, 2 + 2 is an expression that evaluates to 4. An expression can be made up of variables, literals, constants, and operators. Figure 4.14 shows some examples of expressions.

Figure 4.14 uses literals such as 5 and 7, variables such as *Value*, and operators such as =, *, and +. Operators are important for creating expressions. One of the most commonly used operators is the equality operator (=), which is often used with Boolean variables. Boolean values are either True or False. Figure 4.15 shows an example in which a Boolean value is created by testing the equality of two values.

In this example, *Value_1* does not equal *Value_2*. So, *Boolean_Value* is False. The next section explains how this type of Boolean expression is used to control the flow of a VBScript program.

■■■■■■■■ **Figure 4.14** Sample expressions.

```
Literals:
5 + 7


Literals and variables:
Value = 7
5 + Value


Variables and constants:
PI = 3.142
Radius = 7
Area = PI * (Radius * Radius)
```

■■■■ **Figure 4.15** Using the equality operator versus assigning values to variables.

```
Value_1 = 5
Value_2 = 7
```

Operators

Operators are the workhorses of any programming language. VBScript has a large number of operators for constructing expressions. Table 4.3 lists the different operators and their function.

■■■■ **Table 4.3** VBScript Operators

Operator	Function
+	Numeric addition
-	Subtraction or negation (making a number negative)
/	Division
*	Multiplication
=	Equality or instantiation (storing a value in a variable)
<>	Inequality (not equal to)
>	Greater than
<	Less than
>=	Greater than or equal to
<=	Less than or equal to
And	Logical conjunction (putting two logical values together)
Or	Logical disjunction (Either one value or the other value)
Xor	Exclusive Or, logical exclusion

■■■■ **Table 4.3** Continued

Operator	Function
^	Exponent
Eqv	Logical equivalence (one value is the equivalent of the other value)
Imp	Logical implication
Mod	Modulo arithmetic
Is	Object equivalence (do two object references point to the same object?)
&	String concatenation (putting two strings together)

One thing to keep in mind when constructing expressions is that operators have an order of precedence. Just like arithmetic, in which numbers in a mathematical expression are multiplied before they're added, some programming processes happen before others. When operators have equal precedence, they are executed from left to right. You can use parentheses to override an operator's precedence. Operators within parentheses are executed before operators outside the parentheses. In the case of multiple parentheses, the precedence starts with operators in the innermost parentheses and works its way to the outer parentheses.

Controlling the Flow of a VBScript Program

Life would be pretty boring if no one could make a decision, any decision at all. If we had to live unerringly by a prewritten script, we wouldn't be very dynamic, and probably not too happy. Computer programs probably don't care much about the happy part; but to be dynamic, programs must have the ability to respond by making decisions on the fly.

If I Had a Hammer...

The ability of your VBScript program to make decisions lies in a special program statement called an *If Then* statement. The way it works is simple. If an expression evaluates to True, then the code that follows the *If* statement and comes before the *End If* statement is executed. If the expression evaluates to False, the program continues execution after the *End If*, skipping the code between the *If* and the *End If* statements.

There's one more important statement related to the *If* statement: *Else*. When the *If* expression evaluates to False, a second branch, following the *Else* statement, rather than merely continuing onward with the code after the *End If*. Figure 4.16 is an example in which a program makes a decision about whether to return the area of a circle or the circumference.

■■■■■■■ **Figure 4.16** Programs make decisions using *If, Else,* and *End If* statements.

```
<SCRIPT LANGUAGE="VBS">
      <!--
      PI = 3.141592654
      Dim Value, which_choice, Radius
      which_choice = "Area"

      If which_choice = "Area" Then
            Value = PI * Radius^2
      Else
            Value = (2 * PI) * Radius
      End If
      -->
</SCRIPT>
```

A Loop Is a Loop Is a Loop Is a Loop

At times, you will want part of a VBScript program to repeat. This is accomplished using a *loop*. A loop repeats a block of code (one or more lines of VBScript code) until the expression that is used to evaluate when the loop has completed becomes True. There are four different ways to create loops in VBScript:

- *Do While.* Loops until an expression evaluates to True
- *Do Until.* Loops until an expression evaluates to False
- *For.* Loops a specific number of times using an automatic counter
- *For Each.* Loops for each object in a collection

Using Loops

The *Do While* loop, sometimes just known as a *Do* loop, repeats a block of code until an expression supplied as part of the loop evaluates to True. Remember that this is a Boolean expression. There are two ways to construct a *Do While* loop. The first is to evaluate the expression at the beginning of the loop, and the other is to evaluate the loop at the end. The major difference is that you know that if you evaluate the expression at the end of the loop, the block of code will always be executed at least once, even if the *Do While* expression evaluates to False. If you check the expression at the beginning of the loop and the expression evaluates to False, the loop will never be executed.

Figure 4.17 is an example of a *Do While* loop in which the expression being evaluated is at the beginning of the loop.

The loop in this example doesn't really do anything meaningful. It simply scans through the array of vacation choices until it hits Cleveland, where it's stopped cold (sorry couldn't help the pun). If the expression in Figure 4.17 had been set equal to "freezing," the program would never

```
<SCRIPT LANGUAGE="VBS">
        <!--
        Dim VacationChoices(3), Weather, Counter, Choice
        VacationChoices(0) = "Puerto Vallarta"
        VacationChoices(1) = "San Diego"
        VacationChoices(2) = "Honolulu"
        VacationChoices(3) = "Cleveland"
        Weather = ""
        Counter = 0

        Do While Weather <> "freezing"
                Choice = VacationChoices(counter)
                If Choice = "Cleveland" Then
                        Weather = "freezing"
                Else
                        Weather = "Warm"
                End If
                Choice = Choice + 1
        Loop
        -->
</SCRIPT>
```

have entered the loop. Processing would have continued after the *Loop* statement.

There are occasions when you want a loop to happen at least once before checking to see if you want it to loop again. This circumstance is covered by the code in Figure 4.18.

Figure 4.18 Place the *While* at the end of the loop to allow
at least one pass before testing the expression.

```
<SCRIPT LANGUAGE="VBS">

    <!--

    Dim PayAmount, TaxAmount

    Do

            PayAmount = PayAmount + 50000

            TaxAmount = .33 * PayAmount

    Loop While TaxAmount < 40000

    MsgBox "You'll earn  " & str(PayAmount) & " without paying over
$40,000 in tax"

    -->

</SCRIPT>
```

Whenever you want to construct a loop that continues looping until an
expression becomes True, use the *Until* keyword, rather than *While*. Your
loop will repeat while the expression is False, and stop whenever it becomes
True (see Figure 4.19).

Figure 4.19 Use *Until* to stop the loop when the expression
becomes True.

```
<SCRIPT LANGUAGE="VBS">

    <!--

    Dim Temperature, ThingCounter, ThingsAccomplished

    Temperature = 77

    ThingCounter = 1

    ThingsAccomplished = ""
```

Continued...

Figure 4.19 Continued

```
            Do Until Temperature = 107
                If ThingCounter = 1 Then
                        ThingsAccomplished = ThingsAccomplished +
"Tennis "
                End If
                If ThingCounter = 2 Then
                        ThingsAccomplished = ThingsAccomplished +
"Gardening "
                End If
                If ThingCounter = 3 Then
                        ThingsAccomplished = ThingsAccomplished +
"Swimming "
                End If
                If ThingCounter = 4 Then
                        ThingsAccomplished = ThingsAccomplished +
"Diving "
                End If

                ThingCounter = ThingCounter + 1
                Temperature = Temperature + 10
        Loop

        MsgBox "I managed to: " & ThingsAccomplished
    -->
</SCRIPT>
```

A Way Out

Have you ever played Monopoly, and had your piece put in jail? You can either sit there for several turns, roll a double, or have a "Get out of jail free" card. The point is that there is more than one way of getting out of jail without having to sit there for several turns.

You can also exit out of your loops before their expressions would normally let you out. The VBScript statement that lets you out of the loop is *Exit Do*. You can use *Exit Do* to jump out of any loop. It's a great way to shorten loops that have completed their tasks. Some people recommend it as a way to avoid *endless loops*. Endless loops, which are loops that never end, are accidents of programming. It's better, however, to find these potential endless loops and fix their expressions than use the *Exit Do* statement as a crutch (see Figure 4.20).

And For the Next Loop We Have...

The previous section contained examples of the *Do* loop, which is a very powerful programming device. The last example used a numeric variable to keep track of how many loops had been made. There's certainly nothing wrong with that example, except that there's a better way. The *For Next*

Figure 4.20 Exit a *Do* loop using the *Exit Do* statement.

```
<SCRIPT LANGUAGE="VB">
        <!--
        Dim SomeNumber
        SomeNumber = 1
        Do While SomeNumber <= 100
                SomeNumber = SomeNumber + 1
                If SomeNumber = 50 Then Exit Do
        Loop
        MsgBox "The loop exited while SomeNumber =  " & SomeNumber
        -->
</SCRIPT>
```

loop automatically changes your counter variable and is perfect for looping a specific number of times. Counter variables can be:

- Incremented (increased)
- Decremented (decreased)
- Incremented or decremented in steps larger or smaller than one

A *For Next* loop begins with *For*, followed by a specially formatted expression, and ends with *Next*. The expression sets a numeric variable with an initial value, tells the loop the maximum value to reach, and optionally sets the value by which the counter should step.

When creating a *For Next* loop, you typically use a one-character variable, such as *i*. The statement that follows the word *For* first sets the variable to its initial value ($i = 1$). Follow this with the word *To* and the value you want your counter to eventually reach. To have the counter count by twos, threes, or fours, add the keyword *Step* followed by the value you want your counter to increment or decrement each time it loops. Let's put it all together in Figure 4.21.

Figure 4.21 Loop a predetermined number of times using the *For* loop.

```
<SCRIPT LANGUAGE="VBS">
        <!--
        Dim i
        Dim AnArray(4)


        AnArray(0) = "Zero"
```

```
        AnArray(1) = "One"

        AnArray(2) = "Two"

        AnArray(3) = "Three"

        AnArray(4) = "Four"


        For i = 0 To 4

                MsgBox "The value is now at " & AnArray(i)

        Next

        -->

</SCRIPT>
```

As you can see from this example, the *For Next* loop is an excellent way to increment through an array. For instance, you can look for values in an array using an *If* statement, as shown in Figure 4.22.

■■■■ **Figure 4.22** Use the *For* loop to navigate through an array.

```
<SCRIPT LANGUAGE="VBS">

        <!--

        Dim i

        Dim AnArray(4)


        AnArray(0) = "Zero"

        AnArray(1) = "One"

        AnArray(2) = "Two"
```

Continued...

■■■■■ **Figure 4.22** Continued

```
        AnArray(3) = "Three"
        AnArray(4) = "Four"


        For i = 0 To 4
                If AnArray(i) = "Three" Then MsgBox "The value is now
at " & AnArray(i)
        Next
        -->
</SCRIPT>
```

■■■■■

The optional *Step* keyword is used when you want the counter to increment or decrement by amounts other than 1 (see Figure 4.23).

■■■■■ **Figure 4.23** Step through in increments larger or smaller than one using the *Step* keyword.

```
<SCRIPT LANGUAGE="VBS">
        <!--
        Dim i
        Dim AnArray(4)


        AnArray(0) = "Zero"
        AnArray(1) = "One"
        AnArray(2) = "Two"
        AnArray(3) = "Three"
```

```
        AnArray(4) = "Four"


    For i = 0 To 4 Step 2
            MsgBox "The value is now at " & AnArray(i)
    Next
    -->
</SCRIPT>
```

Figure 4.24 is an example in which the *For Next* loop counts down instead of up. Remember to set the value to which the counter is going to count to a number less than the starting value, or else not much looping will happen.

■■■■■■ **Figure 4.24** Step backwards by using a negative *Step* value.

```
<SCRIPT LANGUAGE="VBS">
    <!--
    Dim i
    Dim AnArray(4)
    AnArray(0) = "Zero"
    AnArray(1) = "One"
    AnArray(2) = "Two"
    AnArray(3) = "Three"
    AnArray(4) = "Four"


    For i = 4 To 0 Step -1
```

Continued...

Figure 4.24 Continued

```
            MsgBox "The value is now at " & AnArray(i)
        Next
        -->
</SCRIPT>
```

You can exit from the *For Next* loop before the counter reaches its end number by using the *Exit For* statement. This is really handy when you are looking for values in an array. Once you've found the value you want, there's absolutely no reason why you have to look at any other values in the array (see Figure 4.25).

Figure 4.25 Exit a *For* loop using the *Exit For* statement.

```
<SCRIPT LANGUAGE="VBS">
    <!--
    Dim i
    Dim AnArray(4)

    AnArray(0) = "Zero"
    AnArray(1) = "One"
    AnArray(2) = "Two"
    AnArray(3) = "Three"
    AnArray(4) = "Four"
```

```
         For i = 0 To 4
                 if AnArray(i) = "Two" Then Exit For
         Next
         MsgBox "We found" & AnArray(i) & " and exited."
         -->
   </SCRIPT>
```

▬▬▬▬

Using For Each—Next

There is a special kind of loop used in VBScript to set values in objects within a group. Because objects and groups have not yet been defined in this book, you may want to come back to this section once you've read about them.

For Each - Next statements loop for each object in a group or collection. VBScript automatically sets an object variable each time the loop repeats (see Figure 4.26).

▬▬▬▬ **Figure 4.26** Step through objects in a group using the *For Each* statement.

```
<SCRIPT LANGUAGE="VBS">
     <!--
     Dim Counter
     Counter = 1
     For Each Turtle in TheSea
             Turtle.Name = "Touche" & Counter
```

Continued...

Figure 4.26 Continued

```
            Counter = Counter + 1
    Next
    -->
</SCRIPT>
```

"As always, Mr. Phelps, if you or any of your programmers decide to exit the *For Each - Next* loop before it is finished, use the *Exit For* statement." There's nothing "impossible" about exiting from a *For Each - Next* loop. Just as when you are looking for values in an array, when you've found a value within a group of objects, there's no reason to keep looking. Go ahead and exit the loop. Figure 4.27 tests for the names of turtles, named in the last example. When the correct turtle is found, the loop exits.

Organizing Your VBScript Program

VBScript programs are organized into small blocks of code called procedures. As a result, you can perform tasks by calling a procedure, rather

Figure 4.27 Exit a *For Each* loop using the *Exit For* statement.

```
<SCRIPT LANGUAGE="VBS">
    <!--
    For Each Turtle in TheSea
```

```
                If Turtle.Name = "Touche123" Then Exit For
        Next
        MsgBox "I found the correct turtle."
        -->
</SCRIPT>
```

than by repeating the same code over and over in your program. You can think of procedures as miniprograms. Effectively using procedures makes your program more compact and easier to debug (for those of us who aren't perfect). Each procedure is given a name, so that you can call on it to run within your program.

VBScript programs are made up entirely of two kinds of procedures, the *Sub* procedure and the *Function*. There is very little difference between the two types of procedures. Functions return values to the procedure that called it, and *Sub* doesn't. That's the only difference.

Programming with *Sub* Procedures

A *Sub* procedure is a group of VBScript statements, beginning with the keyword *Sub* and ending with *End Sub*. *Sub* procedures are given names and can accept parameters that appear in parentheses after the *Sub* keyword (see Figure 4.28).

Figure 4.28 Define small executable blocks of code using the *Sub* keyword.

```
<SCRIPT LANGUAGE="VBS">
    <!--
```

Continued...

■■■ ■■■■ **Figure 4.28** Continued

```
        Sub DisplayFishType (Fish)
                If Fish = "Trout" Then MsgBox "We have a freshwater
    fish"
        End Sub
        -->
</SCRIPT>
```

In the procedure, DisplayFishType, the variable *Fish* has been passed as a parameter. Passing parameters is how you communicate information to *Sub* procedures. A *Sub* procedure can accept constants, variables, or expressions as parameters. If your procedure doesn't need information, it isn't mandatory that you pass it parameters. But, when parameters are omitted, you must still include an empty set of parentheses. The example, DisplayFishType, has only a few lines of code. You can have as many lines of code as you need between the *Sub* and *End Sub* statements.

Figure 4.29 is an example of how you would call the DisplayFishType from another *Sub* procedure.

■■■■ ■■■■ **Figure 4.29** Call *Sub* procedures from within <SCRIPT> tags.

```
        <SCRIPT LANGUAGE="VBS">
            <!--
            Sub DisplayFishType (Fish)
                    If Fish = "Trout" Then
                            MsgBox "We have a freshwater
```

```
     fish."
               Else
                         MsgBox "We have a saltwater fish."
               End If
       End Sub
       Sub GoneFishing ()
               Dim PoorFish


               PoorFish = "Bass"


               DisplayFishType PoorFish
       End Sub


       -->
   </SCRIPT>
```

There is an alternative way of calling procedures using the *Call* statement. This is a throwback to older programming styles and should probably be avoided. If you end up using the *Call* statement, you'll need to enclose the parameters within parentheses.

Using Function Procedures

A function differs from a *Sub* procedure in that it returns a value to the procedure that called it. This may not seem significant, but it changes the reasons for writing a function rather than a *Sub* procedure. Think of *Sub* procedures as "command-based" and functions as "result-based." When you want the computer to change the colors of your Web page or display information, that is command-based. When you want the computer to process information and return an answer, that need is result-based.

Functions start with the a *Function* statement and end with *End Function*. Just like *Sub* procedures, parameters must be enclosed in parentheses. Remember that these parentheses must be there, whether or not they contain a parameter.

Figure 4.30 shows a very simple multiplication example. To return a value from the function, simply save the value into a variable with the same name as the function. Remember from earlier in the chapter that all variables in VBScript are variants. VBScript functions return all their variables as variants.

Declaring Procedures

VBScript is a powerful language, just like its parent, Visual Basic. But VBScript is embedded in the HTML of your Web page. This section dis-

■■■■■ **Figure 4.30** Functions return values as variants.

```
<SCRIPT LANGUAGE="VBS">
    <!--
    Function Multiply (a, b)
            Multiply = a * b
    End Function


    Sub MainProc ()
            Dim Var1, Var2, Answer
            Var1 = 5
            Var2 = 7
            Answer = Multiply a,b
```

```
       End Sub

       -->

</SCRIPT>
```

cusses how and where you should place VBScript procedures in a Web page.

Before a procedure can be called, regardless of whether it's a function or a *Sub* procedure, it must be *declared*. Declaring a procedure means that your computer must have it loaded into memory and ready to use. There is a special part of your Web page called the HEAD. Anything in this section of an HTML page is loaded first. This is a great place to place your procedures. When your functions and *Sub* procedures are placed in the HEAD portion of a Web page, you know they are loaded and ready to use. The HEAD portion of a Web page begins with the <HEAD> tag and ends with the </HEAD> tag. This is typically where the title of your page appears within <TITLE></TITLE> tags (see Figure 4.31).

Figure 4.31 Place scripts in the <HEAD> portion of a Web page to make them accessible.

```
<HTML>
<HEAD>
<TITLE>My Math Web Page</TITLE>
<SCRIPT LANGUAGE="VBS">
       <!--
```

Continued...

■■■■■■■ **Figure 4.31** Continued

```
        Function Multiply (a, b)
                Multiply = a * b
        End Function
        -->
</SCRIPT>
</HEAD>
<BODY>
..Body and any forms go here...
</BODY>
</HTML>
```

The Fun Part

VBScript wouldn't be much fun if you couldn't call all the procedures and functions you've created. VBScript is designed to be used in Web pages, and most often this means a Web page with a form.

Use VBScript to:

- Validate information entered into a form
- Process information without having to rely on server CGI programs
- Create dynamic Web pages

Validation Using VBScript

Making certain viewers of your Web page enter information correctly into forms has historically been difficult in a Web page. Validating information was either not done, or done by the server. This means that after users entered their data and submitted it to the server, they would have to wait for the server to process the information and return results before they could find out if everything had been entered correctly. You can shorten this lengthy process by writing VBScript to validate data before it's sent to the server.

Constructing the Form

If you've created a few Web pages, you probably know how to create basic input forms in HTML. This is a headstart, but there are a few other important things you should know. First of all, name everything! This is just as important as naming the kids in your family. Can you imagine calling one of your kids by hollering, "Hey kid, come here." If you have more than one, say the average 2-1/2 kids in the American family, it gets tough to get the right one to come running without calling them distinctive names. All the elements of a form, and even the form itself, can and should be given a name. When you name the form by using the NAME attribute of the FORM tag, think of it as similar to a family name.

```
<FORM NAME="InputForm">
```

Once you've named your form, you refer to it using the name you've given it. As you add the elements that appear on your Web page, such as menus, lists, text entry controls, and checkboxes, each should have its own name.

```
<INPUT NAME="FirstName" TYPE="TEXT" SIZE="10">
```

Dot Notation

Using *objects* in your Web page is an important concept that is discussed later in this chapter. In many languages today, programming constructs such as your Web page are considered to be objects. Your Web page is a document just like your car or your refrigerator is an object. You can't name your Web page, so it has the boring, yet effective, name *document*. To refer to the form, InputForm, on your Web page, you precede it with the name of your Web page. Separate the two names with a dot (.) like this: document.InputForm.

To refer to a named element in a form, add it to the name of the form, separated by a dot. This is how you would refer to the text input element, FirstName:

```
document.InputForm.FirstName
```

The Big Event

Creating a form that places interesting controls on your Web page is only half the fun. Making them do something is the other half. In the past, there was only one option: add a **Submit** button to send the data off to the server to be processed by a CGI (Common Gateway Interface) program. The advantage of using VBScript is that you can process information locally using the Internet Explorer Web browser. You then have the option of sending the processed information to the server, or simply using the data locally.

To trigger VBScript procedures to start running, a Windows *event* is triggered. Windows operates by sending messages to programs notifying them when something, almost anything, has occurred. Windows is the ultimate gossip. When programs receive these messages, it's considered an event. For example, when the mouse is clicked on a form button, Windows sends a mouse click message that triggers the button's On_click event. When VBScript procedures are associated (mapped) with these events, they begin running when the event is triggered by a message from Windows.

Different form elements have different sets of events associated with them. For example, a text entry element doesn't have an On_click event, where a button does. To associate a VBScript procedure with an event, name the procedure with the name of the control followed by the name of the event. Notice in Figure 4.32, that the **EnterMe** button has an event script called EnterMe_OnClick.

In the procedure, you create a variable that refers to the form using the *Set* statement. Your form is considered an object and you can only create variables with an object subtype using the *Set* statement. This new variable is not a different form object; it is a new reference to the same object. Once again, every kid has their own name, but often times you refer to them using other affectionate terms. In fact, you may have many different references to the same kid depending on your mood.

The sample HTML file in Figure 4.32 doesn't do very much. When the **EnterMe** button is clicked, the *Sub* procedure validates the data by checking to make sure that the value entered is a valid month. So far, nothing else is done with the data. You have a choice at this point: You can use the information entered in the form in more VBScript procedures and functions, or you can choose to send it on to the server for processing.

Figure 4.32 Use the *Set* statement to create a reference to the form.

```
<HTML>
<HEAD>
<TITLE>My Little Web Page</TITLE>
<SCRIPT LANGUAGE="VBS">
        <!--
        Sub EnterMe_OnClick
        Dim TempForm
        Set TempForm = Document.MyForm
        If TempForm.Month.Value < 1 Or TempForm.Month.Value > 12 Then
                MsgBox "Please enter a valid month."
        End If
        End Sub
        -->
</SCRIPT>
</HEAD>
```

Continued...

■■■■■ **Figure 4.32** Continued

```
<BODY>
<H1>This is my data entry page</H1>
<FORM NAME="MyForm">
Enter the month of your birth. (1 through 12):
<INPUT NAME="Month" TYPE="TEXT" SIZE="2">
<INPUT NAME="EnterMe" TYPE="BUTTON" VALUE="Enter Me">
</FORM>
</BODY>
</HTML>
```

■■■■■

Sending Form Data to the Server

The previous section explains how you can collect data from a form and validate it. When you choose to send the validated information to the server, you need only a few additional lines in your program. Notice in the next example that there is now an *Else* to the *If* statement. So, when the data is correct, the *TempForm.Submit* statement is executed. Remember that TempForm refers to your form object and form objects have a special function called **Submit** built into them. You refer to built-in functions, called *methods*, by using the dot notation described earlier in this chapter (see Figure 4.33).

VBScript and ActiveX

This chapter introduces the VBScript language and how to write VBScript programs using forms. Form objects have been an important

▬▬▬▬ **Figure 4.33** Use dot notation to reference methods and object variables.

```
<SCRIPT LANGUAGE="VBS">
      <!--
      Sub EnterMe_OnClick
      Dim TempForm
      Set TempForm = Document.MyForm
      If TempForm.Month.Value < 1 Or TempForm.Month.Value > 12 Then
            MsgBox "Please enter a valid month."
      Else
            TempForm.Submit      ' Data correct; send to server.
      End If
      End Sub
      -->
</SCRIPT>
```

part of integrating VBScript into your Web page. Microsoft has introduced a way to include a special type of object into your Web page called ActiveX controls. The simple form controls you've used in the past are nothing like ActiveX controls, what were once called OLE controls. (OLE stands for Object Linking and Embedding.)

Microsoft has provided several exciting ActiveX controls (described in Chapter 2) that you can drop right into your Web page and communicate with using VBScript. Some of the abilities provided by the built-in controls include:

- Create powerful charts
- Present new items automatically

- Preload designated Web pages into a cache directory
- Automatically trigger events based on a timer

Unlike the form controls, ActiveX controls, and other supported object types like Java objects, are added to your Web page using an <OBJECT> tag. This tag, along with the <PARAM> tag used to set properties of the object, are all you need to embed powerful abilities in your HTML. Figure 4.34 shows the <OBJECT> tag for embedding the Microsoft Label control.

Use VBScript to set properties dynamically from within your Web page. For example, you can have the user set properties using a form. Once you have the value entered in the form, you can easily set the property to its new value. Reference the property by beginning with the ID of the object. (See the ID parameter of the <OBJECT> tag.) Using dot notation, enter the name of the property you want to change, and set the new value to the form element containing the new value:

```
lblActiveLbl.Caption = MyForm.NewProperty.Value
```

Not only does VBScript allow you to expand the capabilities of your Web page, but you can also greatly expand the capabilities of the ActiveX controls integrated into your Web pages.

■■■■■■ **Figure 4.34** ActiveX controls have documentation about how to format the <OBJECT> tag.

```
<OBJECT    classid="clsid:{99B42120-6EC7-11CF-A6C7-00AA00A47DD2}"
   id=lblActiveLbl  width=250  height=250  align=left  hspace=20
vspace=0 >
<PARAM NAME="Caption" VALUE="ActiveX Label">
```

CHAPTER 5

EXPLORING ACTIVEX

The cornerstone of Microsoft's Active Web technology is ActiveX controls. ActiveX controls are basically OLE controls, but they are faster and smaller than OLE controls so that they can be used across the Internet. The ActiveX Control technology lets you incorporate content into your Web pages that ranges from multimedia sound and video, interactive charts, and a multitude of other exciting and useful applications.

Because Microsoft has built several ActiveX controls into the Internet Explorer 3.0, you can drop controls right into your Web page. Some of the capabilities provided by the built-in controls include:

- Creating powerful charts
- Presenting new items automatically

- Preloading designated Web pages into a cache directory
- Automatically triggering events based on a timer

Placing these ActiveX controls in your Web pages doesn't require the skill of a programmer. In fact, within minutes you can provide ActiveX content on your Web site using the <OBJECT> HTML tag. Microsoft has even created development tools, such as the ActiveX Control Pad, which eliminate the need to even write the HTML code. Once you have the ActiveX controls placed in your Web pages, you can use ActiveX scripting to create user interactivity with the ActiveX controls. Now it's time to truly explore ActiveX controls.

Object Tag

For some time now, companies such as Netscape, Sun, and Microsoft have been evangelizing the incorporation of their different technologies into Web documents. Netscape is promoting inline plug-ins that are inserted in HTML pages with the <EMBED> tag, Sun has Java applets that are inserted in HTML pages with the <APPLET> tag, while Microsoft has recently been promoting the ActiveX control technology.

Rather than have a variety of different tags for each of these components the W3C consortium, the organization that sets the HTML standards, has created the <OBJECT> tag to replace all of the following HTML tags.

- <EMBED>
- <APPLET>
- <IMG>

As with any new HTML tag, the <OBJECT> tag is designed to handle existing components, future components, and at the same time to be backward-compatible with current browsers. The new <OBJECT> tag can be used to incorporate all of the following components within Web pages:

- ActiveX controls
- Java applets
- Images

Because there is a wide diversity of components that are used in conjunction with the <OBJECT> tag, it has significant number of attributes associated with it, as shown in Table 5.1.

■■■■■■■ **Table 5.1** Attributes of the <OBJECT> tag

Attribute	Description
DATA	Used to point to location for data that will be used to initialize the object. This could be an .AVI file when incorporating an AVI object.
WIDTH	Width in number of standard units.
HEIGHT	Height in number of standard units.
ID	The name token given to a particular object that other objects can reference. This allows objects to communicate with each other.
CLASSID	Class identifier number for ActiveX control objects.
CODEBASE	Specifies URL location where browser can download ActiveX control, if one isn't currently loaded.
NAME	A way for a browser to determine if an object found in a FORM block will participate in the "submit" process.
DECLARE	Indicates that an object is to be declared, but not instantiated.

Continued...

Table 5.1 Continued

Attribute	Description
ALIGN	Designates the location of the object on the Web page. The values for this attribute are the same as those available for placing images on Web pages.
TYPE	Used to ensure that the viewing agent can recognize the program type.
CODETYPE	Used to ensure that the viewing agent is compatible with the indicated object. If the code isn't compatible with the indicated object it won't be loaded and an apology section will be loaded.
STANDBY	Specifies text string that is displayed while the object is being loaded.
BORDER	Width of border around object in standard units.
HSPACE	Space to keep between the left and right sides of the visible area of the object, and other objects or text on the page. Defined in standard units.
VSPACE	Space to keep between the top and bottom sides of the visible area of the object, and other objects or text on the page. Defined in standard units.
SHAPES	Indicates that some part of the OBJECT contains anchors in various shapes on the visible area of the OBJECT.

The <OBJECT> tag uses these attributes to indicate the type of component that will be used or needs to be downloaded, the file that contains the data, and the specific parameters associated with the component. Following is an example of the HTML source code that would be used to insert an ActiveX Animation Button control in a Web page.

```
<OBJECT
CODEBASE="http://www.science.org/ieanbtn.ocx"
```

```
ID=anbtn
CLASSID="clsid:0482B100-739C-11CF-A3A9-00A0C9034920"
WIDTH=300
HEIGHT=400
ALIGN=center
HSPACE=0
VSPACE=0>
</OBJECT>
```

The uses of attributes such as WIDTH, HEIGHT, HSPACE, and VSPACE
are obvious to any Web developer. The values for these dimension attributes can be defined using standard units. There are several different types of
values that you can use when you specify these attributes.

- An integer number that represents the number of pixels.
- A percentage value to indicate the percentage of the display area, such
  as 25%.
- Fixed units of measure identified by a suffix following the desired
  floating-point number (the available units of measure and their
  suffixes include centimeters (cm), inches (in), points (pt), and
  picas (pi)).

When you place ActiveX controls in Web pages, the two most important
attributes you must be concerned with are CLASSID and CODEBASE.
These attributes are used to identify the control to the user's system, and
indicate a location to download the control from if it isn't already present
on the user's system.

CLASSID Attribute

Several of the ActiveX controls that are featured in this chapter come pre-
built in Internet Explorer 3.0. When Internet Explorer 3.0 is installed, these
controls are placed in the *C:\Windows\System* directory of your computer,
and they are registered in the system registration database.

When you place an ActiveX control in a Web page, you must use the CLASSID attribute and specify the global unique identifier (GUID) value for the desired control. This tells the user's computer what Common Object Model (COM) class needs to be instantiated to create the desired object. The GUID is the ID (typically a large 128-bit identifier) used to identify OLE controls that are already present in the system registration database. The creator of a particular ActiveX control uses the ActiveX SDK to assign the control a GUID.

CODEBASE Attribute

Suppose you have found one of the greatest new ActiveX controls that has just become available, and you want to incorporate it into your Web pages. What will happen when a user visits your Web pages but doesn't have this newly released control loaded? The answer to your dilemma is the CODEBASE attribute.

The CODEBASE attribute is used to specify the URL location from which controls that are not currently loaded on the user's computer can be down-loaded. This attribute can be used to specify three different file types.

- *Portable Executable file formats such as .EXE, .DLL, or .OCX.* The designated file is automatically downloaded, installed, and registered when specified by the CODEBASE attribute.
- *.CAB.* A file, referred to as a cabinet, that contains one or more files compressed together, including an .INF file that contains installation information.
- *.INF.* A file that contains installation information. This file typically contains information on the files that need to be downloaded for a particular ActiveX control to be executed.

The CODEBASE attribute gives Web developers a simple way to ensure that users visiting their Web site with the Internet Explorer (or any browser that supports ActiveX controls) can view ActiveX content, even when the ActiveX control isn't currently loaded on the user's computer. This can happen behind the scenes, depending on the Trust Verification settings that the user has in the Internet Explorer. To protect your computer from downloading potentially mischievous content, you should set your trust verification settings accordingly (see Chapter 2). Of course, this system only tells you who created the ActiveX control you will be downloading, not if it is harmful in any way.

The following sample code illustrates an example of using the gradient control. The CODEBASE attribute specifying the URL is included within the <OBJECT> tag.

```
<OBJECT ID="iegrad1" WIDTH=100 HEIGHT=51

CLASSID="CLSID:017C99A0-8637-11CF-A3A9-00A0C9034900"

CODEBASE="http://www.microsoft.com/ie/download/activex/iegrad.ocx#Version=4,70,0
,1086">
```

In this example, the Internet Explorer browser contacts the indicated URL to download the particular ActiveX control needed. As you can see, you can also specify the version number of the ActiveX control. The user's browser will first check to see if the user's system has the current ActiveX control loaded, and then will download the control only if the version number specified is more recent than the control currently loaded. You can also ensure that the specified control is always downloaded no matter what version number is currently loaded by making the version number equal to "-1,-1,-1,-1." Before you do this, you may want to consider the consequences of everyone having to download the ActiveX control from your Web server every time they contact that particular Web page.

If no CODEBASE attribute is specified, and the user's computer doesn't have the indicated ActiveX control, nothing is displayed. The user won't know what they are missing.

Param Tag

Every control has several additional parameters that must be defined for it to produce the desired content. For example, when using the Chart control, you need to specify properties such as the type of chart to display, colors used, and the data that it contains. The <PARAM> tag is used in combination with the <OBJECT> tag to specify these additional NAME|VALUE pairs that are passed to the control for it to execute properly. The NAME attribute defines the property name, while the VALUE attribute defines the property value. Following is an example of the HTML code used to place an ActiveX Animation Button control within a Web page, and the parameters this control requires.

```
<OBJECT
CODEBASE="http://www.science.org/ieanbtn.ocx"
ID=anbtn
CLASSID="clsid:0482B100-739C-11CF-A3A9-00A0C9034920"
WIDTH=300
HEIGHT=400
ALIGN=center
HSPACE=0
VSPACE=0>
<PARAM NAME="defaultfrstart" VALUE="0">
<PARAM NAME="defaultfrend" VALUE="7">
<PARAM NAME="mouseoverfrstart" VALUE="8">
<PARAM NAME="mouseoverfrend" VALUE="15">
<PARAM NAME="focusfrstart" VALUE="16">
<PARAM NAME="focusfrend" VALUE="23">
<PARAM NAME="downfrstart" VALUE="24">
<PARAM NAME="downfrend" VALUE="34">
<PARAM NAME="URL"
VALUE="http://www.microsoft.com/ie/download/activex/cool.avi">
</OBJECT>
```

In this example, the <PARAM> statements are placed between the start and end <OBJECT> tags. It is important to remember that in some cases the NAME and VALUE attributes that are passed to the object are case sensitive. Case sensitivity is determined by the developer when the particular control created. You can assume no case sensitivity unless specified otherwise.

There are several attributes, known as VALUETYPE attributes, that can be used to further specify the type of the VALUE attribute in a <PARAM> tag (see Table 5.2).

The desired VALUETYPE attribute is specified before the VALUE attribute, as shown in the following code example:

```
<PARAM  NAME="coolguy"   REF VALUE="http://www.science.org/don">
```

The <PARAM> tag is the way that you will customize the ActiveX controls placed within your Web pages.

Alternate Tags

When you include various ActiveX controls in your Web pages, you should provide content that will be visible to people using Netscape or Mosaic browsers. The <OBJECT> tag allows you to place these backward compatible tags within it. This allows browsers that don't support the <OBJECT> tag, or support the components specified by the <OBJECT> tag to still view some content on your Web page.

▬▬▬▬▬ **Table 5.2** VALUETYPE Attributes for Use with the <PARAM> tag

Attribute	Description
DATA	Denotes that the value is a string that should be passed directly to the object. This is the default when no VALUE-TYPE is specified.
OBJECT	Denotes that the value is an URL to an OBJECT element in the same document.
REF	Denotes that the value attribute specifies an URL.

▬▬▬▬▬

In the following example, a Surround Video ActiveX control is being placed in a Web page using the <OBJECT> tag. For those using a browser that doesn't support ActiveX controls, the <IMG> is used so that they can at least view a picture with similar content.

```
<OBJECT ID="SVControl1" WIDTH=100 HEIGHT=51
CLASSID="CLSID:7142BA01-8BDF-11CF-9E23-0000E8A37440">
<PARAM NAME="_ExtentX" VALUE="2646">
<PARAM NAME="_ExtentY" VALUE="1323">
<IMG SRC="/images/city.gif" ALIGN=left  WIDTH=200 HEIGHT=50>
</OBJECT>
```

Some Web developers may remember a time not so long ago when many browsers could not display images. When placing an image in your Web pages using the <IMG> tag, you had to add the ALT attribute. The ALT attribute would be a string of text that would be displayed for browsers that didn't support images. Microsoft has changed the capabilities of the ALT attribute for the Internet Explorer. Now you can use this attribute with a <IMG> tag to display a pop-up window when a mouseover event occurs. Here is an example of HTML code that includes the ALT attribute:

```
<IMG SRC="/library/images/gifs/general/sebug.gif" WIDTH=61 HEIGHT=64 BORDER=0
ALT="Search" HSPACE=0>
```

Figure 5.1 shows the Microsoft home page, which displays a text message in a pop-up window when a mouseover event occurs.

ActiveX Control Pad

Now that you know the long and difficult way of placing ActiveX controls in Web pages, by writing HTML code with the <OBJECT> tag, it's time to learn the easy way using ActiveX Control Pad. The ActiveX Control Pad makes the insertion of ActiveX controls in Web pages a simple point-and-click operation,

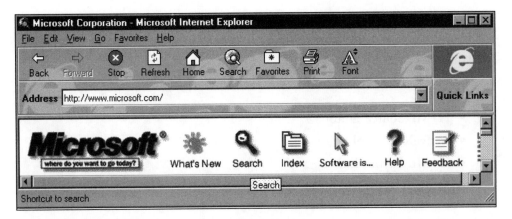

Figure 5.1 Use the ALT attribute to present timely information to a user browsing your Web pages.

rather than one that requires many laborious hours of writing HTML code. Here are just some of the features of the ActiveX Control Pad:

- Displays all of the ActiveX controls currently registered on your system that you can insert in the Web pages you create
- Allows simple and exact drag-and-drop placement of controls on a Web page
- Generates all of the HTML code needed for ActiveX control insertion
- Allows you to assign actions to the ActiveX controls using simple scripting

Using the ActiveX Control Pad, you don't have to remember the long GUID for every control or the numerous attributes of each control. The ActiveX Control Pad retrieves the CLASSID information on the control you want to use and then generates the necessary HTML code with the <OBJECT> tag. Considering there are over 1,000 existing ActiveX controls, each with its own distinct 128-bit GUID, the usefulness of the ActiveX Control Pad becomes readily apparent. There are four main utilities that constitute the ActiveX Control Pad:

- HTML Source Editor
- ActiveX Control Editor
- HTML Layout Editor
- Script Wizard

You can explore the capabilities of each of these utilities after you download the ActiveX Control Pad from the following URL:

    http://www.microsoft.com/workshop/author/cpad/

Before you install the ActiveX Control Pad, you should have Internet Explorer 3.0 already installed. Microsoft also recommends that you have 16 MB of RAM, but the ActiveX Control Pad can be run with only 8 MB of RAM, albeit a little slower.

HTML Source Editor

When you first run the ActiveX Control Pad, it opens into the main text editor window shown in Figure 5.2.

The HTML Source Editor is the main window of the ActiveX Control Pad, and it provides a simple environment in which you can add either ActiveX controls or HTML layout controls to a Web page. In this text environment you can create or modify HTML code.

Before you add either ActiveX controls or HTML layout controls, you must position the HTML Source Editor cursor in the location of the Web page where you want the control added. When you add ActiveX controls, you can add them to either the <HEAD> or <BODY> of the Web page; but HTML layout controls can only be placed in the <BODY> of the Web page.

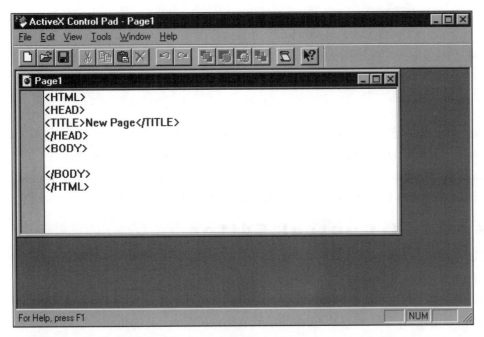

Figure 5.2 When the ActiveX Control Pad is started, a new HTML document is created.

Here is the basic procedure for creating Web pages containing ActiveX controls using the ActiveX Control Pad:

1. Create a new HTML document by selecting the **File|New HTML** command, or open an existing HTML document by selecting the **File|Open** command.

2. Insert either ActiveX controls or HTML layout controls in your Web page. Position your cursor in the HTML Text Editor where you want the desired control to be placed. Then choose either the **Edit|Insert ActiveX Control** or **Edit|Insert HTML Layout** command. Modify the properties, appearance, and size of the controls that you insert into the Web page, and close the Edit ActiveX Control window.

3. Create script to modify the actions of the control by choosing the **Tools|Script Wizard** command.

4. View the Web page in Internet Explorer to test its appearance and functionality.

When an ActiveX control or HTML layout control is added to the Web page, you will see a small icon to the left of the <OBJECT> tag for that particular control. You can modify the properties of a particular control by clicking on this icon, which will launch the appropriate editor.

ActiveX Control Editor

The ActiveX Control Editor is the utility that allows you to choose the ActiveX control to add, and then modify its properties and size. The Insert ActiveX Control window appears when the ActiveX Control Editor is activated, by selecting the **Edit|Insert ActiveX Control** command. The Insert ActiveX Control window displays all of the ActiveX controls registered on your system and available for placement in a Web page, as shown in Figure 5.3.

After you choose the ActiveX control, both the Edit ActiveX Control window and Properties window are opened (see Figures 5.4 and 5.5).

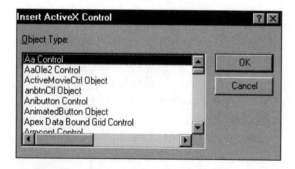

▬▬▬▬ **Figure 5.3** Choose the ActiveX control you want to add to your Web page.

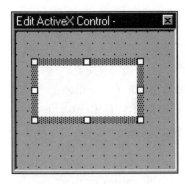

Figure 5.4 Use the mouse to position and set the desired size of the ActiveX control in the Edit ActiveX Control window.

The control appears in the Edit ActiveX Control window exactly as it will appear on your Web page. For example, when you choose the Chart control, you should see the chart displayed in the Edit ActiveX Control window. When you vary any of the chart properties, the displayed chart should change appropriately.

Properties	
Apply	
BackColor	
BackStyle	1 - Opaque
ChartData	0
ChartType	8 - Simple Area Chart
CodeBase	
ColorScheme	0 - Color Scheme 1
ColumnIndex	0
ColumnName	C 0
Columns	3
DataItem	9
DisplayLegend	1 - On
ForeColor	
GridPlacement	0 - Bottom
Height	37.5
hgridStyle	0 - No Grid
HorizontalAxis	0

Figure 5.5 Customize the properties of the ActiveX control to present the desired content.

Oftentimes when you first choose a particular control to add to a Web page, the box representing the control appears empty. Sometimes the ActiveX Control Pad displays the control if you close your ActiveX Control Editor and then choose to edit the same control by clicking on the edit object icon in the HTML Source Editor.

Of course, when you vary the dimensions of a control, the values in the Properties window also change. The Properties window displays all of the properties that can be defined for a control. These properties represent NAME|VALUE pairs that will be defined with the <PARAM> tag when the HTML code is generated for the ActiveX control.

Make sure that you click on the **Apply** button in the Property window after you have modified a particular property to ensure that the property value has been changed.

When you are done modifying the ActiveX control for insertion, close the Edit ActiveX Control window. The Property window automatically closes when the Edit ActiveX Control window is closed. The HTML code for the ActiveX control is then created or modified, and placed in the chosen location in the HTML Source Editor. The ActiveX Control Editor provides a simple way to include ActiveX controls in your Web pages, eliminating the need for writing the actual HTML code.

Setting Color Properties

The days of black and white are over. Nowadays people like color, including colored cars, colored TVs, and even colored Web pages. Most ActiveX controls have several properties through which you can define the color that appears, such as BackColor, ForeColor, or FontColor. When inserting an ActiveX control in a Web page using the ActiveX Control Pad, you set the color characteristics in the Properties window. In this window you must define the color you want using either the integer or the RGB value for the desired color.

The RGB color code system is based on three color components: red, green, and blue. A value ranging from 0-255 is used to define the particular intensity of the component. Here are some examples of RGB values for different colors.

- Black: 0, 0, 0
- White: 255, 255, 255
- Bright purple: 255, 0, 255

When you define colors using the RGB color code in the ActiveX Control Pad Property window, all you need is the values in the same format as they appear in the color examples above (for example, 15, 100, 75). In addition to using the RGB color code, you can also define colors using the appropriate integer. An integer value for a particular color is defined by taking the decimal number created by adding together the different RGB binary values. The following example illustrates how you can determine the integer number for a color defined with the RGB color code (100, 125, 200).

Using the calculator accessory, you can easily determine the binary number for each of the RGB color codes. Enter the number, such as 200, while in decimal (Dec) mode, and then click on the binary mode (Bin) radiobutton. The entry field then displays the binary number.

- The binary number for 200 is 11001000.
- The binary number for 125 is 1111101.
- The binary number for 100 is 1100100.

These binary numbers are then concatenated together (the number created is 11000100001111110101100100, because the number is in the order BGR with a zero added to make all numbers 8 bits long) and evaluated in decimal mode. The resulting integer can be used in place of the three RGB color codes, which in this example would be equal to 25722212.

When you have finished editing a particular ActiveX control and return to the HTML Source Editor, the ActiveX Control Pad converts either the integer or the RGB color code into a RGB hex triplet color code. The color must be specified in HTML code with the RGB hex triplet color code to be displayed on the Web.

You can edit the color displayed for a particular ActiveX control either with the Property window or directly in the HTML Source Editor. If you don't remember the RGB hex triplet color code values for a color, you can check out the following URL, which shows a RGB hex triplet color chart:

```
http://www.phoenix.net/~jacobson/rgb.html
```

HTML Layout Editor

Exact placement of objects on a Web page using HTML can often be a time-consuming exercise. The poorly designed HTML language simply doesn't allow for easy object layout. The HTML layout control solves this problem. Now you can place all of your ActiveX controls, such as radiobuttons, ActiveMovies, and text entry fields, in any location you want using a WYSIWYG layout screen. The HTML layout control features several capabilities.

- Point-and-click insertion of one or many ActiveX controls on Web pages in the same way you create forms in Visual Basic
- Setting the properties of the ActiveX control
- Setting control transparency allowing controls to overlap each other

The HTML layout control acts as a container for all of the controls you place in it. When you complete a HTML layout, it is saved as a document with an .ALX file extension. The HTML layout is then incorporated at run-time, in the same way that image files are loaded. Because the information on a particular HTML layout is saved as a separate .ALX file, you can incorporate the same HTML layout multiple times in the same Web document, or in multiple Web documents. You do not need to create a new HTML layout file to have the same functionality in different Web documents. Of course, the HTML Layout control is needed to view these .ALX files.

■■■■■■■ **TIP**

In the beta releases of Internet Explorer 3.0 the HTML Layout control is not built-in, but it will be in the final release of Internet Explorer 3.0. When you install the ActiveX Control Pad the HTML Layout control is also installed.

■■■■■■■

Now you are ready to create a new HTML layout. Select the **File|New HTML Layout** command, which opens the Layout window in addition to the Toolbox window. With a simple point-and-click, you can select from a variety of different controls in the Toolbox. After you choose the desired control, either click on the Layout window in the location where you want the control to be placed, or drag the control to the Layout window. You can change the properties of the particular control by double-clicking on it, which opens the Properties window. These various windows can be seen in Figure 5.6.

The Properties window lets you modify the properties for each control. Here are some of the customizations for the radiobutton control:

- If the radiobutton should initially be checked or not

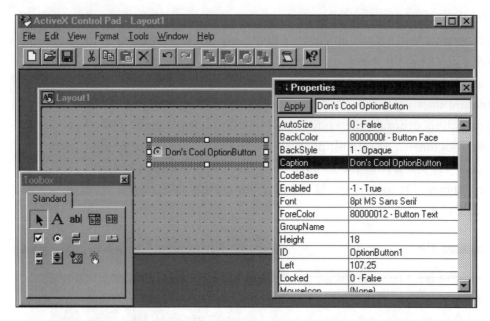

Figure 5.6 Modify the desired properties of the control in the Property window.

- If there is a caption displayed next to the radio control
- Size of font for the caption

Here is an example of the HTML code produced when the HTML layout containing the simple radiobutton control is inserted into an HTML document.

```
<HTML>
<HEAD>
<TITLE>Simple Control</TITLE>
</HEAD>
<BODY>
<OBJECT CLASSID="CLSID:812AE312-8B8E-11CF-93C8-00AA00C08FDF"
ID="test1" STYLE="LEFT:0;TOP:0">
```

```
<PARAM NAME="ALXPATH" REF
VALUE="file:C:\DON\BOOK\ActiveX\Chapter2\WebPages\test1.alx">

</OBJECT>

</BODY>

</HTML>
```

The usefulness of the HTML Layout control is that you can easily design the exact layout of controls placed on a Web page. Here is an illustration of the text information contained within the TEST1.ALX file generated for the Simple Control example.

```
<DIV STYLE="LAYOUT:FIXED;WIDTH:362pt;HEIGHT:134pt;">

    <OBJECT ID="OptionButton1"

     CLASSID="CLSID:8BD21D50-EC42-11CE-9E0D-00AA006002F3"
STYLE="TOP:33pt;LEFT:107pt;WIDTH:108pt;HEIGHT:18pt;TABINDEX:0;ZINDEX:0;">

        <PARAM NAME="BackColor" VALUE="-2147483633">

        <PARAM NAME="ForeColor" VALUE="-2147483630">

        <PARAM NAME="DisplayStyle" VALUE="5">

        <PARAM NAME="Size" VALUE="3810;635">

        <PARAM NAME="Caption" VALUE="Don's Cool OptionButton">

        <PARAM NAME="FontCharSet" VALUE="0">

        <PARAM NAME="FontPitchAndFamily" VALUE="2">

        <PARAM NAME="FontWeight" VALUE="0">

    </OBJECT>

</DIV>
```

Toolbox Time

As illustrated in Figure 5.6, the Toolbox is initially loaded with several standard controls. As new ActiveX controls are created, many developers will want to use them in the HTML Layout Editor environment. The HTML Layout Editor allows you to add new controls to the Toolbox. Right-click on the Toolbox window to open the pop-up menu. When you select the **Additional Controls** command, the window shown in Figure 5.7 opens.

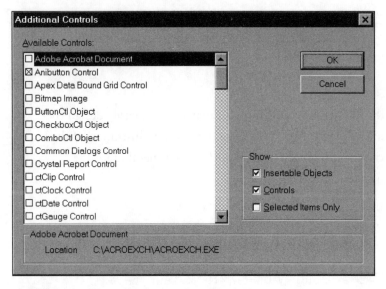

Figure 5.7 Choose the controls you want to add, and click **OK.**

Click on the check box for every control you want added to the Toolbox, and press **OK.** Now you can use all of the ActiveX controls with the HTML Layout Editor. You can also delete controls from the Toolbox in seconds. Right-click on the control you want to delete. Then choose the delete option. Now you have the tools to activate your Web pages with ActiveX controls.

There are already an endless number of ActiveX controls. Organization of these controls in the Toolbox window is a necessity. When you first open the Toolbox window, you can see that the only existing page is labeled Standard. The Toolbox lets you add additional pages to keep a better organization of the ActiveX controls you will use in development. Right-click on the Standard page, and choose **New Page.** Then enter the name of the new page you want to create. Now add the desired controls to this new page.

Control Appearance

Bitmaps are assigned to controls by selecting either the Picture or PicturePath property and indicating the path to the desired image file. The image will be scaled to the size of the control when it is displayed on a Web page.

In addition to defining a particular image to be displayed for an ActiveX control, you can also assign bitmap *transparency* to many controls. Transparency allows the background or other controls that lie behind a particular control to be seen. You can assign transparency to a control by choosing the BackStyle property. There are several controls that are part of the Microsoft form controls that are always transparent:

- OptionButton
- Label
- ToggleButton
- CheckBox
- CommandButton

As you place ActiveX controls on a HTML layout, their relative locations can be set using four of the WYSIWYG buttons on the ActiveX Control Pad toolbar:

- Bring to Front
- Move Forward
- Move Backward
- Send to Back

Select the control you want to move, and then choose the appropriate button. This capability combined with the ability to set the transparency and appearance of controls allows you to produce an impressive control layout.

Script Wizard

The real usefulness of ActiveX controls lies in the ability to link them together using ActiveX scripting. Many of the ActiveX controls that you use in your Web pages have both actions and events associated with them. Using ActiveX scripting in combination with your ActiveX controls allows you to add user interactivity. For example, now you can allow the user to vary the properties of a particular ActiveX control, such as the chart control. You could link together a Command button with a chart control. Now when the Command button is clicked, the ChartStyle property of a Chart control is changed to present a Point chart, rather than a Line chart. Another example could allow a user to type a text string in a Textarea control, which is then displayed by the Marquee control.

The Script Wizard can be started whether you are in the HTML Source Editor or the HTML Layout Editor by selecting the **Tool|Script Wizard** command or clicking on the **Script Wizard** button on the main toolbar. When you activate the Script Wizard while in the HTML Source Editor, you can edit the actions and scripts for all of the ActiveX controls in a particular Web page, including any HTML layout controls. When you activate the Script Wizard while in the HTML Layout Editor, you can edit the scripts for only those ActiveX controls placed in that particular HTML layout.

The Script Wizard in the ActiveX Control Pad allows you to quickly add ActiveX scripting to the controls in a Web page you create. When you first run the Script Wizard, you will see it consists of three main windows, as shown in Figure 5.8.

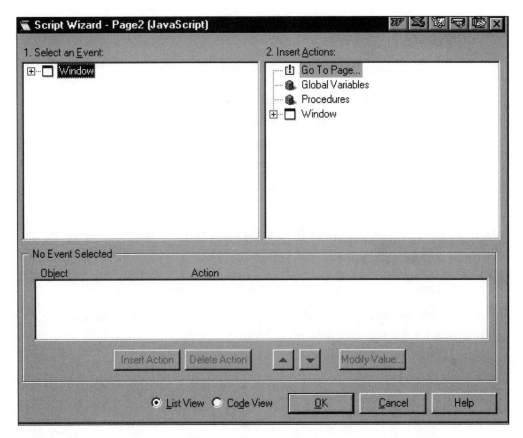

- *Event pane.* Displays the events available for each of the controls placed in a Web page or in a HTML layout. For example, a CommandButton control will have click, doubleclick, mouseover, and numerous other events associated with it.

- *Action pane.* Displays the various properties, methods, or variables for the available controls.

- *Script pane.* There are two display modes for the script pane: List and Code. When in List mode, the action or actions assigned to specific events are displayed whenever the event is selected in the Event pane. When in Code mode, the actual ActiveX scripting code, either VBScript or JavaScript, is displayed.

The Script Wizard generates the ActiveX scripting for the events and actions you specify. The ActiveX scripting that is created can be either VBScript or JavaScript, depending on the option settings for the Script Wizard. You can modify the Script Wizard settings by selecting the **Tools|Options** command and choosing the **Script** option, which will open the window shown in Figure 5.9.

Here is the typical procedure to follow to create ActiveX scripting for an ActiveX control using the Script Wizard:

1. Click on the (+) sign in the Event pane to display all of the available events for a particular control.
2. Select the event that you want to script.
3. In the Action Pane double-click on the property, method, or variable that you want to add to the chosen event.

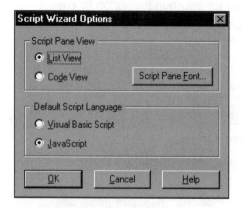

■■■■■ **Figure 5.9** Select the default scripting language you want the Script Wizard to generate.

4. The script for linking the event to the property, method, or variable is illustrated in the Script pane.

5. You can then modify the event-action relationship created in the Script pane using either the List mode or Code mode. In List mode (see Figure 5.10), you can insert actions, delete actions, or vary the order of actions that occur for a particular event. In Code mode (see Figure 5.11) you can actually modify the ActiveX scripting.

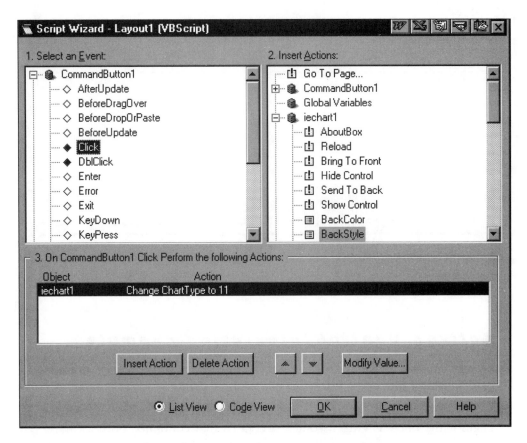

▬▬▬▬ **Figure 5.10** Choose an event and then an appropriate action to instantly create the scripting for control integration.

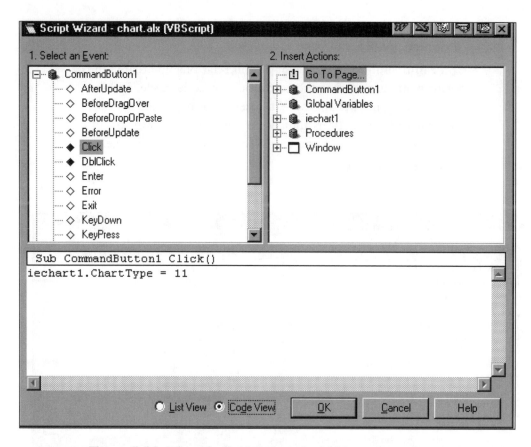

Figure 5.11 When Code View is selected, you can write new VBScript or modify existing code.

ActiveX Control Integration Example

The true interactivity of ActiveX controls is achieved using the scripting capabilities of the Script Wizard. This example demonstrates the integration of the Chart control with a Command button in a HTML layout. To begin with, a new HTML layout was created that contained both a Chart control and CommandButton control. The Script Wizard was then launched while the HTML layout was still open, and it appeared as shown in Figure 5.10.

The Click event of the CommandButton control was selected, and the ChartStyle property of the Chart control was chosen as the action. The Script pane in Figure 5.10 displays the event-action relationship which indicates that when the user clicks the CommandButton on the Web page, the Chart displayed will change from a Simple Bar Chart (14) to a Simple Column Chart (11). When the Code mode in the Script Wizard is chosen, the actual ActiveX scripting code generated is displayed (see Figure 5.11).

Once completed with the Script Wizard, the HTML layout control can be added to a new HTML document using the Edit|Insert HTML Layout command, as shown in the following code example.

```
<HTML>
<HEAD>
<TITLE>Chart And Command Button Integration</TITLE>
</HEAD>
<BODY>
<OBJECT ID="chart"
CLASSID="CLSID:812AE312-8B8E-11CF-93C8-00AA00C08FDF">
<PARAM NAME="ALXPATH" REF VALUE="file:C:\DON\BOOK\ActiveX\Chapter5\chart.alx">
</OBJECT>
</BODY>
</HTML>
```

Because the ActiveX scripting was created for controls contained in the HTML Layout control, the actual script code is placed in the .ALX file (see Figure 5.12).

▬▬▬▬▬▬ **Figure 5.12** The HTML code for both the Chart and CommandButton controls and script code are contained in the .ALX file.

```
<SCRIPT LANGUAGE="VBScript">
<!--
```

Continued...

■■■■■ **Figure 5.12** Continued

```
Sub CommandButton1_Click()
iechart1.ChartType = 11
end sub
-->
</SCRIPT>

<DIV STYLE="LAYOUT:FIXED;WIDTH:240pt;HEIGHT:180pt;">
    <OBJECT ID="CommandButton1"
    CLASSID="CLSID:D7053240-CE69-11CD-A777-00DD01143C57"
STYLE="TOP:116pt;LEFT:66pt;WIDTH:83pt;HEIGHT:25pt;TABINDEX:0;ZINDEX:0;">
        <PARAM NAME="Caption" VALUE="Change ChartStyle">
        <PARAM NAME="Size" VALUE="2911;873">
        <PARAM NAME="FontCharSet" VALUE="0">
        <PARAM NAME="FontPitchAndFamily" VALUE="2">
        <PARAM NAME="ParagraphAlign" VALUE="3">
        <PARAM NAME="FontWeight" VALUE="0">
    </OBJECT>
    <OBJECT ID="iechart1"
    CLASSID="CLSID:FC25B780-75BE-11CF-8B01-444553540000"
STYLE="TOP:25pt;LEFT:41pt;WIDTH:132pt;HEIGHT:79pt;TABINDEX:1;ZINDEX:1;">
        <PARAM NAME="_ExtentX" VALUE="4657">
        <PARAM NAME="_ExtentY" VALUE="2778">
        <PARAM NAME="Rows" VALUE="4">
        <PARAM NAME="Columns" VALUE="3">
        <PARAM NAME="ChartType" VALUE="14">
        <PARAM NAME="Data[0][0]" VALUE="9">
        <PARAM NAME="Data[0][1]" VALUE="10">
        <PARAM NAME="Data[0][2]" VALUE="11">
        <PARAM NAME="Data[1][0]" VALUE="7">
        <PARAM NAME="Data[1][1]" VALUE="11">
        <PARAM NAME="Data[1][2]" VALUE="12">
```

```
        <PARAM NAME="Data[2][0]" VALUE="6">

        <PARAM NAME="Data[2][1]" VALUE="12">

        <PARAM NAME="Data[2][2]" VALUE="13">

        <PARAM NAME="Data[3][0]" VALUE="11">

        <PARAM NAME="Data[3][1]" VALUE="13">

        <PARAM NAME="Data[3][2]" VALUE="14">

        <PARAM NAME="HorizontalAxis" VALUE="0">

        <PARAM NAME="VerticalAxis" VALUE="0">

        <PARAM NAME="hgridStyle" VALUE="0">

        <PARAM NAME="vgridStyle" VALUE="0">

        <PARAM NAME="ColorScheme" VALUE="0">

        <PARAM NAME="BackStyle" VALUE="1">

        <PARAM NAME="Scale" VALUE="100">

        <PARAM NAME="DisplayLegend" VALUE="0">

        <PARAM NAME="BackColor" VALUE="16777215">

        <PARAM NAME="ForeColor" VALUE="32768">

    </OBJECT>

</DIV>
```

■■■■■■

Now the HTML document can be provided to a user. When the Web
page is first loaded, the Chart will appear as a Simple Bar Chart (see
Figure 5.13), but when the user activates the Click event of the
CommandButton, the chart changes to a Simple Column Chart (see
Figure 5.14).

This example clearly demonstrates the endless number of different event
and action relationships you can design for ActiveX controls in your
Web pages. You can create this kind of interactivity in seconds using the

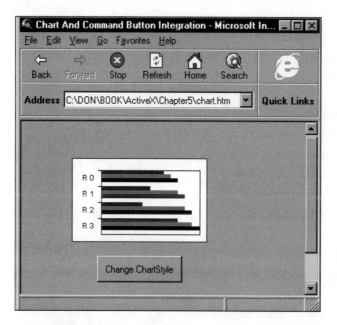

■■■■■■■ **Figure 5.13** The user can click on the CommandButton to change
the chart style.

Script Wizard as part of the ActiveX Control Pad development
environment.

Internet Explorer ActiveX Controls

There are already numerous existing ActiveX controls that you can immediately begin experimenting with and including in your Web site. The following are ActiveX controls that are built into Internet Explorer 3.0:

- *Intrinsic controls.* Typical form components such as radiobuttons and checkboxes

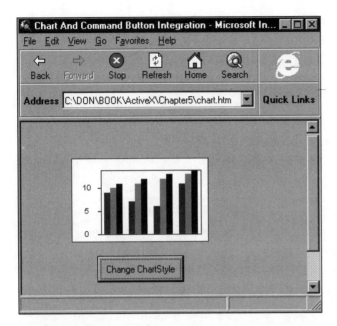

Figure 5.14 The chart is dynamically changed to a Simple Column chart.

- *Chart.* Allows you to create and display a variety of different charts on a Web page
- *Label.* Displays text at any angle on a Web page
- *StockTicker.* Allows you to display real-time data, such as stock quotes, temperatures, and so forth
- *Animation Button.* Displays various frames of an .AVI sequence depending on the state of the button
- *New Item.* Inserts images that appear and disappear after a designated time period
- *Marquee.* Allows you to place scrolling text within your Web pages
- *Preloader.* Downloads designated URLs into the cache directory, while the user is viewing another Web page

- *Timer.*   Initiates various actions on a Web page when the user performs some specific action
- *Popup Menu.*   Displays a pop-up menu on a Web page

Because these controls are built into Internet Explorer 3.0, the user doesn't need to download any additional controls.

■■■■■■■ TIP

At the time this book was written, several of these controls were not yet implemented in the Internet Explorer 3.0. They were in fact called "Cool Controls" that had to be downloaded from the following URL, referred to as the ActiveX Gallery. Web page examples of these controls can also be found in the ActiveX Gallery:

http://www.microsoft.com/workshop/

When you implement these controls in your Web pages, reference the "Cool Control" URL for the CODEBASE attribute. This will ensure that even if Microsoft hasn't built these controls into the Internet Explorer 3.0, users visiting your site will still have the controls downloaded and installed on their computers and can therefore view your ActiveX content.

■■■■

Intrinsic Controls

In previous Web page creation, you've probably placed various FORM elements on Web pages, ranging from radiobuttons to text area input. These standard HTML form tags are now controls in the Internet Explorer environment. When Internet Explorer is downloaded and installed, these controls are contained in the HTMLCTL.OCX, which is installed with Internet Explorer 3.0. Here is a list of the various Intrinsic controls:

- Password
- Radio
- List
- Button
- CheckBox
- Combo
- Text
- Textarea

Many of these intrinsic controls are shown as standard controls in the Toolbox window, which is part of the HTML Layout Editor. The functions of these controls should be familiar to all Web developers.

Chart Control

When displaying and creating charts, you are no longer limited to using only Excel. With the Chart control, you can quickly insert charts within your own Web pages in seconds. The Chart control provides several different types of charts:

- Bar
- Line
- Area
- Point
- Pie
- Column
- Stock

The list of these different charts can be found by choosing the ChartType property in the Property window after the Chart control has been selected for insertion in the ActiveX Control Pad. Almost all of these different chart types can exist in three different styles: single, stacked, and full.

The Property window shown in Figure 5.15 displays nearly all of the different properties for the Chart control. The properties Rows and Columns define the number of rows and columns in a chart. You can define the

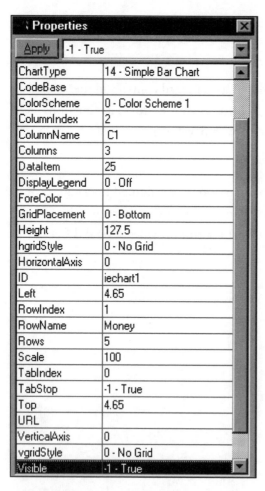

Properties	
Apply	-1 - True

ChartType	14 - Simple Bar Chart
CodeBase	
ColorScheme	0 - Color Scheme 1
ColumnIndex	2
ColumnName	C1
Columns	3
DataItem	25
DisplayLegend	0 - Off
ForeColor	
GridPlacement	0 - Bottom
Height	127.5
hgridStyle	0 - No Grid
HorizontalAxis	0
ID	iechart1
Left	4.65
RowIndex	1
RowName	Money
Rows	5
Scale	100
TabIndex	0
TabStop	-1 - True
Top	4.65
URL	
VerticalAxis	0
vgridStyle	0 - No Grid
Visible	-1 - True

■■■■ **Figure 5.15** Click on a chart property and modify it in the text entry window on top of the Properties window.

name of a row by first specifying the row with the RowIndex property, and then modifying the RowName property. The same procedure can be done to name columns using the ColumnName property.

Inserting Chart Data

Before you can display a Chart control, you must define the data that will be displayed. You can insert the data displayed by a Chart control using a combination of several Chart properties.

- *RowIndex*. Specifies a particular row beginning with 0 up to the number specified by the Rows property
- *ColumnIndex*.   Specifies a particular column beginning with 0 up to the number specified by Column property
- *DataItem*.   Specifies a data value for a particular Row|Column pair

It is very simple to define the data in your chart. For example, to define the data in row 3 and column 0, you would insert 3 in the RowIndex, and 0 in the ColumnIndex. Then you would indicate the desired data value for the DataItem property. Figure 5.16 shows a simple bar chart in which the value 25 was entered for the DataItem defined by a ColumnIndex of 2, and a RowIndex of 1.

Figure 5.17 shows the HTML generated by the ActiveX Control Pad for the sample chart defined by the properties in Figure 5.15, and shown in Figure 5.16.

You can see in the HTML code shown in Figure 5.17 how the data is defined with the <PARAM> tag as a NAME|VALUE pair. The NAME is in the form Data[RowIndex][ColumnIndex], and the VALUE is the numerical value for the designated DataItem property.

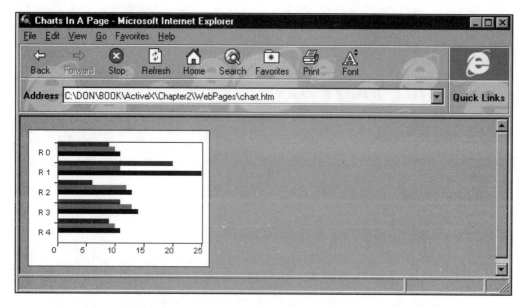

Figure 5.16 The chart that appears on the Web page when defined by the properties shown in Figure 5.15.

Figure 5.17 HTML code generated by the ActiveX Control Pad for insertion of the chart control.

```
<HTML>
<HEAD>
<TITLE>Charts In A Page</TITLE>
</HEAD>
<BODY>
<OBJECT ID="iechart1" WIDTH=236 HEIGHT=171
 CLASSID="CLSID:FC25B780-75BE-11CF-8B01-444553540000">
    <PARAM NAME="_ExtentX" VALUE="6244">
    <PARAM NAME="_ExtentY" VALUE="4498">
    <PARAM NAME="Rows" VALUE="5">
```

```
        <PARAM NAME="Columns" VALUE="3">
        <PARAM NAME="ChartType" VALUE="14">
        <PARAM NAME="Data[0][0]" VALUE="9">
        <PARAM NAME="Data[0][1]" VALUE="10">
        <PARAM NAME="Data[0][2]" VALUE="11">
        <PARAM NAME="Data[1][0]" VALUE="20">
        <PARAM NAME="Data[1][1]" VALUE="11">
        <PARAM NAME="Data[1][2]" VALUE="25">
        <PARAM NAME="Data[2][0]" VALUE="6">
        <PARAM NAME="Data[2][1]" VALUE="12">
        <PARAM NAME="Data[2][2]" VALUE="13">
        <PARAM NAME="Data[3][0]" VALUE="11">
        <PARAM NAME="Data[3][1]" VALUE="13">
        <PARAM NAME="Data[3][2]" VALUE="14">
        <PARAM NAME="Data[4][0]" VALUE="9">
        <PARAM NAME="Data[4][1]" VALUE="10">
        <PARAM NAME="Data[4][2]" VALUE="11">
        <PARAM NAME="HorizontalAxis" VALUE="0">
        <PARAM NAME="VerticalAxis" VALUE="0">
        <PARAM NAME="hgridStyle" VALUE="0">
        <PARAM NAME="vgridStyle" VALUE="0">
        <PARAM NAME="ColorScheme" VALUE="0">
        <PARAM NAME="BackStyle" VALUE="1">
        <PARAM NAME="Scale" VALUE="100">
        <PARAM NAME="DisplayLegend" VALUE="1">
        <PARAM NAME="BackColor" VALUE="16777215">
        <PARAM NAME="ForeColor" VALUE="32768">
</OBJECT>
</BODY>
</HTML>
```

Label Control

Anyone that has spent time working with the Web recognizes the many limitations in displaying text on a Web page. The Label control lets you customize the display of text on your Web page. Have text appear at angles, or in various fonts and sizes without having to create actual images. The Label control has several properties and events associated with it (see Table 5.3).

PageGen

When you want to produce complex designs using the Label control you can use the PageGen tool, rather than the ActiveX Control Pad. You can download the PageGen tool at the following URL:

```
http://www.rosesoft.com/
```

The PageGen tool lets you design complex presentations of the Label control in seconds. Figure 5.18 illustrates a sample of the Label control produced with the PageGen tool.

■■■■■ **Table 5.3** Important Properties of the Label Control

Property Name	Description
CAPTION	The text string that appears.
ANGLE	The angle that the text is rotated.
MODE	The mode in which the text is rendered such as, normal, normal text with rotation, or text displayed according to user specified lines.
ALIGNMENT	Defines how the text should be aligned in the Label control.

■■■■■

■■■■■■■ **Figure 5.18** Choose **Settings|Properties** to vary the caption and
font size of the text displayed.

The text produced in this example is far more complex than lying at a different angle. To produce this type of text appearance, select the
View|Display Lines command and draw the two lines between which you
want the text displayed. You can modify the properties of the text that is
displayed by selecting the **Settings|Properties** command and then, once you
complete the design, saving the HTML file. You can then cut and paste the
HTML code generated for the Label control into the desired Web page.
Figure 5.19 shows the HTML code generated by the PageGen utility for
this sample Label control.

In the HTML code example shown here, hundreds of lines of code were
removed. The PageGen obviously makes generating complex Label control
presentations much simpler than having to enter these values into the
Properties window of the ActiveX Control Pad.

■■■■■■■ **Figure 5.19** You can edit the various events using the appropriate script editor.

```
<HTML>
<BODY>
<br>This label is designed using IePageGen utility
<OBJECT
classid="clsid:99B42120-6EC7-11CF-A6C7-00AA00A47DD2"
CODEBASE="http://ohserv/ie/download/activex/ielabel.ocx#ver-
sion=4,70,0,1085"
id="IeLabel1"
width=394
height=121>
<param name="Alignment" value="4">
<param name="Angle" value="0">
<param name="BackColor" value="#FFFFFF">
<param name="BackStyle" value="1">
<param name="Caption" value="Don't Try This At Home!">
<param name="FillStyle" value="0">
<param name="ForeColor" value="#000000">
<param name="FontBold" value="1">
<param name="FontItalic" value="0">
<param name="FontName" value="Times New Roman">
<param name="FontSize" value="72">
<param name="FontStrikeout" value="0">
<param name="FontUnderline" value="0">
<param name="Mode" value="3">
<!This data is generated by PageGen Utility.
   While editing these values, do so carefully>
<param name="TopPoints" value="71">
<param name="TopXY[0]" value="(71, 109)">
<param name="TopXY[1]" value="(74, 109)">
```

```
<param name="TopXY[2]" value="(76, 109)">
<param name="TopXY[3]" value="(78, 109)">
.... REPETITIVE LINES DELETED
<param name="BotPoints" value="153">
<param name="BotXY[0]" value="(59, 167)">
<param name="BotXY[1]" value="(60, 167)">
<param name="BotXY[2]" value="(60, 168)">
<param name="BotXY[3]" value="(62, 169)">
... REPETITIVE LINES DELETED
</OBJECT>
<SCRIPT LANGUAGE="VBSCRIPT">
Sub IeLabel1_Change()
        ' Change Event Code Goes Here
End Sub
Sub IeLabel1_Click()
        ' Click Event Code Goes Here
End Sub
Sub IeLabel1_DblClick()
        ' DblClick Event Code Goes Here
End Sub
Sub IeLabel1_MouseDown(ByVal Button, ByVal Shift, ByVal x, ByVal y)
        ' MouseDown Event Code Goes Here
End Sub
Sub IeLabel1_MouseMove(ByVal Button, ByVal Shift, ByVal x, ByVal y)
        ' MouseMove Event Code Goes Here
End Sub
Sub IeLabel1_MouseUp(ByVal Button, ByVal Shift, ByVal x, ByVal y)
        ' MouseUp Event Code Goes Here
End Sub
</SCRIPT>
</BODY>
</HTML>
```

Stock Ticker

Today you don't have a Web site of any significance if you don't have a stock ticker. That statement that may not be completely true, but the Stock Ticker ActiveX control does give you the ability to place continuously changing data on your Web site. This data could range from stock prices to temperatures in major cities (see Table 5.4).

Here is an example of the HTML code produced by the ActiveX Control Pad to include the Stock Ticker control in a Web page:

```
<HTML>
<HEAD>
<TITLE>Chart And Command Button Integration</TITLE>
</HEAD>
<BODY>
<OBJECT
ID=iexr2
TYPE="application/x-oleobject"
CLASSID="clsid:0CA4A620-8E3D-11CF-A3A9-00A0C9034920"
WIDTH=300
HEIGHT=50>
<PARAM NAME="DataObjectName" VALUE="http://www.microsoft.com/ie/appdev/con-
trols/iexrt.xrt">
<PARAM NAME="DataObjectActive" VALUE="1">
<PARAM NAME="scrollwidth" VALUE="5">
<PARAM NAME="forecolor" VALUE="#ff0000">
<PARAM NAME="backcolor" VALUE="#0000ff">
<PARAM NAME="ReloadInterval" VALUE="5000">
</OBJECT>
</BODY>
</HTML>
```

▬▬▬ **Table 5.4** Properties Necessary to Display the StockTicker
Control

Property Name	Description
DATAOBJECTNAME	The name of the URL or ActiveX control that contains the data.
DATAOBJECTACTIVE	Value equals 0 to indicate the data source is not active, and equals 1 to indicate the data source is active.
SCROLLSPEED	Numerical value specifies the interval for the ticker display.
SCROLLWIDTH	The ticker scrolls the indicated numerical SCROLLWIDTH.
RELOADINTERVAL	The specified interval for reloading the data source URL.
BACKCOLOR	RGB hex triplet numerical value to indicate background color.
FORECOLOR	RGB hex triplet numerical value to indicate foreground color.

▬▬▬

If you don't specify either the *Foreground* color or the *Background* color, the default colors will be used. The default colors are black for the foreground and gray for the background. The Stock Ticker control downloads the data at regular intervals from a URL designated by the DataObjectName. This URL contains a file with the data placed in either text or WOSA/XRT format.

WOSA/XRT

Real-time market information, such as stock prices, consists of constantly changing data that needs to be supplied to various software clients. At this time, no standard has been developed controlling how real-time data is transferred. For example, a stock broker may not only be interested in stock prices, but also in the current rates on CDs and treasury bonds. Each of these different types of real-time market data is provided by its own electronic delivery mechanism in its own proprietary format.

The Open Market Data Council has attempted to establish an open standard for providing real-time data to Windows applications. This new standard has been called the Windows Open Services Architecture Extensions (WOSA/XRT) for real-time market data. Now users will be able to access real-time market data with simple, noncustomized software clients, thus lowering the cost of accessing real-time market data and greatly expanding the number of potential users. The Stock Ticker control promises a variety of useful capabilities, because it is capable of displaying information generated according to the open WOSA/XRT standard.

New Item

When you add new items to your Web site, you may want to display an image to indicate to visitors they should check out the new items. The New Item control allows you to specify an image to display for a new item on your Web page.

■■■■ **Table 5.5** Significant Properties of the New Item Control

Property Name	Description
DATE	The date the object should no longer be visible. An example date value would be in the form value ="6/28/96".
IMAGE	The value is the URL for the image that should appear.

■■■■

This object also features the ability to specify a date when the image will no longer be visible. This makes Web page management much easier. Now you won't have a "new product release" advertised on your Web page for a product that has been out for a year or more.

If you don't include a <PARAM> tag identifying a particular image, the default image is a yellow star with "New" written on it.

Preloader

Imagine the situation in which you click for the next Web page, and wait, and wait, and wait. Bandwidth limitations often make it time-consuming to download all of the components of a Web page. The Preload control lets you have specified files or URLs loaded into the cache directory of a browser that is visiting one of your Web pages. For example, while a person peruses your home page, several of the other Web pages present on your Web site could be loaded into the user's cache directory. Then when the user decides to view these other Web pages, they will be instantly retrieved from the cached file. This control runs invisibly, but it does launch a window that indicates to the user whether the designated document was preloaded successfully (see Table 5.6).

■■■■■■■ **Table 5.6** Properties of the Preloader Control

Property Name	Description
URL	The value of this property is the URL of the document that should be preloaded.
ENABLE	When the value of this property equals 1, the control is enabled, and when the value equals 0, the control is disabled.

■■■■■■■

Here is an example of the Preloader control inserted into a HTML document using the ActiveX Control Pad:

```
<HTML>

<HEAD>

<TITLE>Preloader Control</TITLE>

</HEAD>

<BODY>

<OBJECT ID="PreLoader1" WIDTH=100 HEIGHT=51 CLASSID="CLSID:16E349E0-702C-11CF-A3A9-00A0C9034920"

CODEBASE="http://www.microsoft.com/ie/download/activex/ieprld.ocx#Version=4,70,0,1082">

<PARAM NAME="_ExtentX" VALUE="2646">

<PARAM NAME="_ExtentY" VALUE="1349">

<PARAM NAME="URL" VALUE="http://www.science.org/chart.htm">

<PARAM NAME="enable" VALUE="1">

</OBJECT>

</BODY>

</HTML>
```

Marquee Control

Moving text catches a person's attention long before dull, static text. The Marquee control gives you the ability to scroll a message that identifies important or new concepts to visitors on your Web site. When you incorporate the Marquee control into a Web source file, there are several different properties that you can specify to control the appearance of the message.

- How fast the message should scroll
- The direction the message should scroll
- How the message should scroll
- The color of the text displayed
- The color of the background behind the text

You can learn more about using the Marquee control by visiting the Microsoft demonstration page at:

http://www.microsoft.com/ie/showcase/howto_3/pdcdemo5.htm

■■■■■■■ **Table 5.7** Properties of the Marquee Control

Property Name	Description
ALIGN	Specifies how the text should be placed around the marquee, either aligned with the top, middle, or below the marquee.
BEHAVIOR	Specifies how the message text will appear in the marquee.
DIRECTION	Specifies the direction that the message will scroll.
SCROLLDELAY	Number of milliseconds delay you want between each draw of the message text.
SCROLLAMOUNT	Number of pixels between draws of the message text.
BGCOLOR	Specifies the numerical code for the color of the marquee.
HEIGHT	Specifies the height of the marquee. When not specified, the default height is 100% of the Web page.
WIDTH	Specifies the width of the marquee. When not specified, the default width is 100% of the Web page.
HSPACE	Number of pixels for the margin on the left and right side of the marquee.
VSPACE	Number of pixels between the message text and the top and bottom margins of the marquee.
LOOP	Specifies the number of times you want the message to scroll on the Web page, or choose endless scrolling by selecting INFINITE.

Perusing the Web, you may have noticed various scrolling messages that started appearing around November 1995. Most of these scrolling messages were produced using Java applets. The problem is that even a simple scrolling text Java applet can produce a significant drain on your computer resources while it is running. Java applets have impressive capabilities, but using them to scroll a text message on a Web page is like using a bulldozer to make a sand castle. The Marquee control is one simple way to spice up your Web site.

■■■■ **TIP**

> You can see the amount of computing power consumed by a Java applet that produces a scrolling text message by rapidly moving your mouse cursor. When using a Java applet to produce a scrolling text message, the text will actually slow or stop, but when using the <MARQUEE> tag the movement of the text message will not be affected.

■■■■

Popup Menu Control

In a graphical display environment pop-up menus provide a convenient way to display important information when the user executes a particular event. The pop-up menu control allows you to easily add pop-up menu capability to your Web pages.

There are very few properties that you can define for the pop-up menu. The main properties include the size and placement of the pop-up menu easily defined using the Edit ActiveX Control window and the MenuItem. The MenuItem is used to define the different menu selections that appear in the pop-up window. The MenuItem appears in the HTML code as a NAME|VALUE pair with the <PARAM> tag. The syntax for the MenuItem property is shown in this example code:

```
<PARAM NAME="MenuItem[0]" VALUE="Don't vote for">
<PARAM NAME="MenuItem[1]" VALUE="him">
```

The MenuItem[] identifies the row number, while the VALUE for this property is a text string that will appear in the pop-up menu. The pop-up menu control has several methods, which can be integrated with the Script Wizard associated with it, which are used in combination with an ActiveX scripting language such as VBScript or JavaScript.

Providing ActiveX Controls

It is extremely simple to provide ActiveX control content on your Web site. Those users who have provided Netscape plug-ins are familiar with having to configure their server to provide the particular MIME extension before they can provide the desired content on their Web pages. When providing Web pages containing ActiveX controls, you do not need to configure your server in any way. It's that simple.

6

dbWEB

dbWeb is an exciting database gateway product originally developed by Aspect Software Engineering, Inc., and purchased by Microsoft. The product is actually two applications, one an ISAPI Web server extension that provides a gateway between Web browsers and an ODBC data source, and the other product is the dbWeb Administrator, with which you can create powerful Web pages for taking advantage of the data mining capabilities of the dbWeb server.

dbWeb works with a wide range of software. The dbWeb system supports a large number of databases, including Oracle, SQL Server, Access, and, most importantly, any database that supports 32-bit ODBC. Because dbWeb is an ISAPI service, it works with the many ISAPI-compliant Web servers. And, on the client end, dbWeb works in most of the popular Web browsers. Samples in this chapter use Microsoft Internet Explorer.

The dbWeb Service

The Microsoft Internet Information Server is extensible through the ISAPI interface (see Chapter 9 for more information). dbWeb is a product that extends the abilities of Internet Information Server by providing a gateway to an ODBC (Open Database Connectivity) data source. Instead of conventional CGI programs used to process database queries, the dbWeb service intercepts data requests and sends them on to the data source. The dbWeb service also manages sending query results back to the Web browser completely formatted.

dbWeb is installed as an NT service. To start the dbWeb service, you should open the Control Panel and start the Services application. If your dbWeb application has been successfully installed, you will find dbWeb in the list of services. You can modify this service so that it starts automatically when you boot NT, or you can continue to start this service manually. Once the dbWeb service has been started, you shouldn't have to worry about the dbWeb service any longer.

The dbWeb Administrator

The dbWeb Administrator is the application you will use primarily when creating and managing your Web database access. Using the Administrator tools, you can create schemas that define which database columns you use as part of your application. Creating schemas has been made extremely easy using the Schema Wizard.

Using the Wizard you can:

- Construct tabular reports
- Create custom Query by Example Web pages

- Create links from your data record to full-page information displays
- Build skinny clients with complete custom data entry capability

dbWeb lets you build full database applications using a Web browser as the client. Not only can you build reports from the standard tabular formats, you can create custom freeform reports. A special DBX tool allows you to create the HTML pages for freeform reports and data entry screens.

Quick DB Basics

If you've never worked with databases before, you'll want to read this section; otherwise, jump right into "Creating a New Schema." Databases have a single purpose: to hold information. It's the goal of every other program that uses a database to create the easiest way to get information into and back out of the database.

Information is stored in databases in a *column* and *row* format, in which the columns contain unique types of information, such as first names or addresses. Each row of information represents a new record of information. You will often hear the words "row" and "record" used interchangeably.

If you are going to collect information about famous primatologists, you might have a column for first name, last name, birthday, date of death, address, field of study, and so on. A single record might look like this:

FirstName	LastName	ResearchCenter	Country
Dian	Fossey	Karisoke Research Center	Rwanda

FirstName, LastName, ResearchCenter, and Country are all column names. Each subsequent row of information contains the type of data defined by the column name. For example, Dian is stored as the first name of the famous primatologist Dian Fossey.

When creating schemas, in the next section, you will want to become familiar with the columns in your data source (database), and the types of information that are stored in each column. This example has text information stored in each column. Database columns can store numeric, date, True and False (Boolean), and other types of information, depending on the type of database.

The example displays information about Ms. Fossey in *tabular* format, which is the conventional row and column display. Each new row appears beneath the one before it so that data is viewed in a large two-dimensional array. Schemas can be designed so that this information can be displayed in other formats. The tabular format is perfect, and most often used for displaying query results that involve more than one row. When a single row is expected from your query, you may choose to view the data in a more readable format, called *freeform*.

FirstName	Dian
LastName	Fossey
ResearchCenter	Karisoke Research Center
Country	Rwanda

Using the DBX feature explained in this chapter you can embed column information, sometimes called *fields*, within a more complex HTML document, so that data appears embedded in the text.

Creating a New Schema

A schema is a repository of data that dbWeb uses to create queries against data sources. The schema also specifies how the results of a query appear.

To create a new schema, start the dbWeb Administrator and, if the Data Sources dialog box does not open, select **Open** from the Administrator's **File** menu. The data sources will appear in a tree structured diagram, as shown in Figure 6.1.

When creating a new schema, you can either choose to use the Wizard or manually create the schema (see Figure 6.2). Using the Wizard is highly recommended if you're not used to creating database applications. The Wizard takes you through each necessary step.

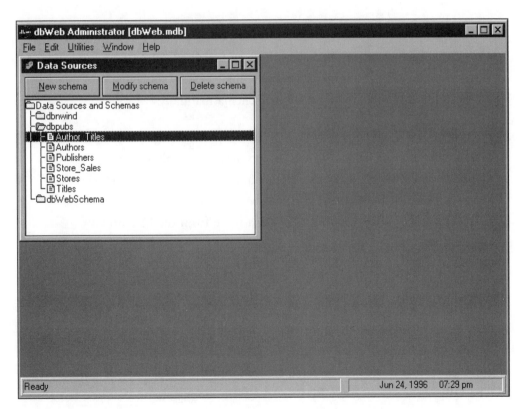

Figure 6.1 Data sources appear in a tree structured diagram.

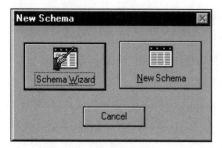

Figure 6.2 Choosing between using the Wizard or manually creating the schema.

Using the Schema Wizard

The Wizard creates a simple database query for which all of the data comes from a single table. If you need a more complex query involving multiple tables and joins, you should create the schema manually.

Choosing a Table

The next step in using the Wizard is to select the database table that contains the data you're allowing users to query, insert, update, or delete. Further along in the process, you will be able to choose which of these features you're going to allow. Choose a table from the list shown in Figure 6.3.

Once you've selected the table, click the **Next** button to continue.

Choosing the Data Columns to Query

You can now select the columns that will appear in your query form. Selecting a column in the Available Fields list (Figure 6.4) and clicking the top-right arrow moves the selected column into the Fields on QBE form. The QBE form is the Query By Example form. Each column that you select here appears on a form on which the user can fill in information to narrow their query. QBE is covered in more detail later in this chapter.

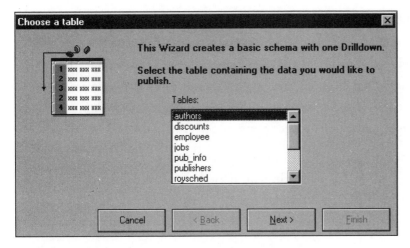

Figure 6.3 Choose a table from the list.

Continue selecting columns or select all the fields simultaneously by clicking the double-right arrow. At this point, you can continue or move back to the table selection dialog box.

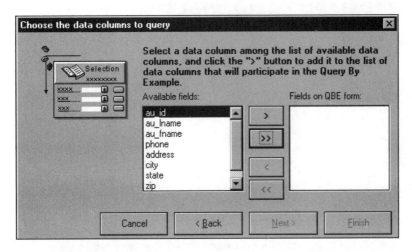

Figure 6.4 Select columns from the Available Fields list.

Choosing Tabular Form Data Columns

The tabular form is the HTML format returned from a database query. The tabular format is a conventional row-and-column format. The tabular form is used by default when multiple rows are returned from a query unless a custom format is requested using one of the dbWeb methods. (See the dbWeb methods for a complete description of each method.)

You do not need to include fields in your query result simply because they were used in the query. For example, you may want a list of names and phone numbers to appear in a tabular form, where the Query By Example form also included the address so the user can query by state and zip code. (See Figure 6.5.)

Specifying a Drill-Down Automatic Link

A drill-down automatic link may evoke painful dental memories. Luckily, drill-down columns are optional. When talking about database queries, *drilling down* into the data refines your search results; you're looking

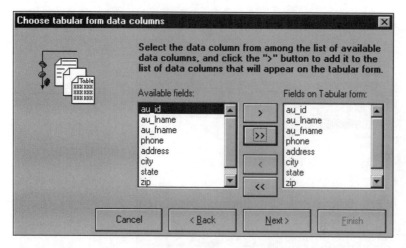

■■■■ **Figure 6.5** Choose the columns you want to appear as results of your query.

deeper into the data. You will be able to specify criteria for a new search when a drill-down column is selected in the search results. This capability is covered in more detail in the next section on automatic links (see Figure 6.6).

Naming Your Schema

You will most likely create many schemas, each one a new view of your data. Give each schema a name that describes the type of information queried from the database. Meaningful names can save you quite a bit of time later when you are trying to figure out which schema delivers what information. Notice in Figure 6.7 that there is a check box for modifying the new schema when the Wizard is finished. Check this box. Many configurable parameters are not set by the Wizard; for example, if you've selected a drill-down column, you'll have to specify the criteria for the drill-down query. Taking a look at your newly created schema, just to make certain that the Wizard has correctly defined your query, is always a good idea.

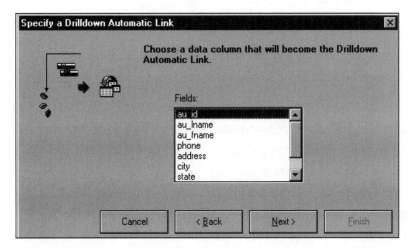

▉▉▉▉▉▉ **Figure 6.6** Choose a column for drill down.

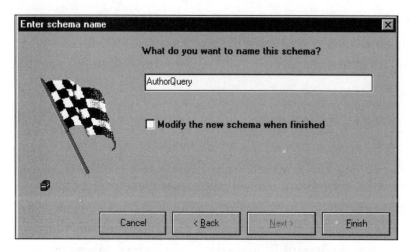

Figure 6.7 Give your schema a meaningful name.

Modifying a Schema

The dbWeb Administrator has made modifying a schema very easy, with each configurable part of your schema in a separate tab (Figure 6.8). Select each tab to configure various portions of the schema.

Schema

The **Schema** tab lets you configure both the way the HTML page appears when a query is returned, and most importantly, the type of access you are allowing users to have over your database.

The dbWeb Administrator creates a professional-looking Web page for query results. You can further customize the output in the **Schema** tab. One of the simple parameters you can set is the e-mail address where you can be reached if a user has a question or problem while using your query. This e-mail address appears at the bottom of the HTML page that is returned with the query. It does not, however, appear in error messages.

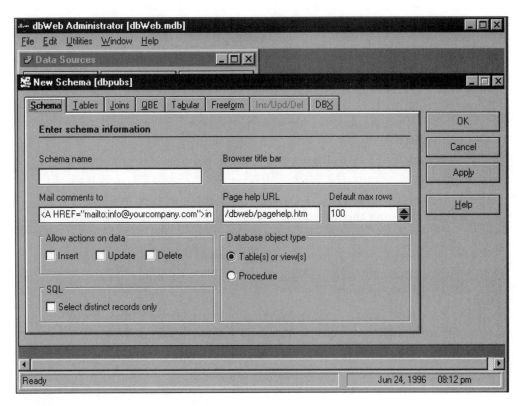

Figure 6.8 Customize your schema.

You can define the title bar of the Web browser when your query is returned. You should make this title meaningful to users so that they can print results, or understand what they're looking at when they are viewing query results. For example, consider including the name of the schema if it isn't too cryptic. If you take this approach, the user can refer to the name of the schema when corresponding with you. Including the schema name in the title results in less handwaving later when you're trying to troubleshoot a problem remotely.

The PageHelp URL is automatically set to the default dbWeb Help page. You aren't stuck with using this page. You can create new Help pages.

When you do create new Help Web pages, or if you move the dbWeb Help pages, you need to change the PageHelp URL to point to the page. One reason why you might want to modify the default Help page, or create a new Help page, is to limit what the user can accomplish using the dbWeb methods.

Other parameters you can set are:

- *Default Max Rows.* The maximum number of rows returned by a query. Setting this parameter avoids having a user try to load 10,000 rows in a Web browser over a 28.8 modem.
- *Database Object Type.* These parameters include normal tables, temporary tables called Views, or the ability to launch database stored procedures.
- *Action on Data.* Specifies whether you are allowing the user to insert, modify, or delete data in the database using dbWeb.
- *SQL Select Distinct Records.* Specifies whether repeating data is allowed, or if only unique data is displayed.

Tables

If you used the Wizard to create your schema, you were allowed to select a single table. Using the **Tables** tab, you can select additional tables to add to your query. Adding tables will not automatically relate the data. You may have to *join* the tables you've selected in the next tab. This is an advanced feature, and you should have some knowledge of how relational databases work before you start selecting additional tables.

Selecting or deselecting tables is similar to using the Wizard. Move tables to and from the tables in the data source using the appropriate buttons.

Joins

Joining tables relates them. If two or more tables share information stored in similar columns, they can be related. For example, if a table that contains employee information has an employeeID column, it can be related to another table containing employee insurance information as long as the insurance table also has an employeeID column. In this way employee information such as name and address can be *joined* to other pertinent information based on columns containing the same information.

To create a join, type the names of the tables and columns you want joined and separate them with an equals sign.

```
titleauthor.au_id = authors.au_id
titles.title_id = titleauthor.title_id
publishers.pub_id = titles.pub_id
```

QBE

The concept of Query By Example is that you fill out a form with information, which gives the database an "example" of the type of information you want included in the result of a query. For instance, if you enter the name "Smith" in a LastName column, you are giving an example of the last name that should appear in the result set. There may be 52 rows with the last name of Smith returned. You can further refine your query by giving examples of first names, cities, zip codes, and so on.

The **QBE** tab lets you choose which columns will appear in your Query By Example form. This tab is very similar to the one you may have used in creating a schema using the Wizard. Move columns to and from the Data Columns in Selected Tables box using the **Add** and **Remove** buttons. The selected columns appear in the QBE data columns box.

When selecting which columns should appear in your QBE form it's easy to just select **Add All**. Not all columns make sense to have in a QBE form. For example, it isn't very common that someone will do a search based on a street address. You may want to search by city or zip code, but rarely will you enter "123 Elm Street". For one reason, "Street" can be entered as "St." and this row would be excluded from a query in which Street was written out. Simply ask yourself what a user might realistically want to use to refine a query.

Tabular Reports

Choose which fields you want to appear in a tabular report. Tabular reports are the results of your query in tabular format (row and column). Keep in mind what will be important to the viewer of the report, and only include that information in the report. Also, wide columns take up room. Columns that do not fit across the page in a Web browser are shown continued after the first tabular report. Because the continued information is not shown with the other reference data it's often very hard to decipher.

If you would like to present more detailed information, limit the tabular report to information from which a user can choose which details to view, and then let them select a hot link option (explained later in this chapter).

Create a computed column by clicking the **Computer Column** button. You can create virtual columns (which are not real columns) by creating expressions with the existing columns. For example, you might choose to display names as first name last name in a single column rather than in separate columns:

```
authors.au_first + authors.au_last
```

Freeform Reports

Freeform reports are used when you know only a single row will be returned in a query. You can still use a tabular format for single rows, but you have much more creative freedom when you can create a freeform report to display the single record.

As in the tabular configuration, select the columns you want to appear in your result. You can be more free with the information you display, as you will only be displaying information for a single data row.

Ins/Upd/Del Tab

If you selected the check box on the schema tag to allow inserts, updates, or deletes, the **Ins/Upd/Del** tab is enabled. On this tab, you can select the columns in which you will allow changes to be made in your database.

- *Insert.* Allow new rows to be inserted into a table
- *Update.* Allow changes to the data that currently exists in the database
- *Delete.* Allow rows to be removed from a table

Select or deselect columns by moving them to and from the Data Columns in Selected Tables box. Once a column has been selected and appears in the box on the right, you can select that column and set its properties (Figure 6.9). You can set properties such as whether you will allow Null values to be entered into the column or whether you want validation to be performed on the information being entered.

DBX Tab

The DBX tab allows you to select custom formats for both single and multiple row outputs. These reports can be created using the DBX editor. To call these custom formats, you must use the appropriate dbWeb method (see the section on dbWeb methods). The methods that will call one of these custom formats have the letter "x" somewhere in the method name.

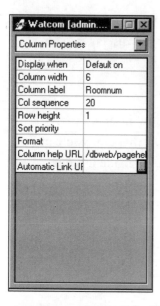

Figure 6.9 Set the properties for columns in which you are allowing changes.

Schema Defaults and Administrator Preferences

The dbWeb Administrator lets you set preferences that make creating multiple schemas easier. There are general preferences, schema creation preferences, server access preferences, and database access preferences.

If you find yourself creating several schemas that share similar properties, you may want to set the default schema values in the Administrator preferences. Select **Preferences** from the Administrator **Edit** menu choice. Then, choose the **Schema Defaults** tab to edit the Schema default preferences, as shown in Figure 6.10.

Set the default URL address values for Help Web pages for both the entire page and specific columns. You can also set your e-mail address, or the e-

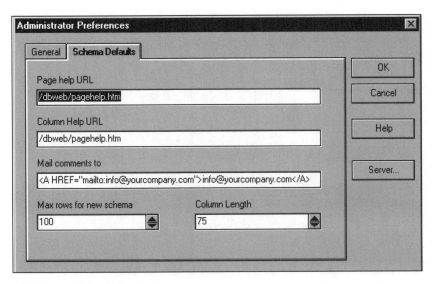

Figure 6.10 Set default values for creating schemas in the Administrator Preferences.

mail address of your technical support department, as a default value in this window.

The general Administrator preferences allow you to set the default database accessed by dbWeb and the name of the dbWeb server (Figure 6.11). If you want to change the default database, click the **Browse** button and select the database from the open files dialog box that appears. This will fill in the Default Schema Database field.

In all likelihood, you are using a local dbWeb server. You can choose to set the default to \\ or leave the default dbWeb serve name field blank. If you are using a remote dbWeb server, clicking the **Browse** button queries the network for remote computers. Select the host that is running the remote server.

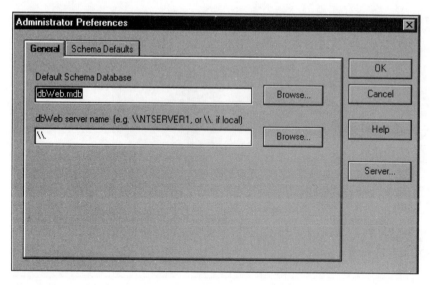

■■■■■ **Figure 6.11** Set the default database and dbWeb server.

Automatic Links

Setting the Automatic Link properties for a column cause it to appear as a hyperlink in either the freeform or tabular display format. As a result, a user viewing this form can click on the data to request additional information. The URL that is activated in the Automatic Link can point to remote Web pages that display additional information, Gopher resources where text documents provide data, FTP servers where files can be downloaded, or even e-mail addresses so that custom e-mail messages can be sent right from the Web browser.

To create an automatic link:

1. Select a schema and click the **Modify schema** button.
2. Select either the **Tabular** or **Freeform** tag.

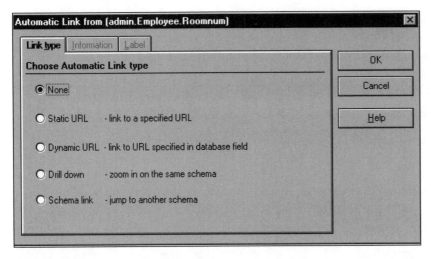

Automatic Link from (admin.Employee.Roomnum)   ⊠

Link type   Information   Label

Choose Automatic Link type

⦿ None

○ Static URL   - link to a specified URL

○ Dynamic URL - link to URL specified in database field

○ Drill down   - zoom in on the same schema

○ Schema link   - jump to another schema

OK

Cancel

Help

▬▬▬▬▬ **Figure 6.12** Select an Automatic Link type by clicking on the radiobutton.

3. Choose a selected column.

4. Click on the **Properties** button.

5. Selecting the Automatic Link property displays a button that you should click. Choose an automatic link from the list. (See Figure 6.12.)

Customize your data presentation by selecting one of the following Automatic Link types:

- *Static URL Automatic Link.* A hotlink in a dbWeb data presentation that points to a custom URL. This is a fixed URL so that every row in a column retrieves the same resource.

- *Dynamic URL Automatic Link.* A hotlink in a dbWeb data presentation that points to a URL that was stored in a database table. This dynamic URL can retrieve a different URL depending on both what column and what row was selected by clicking the hyperlink.

- *Drill Down URL Automatic Link.* A hotlink that causes dbWeb to further filter the results of a query. Choosing this automatic link causes dbWeb to perform an additional query based on the data you have chosen.

- *Schema to Schema Automatic Link.* A hotlink in a dbWeb data presentation that causes dbWeb to formulate a query based on a join between tables in different schemas.

The Automatic Link feature sets dbWeb apart from the many other ODBC data access programs available. This feature allows you to create powerful custom interfaces to your data, rather than presenting static and boring tabular data presentations.

Creating a Custom Format File

dbWeb has the ability to extend its array of display formats by loading a Custom Format File (DBX file). The DBX file is a custom format that you create using the DBX Editor. You can create custom data input (QBE) forms as well as tabular and freeform output display forms. (See Figure 6.13.)

To create a DBX file:

1. After selecting a schema from the data source tree, click on the **Modify schema** button.

2. Select the DBX tag and click on the **Editor** button beside either **the Multi-record** or **Single record** output text boxes. This opens the DBX Editor.

3. Select either **New** or **Open** from the **File** menu of the DBX Editor, depending on whether you are creating a new custom format or editing an existing one.

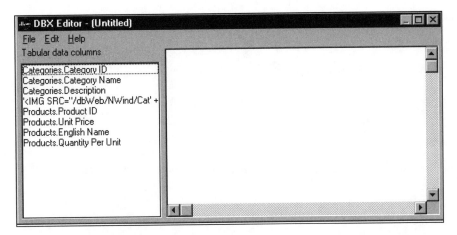

■■■■■■■ **Figure 6.13** Select tabular data columns to insert into the HTML file in the editor.

4. Enter HTML in the editor window on the right. Hint: You can use FrontPage to create the HTML display format, and then use the DBX Editor to insert the DBX tags.

5. Insert DBX tags into the HTML to place formatted column data. (Figure 6.14 shows the DBX tags in bold.)

■■■■■■■ **Figure 6.14** Sample DBX file included with dbWeb.

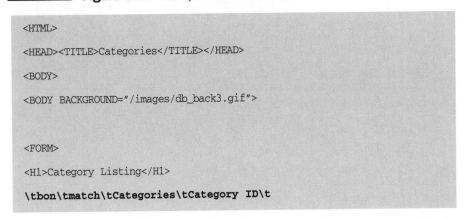

Continued...

Figure 6.14 Continued

```
<TABLE>

<TR><TD COLSPAN=5 VALIGN=BOTTOM><HR></TD></TR>


<TR>

<TH ALIGN=LEFT>Category ID:</TH>

<TD WIDTH=1 ALIGN=LEFT>\tobj\tCategories\tcol\tCategory ID\t</TD>

<TD></TD>

<TD>Picture:</TD>

<TD ROWSPAN=6 VALIGN=TOP>\tobj\tComputed\tcol\tC015813\t</TD>

</TR>


<TR><TD COLSPAN=3 VALIGN=BOTTOM><HR></TD></TR>


<TR><TH ALIGN=LEFT>Category Name:</TH><TD

COLSPAN=2>\tobj\tCategories\tcol\tCategory Name\t</TD></TR>


<TR><TD COLSPAN=3 VALIGN=BOTTOM><HR></TD></TR>


<TR><TH ALIGN=LEFT>Description:</TH>


<TD WIDTH=250 COLSPAN=2 ROWSPAN=2
VALIGN=TOP>\tobj\tCategories\tcol\tDescription\t</TD></TR>


<TR><TD> </TD>

</TR>

</TABLE>
```

```
<TABLE BORDER>

<TR>

<TH>Product ID:</TH>

<TH>Product Name:</TH>

<TH>Unit Price:</TH>

<TH>Quantity Per Unit:</TH>

</TR>


\tbon\tmatch\tProducts\tProduct ID\t

<TR>

<TD ALIGN=RIGHT>\tobj\tProducts\tcol\tProduct ID\t</TD>

<TD>\tobj\tProducts\tcol\tEnglish Name\t</TD>

<TD ALIGN=RIGHT>\tobj\tProducts\tcol\tUnit Price\t</TD>

<TD>\tobj\tProducts\tcol\tQuantity Per Unit\t</TD>

</TR>

\tboff\t

</TABLE>

<BR><BR>

\tboff\t

</FORM>

</BODY>

</HTML>
```

DBX Tag Formats

DBX provides an extension to conventional HTML so that custom representations of data in a database column can be represented anywhere within a DBX file. You can think of these tags like placeholders or custom fields.

Tag format:

```
\tobj\t[Table Name]\tcol\t[Column Name]\t
```

DBX custom formats support *banded data*. Banded data is a group of multiple rows of data. This is inserted into a custom format as a single banded tab beginning with **\tbon** and ending with **\tboff**. Banding displays data in a row-and-column format within a custom format. It's a bit like inserting a table into a word processing document. If you expect your banded data to return a large number of rows, you may want to consider a different display format for your report.

Examining the HTML in Figure 6.14 reveals that table names are preceded with **\tobj**. This represents a database object. Column names are preceded by **\tcol.**

When you insert tags in HTML that are understood by dbWeb, they must follow this format:

```
[object type],[table or object name], [column name]
```

Table 6.1 lists the object types expected by dbWeb. In your HTML you can use either the enumerated object type listed in column one, or the text description of the control type.

■■■■■■■ **Table 6.1** dbWeb Object Types

Object Type	Control Type
1	text
2	radio
3	list
4	combo
5	check
6	operator
7	ontabular
8	onfreeform

▬▬▬▬▬▬ **Table 6.1** Continued

Object Type	Control Type
9	maxrows
10	submit
11	hidden

▬▬▬▬▬▬

You can further format the way your data is displayed within a custom format by using the DBX tab formats shown in Table 6.2. This allows you to format the display of numeric data items, such as time, date, and percentages.

▬▬▬▬▬▬ **Table 6.2** DBX Tag Formats

Formatting Code	Description
%a	Three-letter abbreviation of the day of the week (Mon, Tue, Wed...).
%A	Full name of the day of the week (Monday, Tuesday, Wednesday...).
%b	Three-letter abbreviation of the name of the month (Jan, Feb, Mar...).
%B	Full name of the month (January, February, March...).
%d	Decimal number representing the day of the month (1 - 31).
%H	Hour, in 24-hour format.
%I	Hour, in 12-hour format.
%m	Decimal number representing the month of the year (1 - 12).
%M	Minute (0 - 59).

■■■■■■■ **Table 6.2** Continued

Formatting Code	Description
%p	Modifies time with lowercase a.m. or p.m.
%P	Modifies time with uppercase A.M. or P.M.
%s	Microsecond as a decimal number.
%S	Second as a decimal number.
%w	Decimal number representing the day of the week (0 - 6); Sunday is 0.
%y	Year without displaying the century.
%Y	Year with the century.
%%	Displays a percent sign.
#	When added to another format code, removes leading zeros.

■■■■■■■

Here is a sample: %m%d%y is 12/15/97.

To use the special DBX tags within an HTML tag format the tag like this:

```
<INPUT TYPE = HIDDEN NAME = 11, Column Name, Column Name, VALUE = DBX tag
SIZE = 20>
```

Browsing Data

After creating a schema, you will want to allow others to run your dbWeb queries. The easiest way to present these queries is as anchors in a Web page (See Figure 6.15). Here is the format for embedding your query in a Web page.

```
http://[machines.domain.name]/[ISAPIscriptsFolder]/dbweb/dbwebc.dll/[SchemaName]
?getqbe
```

■■■■■■■ **Figure 6.15** Embed an anchor to call your dbWeb query.

```
<HTML>

<HEAD>

<TITLE>dbTest</TITLE>

</HEAD>

<BODY>

<A
href="http://ebola.science.org/Scripts/dbWeb/dbwebc.dll/test?getqbe">Get
Data</A>


</BODY>

</HTML>
```

Figure 6.16 shows what a dbWeb QBE form looks like. Notice that it is
nicely formatted and customized. The user enters data into the entry
fields and chooses a *comparison operator*. The comparison operator
allows the user to choose whether they want the value they have entered
to equal values in the database, be greater than, less than, or start with
the same letters.

After submitting the query, dbWeb intercepts the data, sends it to the database using ODBC, formats the reply, and displays it in the Web browser (see
Figure 6.17).

dbWeb Methods

In the previous section, the **getqbe** dbWeb method was used to retrieve data
from the database. You aren't restricted to using only one type of request.

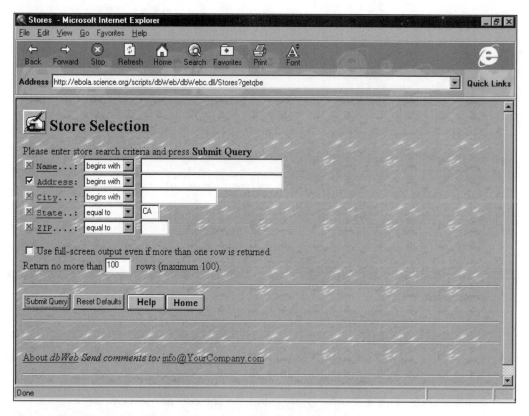

Figure 6.16 Example of a dbWeb QBE form.

There are 17 different methods that can be passed to dbWeb, including requests for Help or the dbWeb version number. Most of the dbWeb methods are designed to specify the format of the result of a query. Some of the methods return data using the default formats and others cause dbWeb to select a custom format. This section discusses each of the methods along with its syntax and use.

getqbe [schema name]?getqbe   This method gets the default dbWeb Query By Example (QBE) form and displays it in the Web browser.

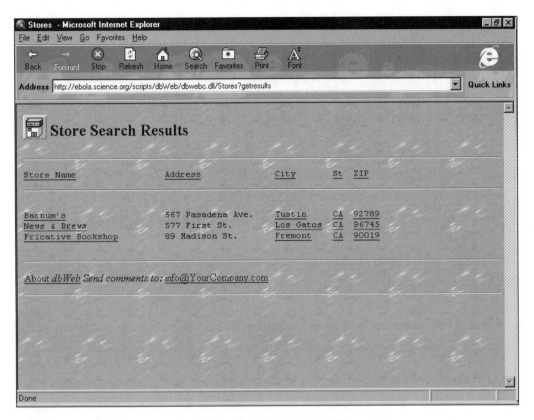

Figure 6.17 Tabular format result of a QBE query.

getresults [schema name]?getresults   This method acts differently depending on whether one data row is retrieved or more than one. If one row is retrieved, this method gets the default freeform form and displays it in the Web browser. If more than one row is retrieved, this method gets the default tabular form and displays it in the Web browser.

link [schema name]?link/[tag]   The link method is called when an automatic link is executed. Depending on the number of rows retrieved, the appropriate form type is displayed in the browser: freeform for one row retrieved and tabular when more than one row is retrieved.

getxqbe [schema name]?getxqbe Clicking on a form's **Submit** button activates the getxqbe method. This method then retrieves the QBE form and displays it in the Web browser.

getxresult [schema name]?getxresult The getxresult method gets a customized form. When one row is retrieved, a custom freeform form is retrieved and displayed in the Web browser. When more than one row is retrieved, getxresult gets a custom tabular form and displays it.

getxtab [schema name]?getxtab Displays a custom tab report in a Web browser regardless of the number of rows retrieved.

getxfree [schema name]?getxfree Displays a custom freeform report in a Web browser regardless of the number of rows retrieved.

linkxresults [schema name]?linkxresults/[tag] When an automatic link is clicked, the linkxresults method gets a customized form. A custom tabular form is retrieved and displayed when more than one row is retrieved. If a single row is retrieved a custom freeform report is displayed.

linkxtab [schema name]?linkxtab/[tag] When an automatic link is clicked, the linkxtab method loads a custom tabular form displaying it in a Web browser.

linkxfree [schema name]?linkxfree/[tag] When an automatic link is clicked, the linkxfree method loads a custom freeform report and displays it in a Web browser.

getinsert [schema name]?getinsert The getinsert method displays the insert form in the Web browser for data entry by the user.

insert   [schema name]?insert   The insert method sends the data in an insert form to the data source, causing the data to be inserted into the database.

getupdate   [schema name]?getupdate   The getupdate method displays the update form in a Web browser, allowing the user to edit data.

update   [schema name]?update   The update method sends data in an update form to the data source, causing existing data to be updated.

delete   [schema name]?delete   The delete method removes the database row referenced by tags in the form.

version   ?version   The version method displays the dbWeb version in the Web browser.

help   ?help   Displays the most current list of methods supported by dbWeb in the Web browser.

ODBC Scalar Functions

This section is a reference that describes all of the ODBC scalar functions. These are functions that can be embedded in expressions sent to the data source. Almost all data sources understand and support scalar functions. These are the scalar functions supported by 32-bit ODBC.

String Functions

These string functions are 1-based, which means that the first character in the string is 1. Any string arguments must be delimited by single quotes.

ASCII(StringExpression)   Returns the ASCII code value of the leftmost character of *StringExpression* as an integer.

CHAR(code)   Returns the character that has the ASCII code value specified by *code*. The value of *code* should be between 0 and 255; otherwise, the return value is data source-dependent.

CONCAT(StringExpression1,String Expression2)   Returns a character string that is the result of concatenating *StringExpression2* to *StringExpression1*. The resulting string is DBMS-dependent. For example, if the column represented by *StringExpression1* contained a NULL value, DB2 would return NULL, but SQL Server would return the non-NULL string.

DIFFERENCE(StringExpression1,String Expression2)   Returns an integer value that indicates the difference between the values returned by the **SOUNDEX** function for *StringExpression1* and *StringExpression2*.

INSERT(StringExpression1,start,length, StringExpression2)   Returns a character string in which length characters have been deleted from *StringExpression1* beginning at start and in which *StringExpression2* has been inserted into *StringExpression*, beginning at start.

LCASE(StringExpression)   Converts all uppercase characters in *StringExpression* to lowercase.

LEFT(StringExpression,count)   Returns the leftmost count of characters of *StringExpression*.

LENGTH(StringExpression)   Returns the number of characters in *StringExpression*, excluding trailing blanks and the string termination character.

LOCATE(StringExpression1,String Expression2[,start])   Returns the starting position of the first occurrence of *StringExpression1* within *StringExpression2*. The search for the first occurrence of *StringExpression1* begins with the first character position in *StringExpression2* unless the optional argument, *start*, is specified. If *start* is specified, the search begins with the character position indicated by the value of *start*. The first character position in *StringExpression2* is indicated by the value 1. If *StringExpression1* is not found within *StringExpression2*, the value 0 is returned.

LTRIM(StringExpression)   Returns the characters of *StringExpression*, with leading blanks removed.

REPEAT(StringExpression,count)   Returns a character string composed of *StringExpression* repeated *count* times.

REPLACE(StringExpression1,String Expression2,StringExpression3)   Replaces all occurrences of *StringExpression2* in *StringExpression1* with *StringExpression3*.

RIGHT(StringExpression,count)   Returns the rightmost *count* of characters of *StringExpression*.

RTRIM(StringExpression)   Returns the characters of *StringExpression* with trailing blanks removed.

SOUNDEX(StringExpression)   Returns a data source-dependent character string representing the sound of the words in *StringExpression*. For example, SQL Server returns a four-digit SOUNDEX code; Oracle returns a phonetic representation of each word.

SPACE(count)   Returns a character string consisting of *count* spaces.

SUBSTRING(StringExpression,start, length)   Returns a character string that is derived from *StringExpression* beginning at the character position specified by *start* for *length* characters.

UCASE(StringExpression)   Converts all lowercase characters in *StringExpression* to uppercase.

Numeric Functions

This section describes numeric functions that are included in the ODBC scalar function set.

ABS(numeric)   Returns the absolute value of the argument.

ACOS(float)   Returns the arccosine of *float* as an angle, expressed in radians.

ASIN(float)   Returns the arcsine of *float* as an angle, expressed in radians.

ATAN(float)   Returns the arctangent of *float* as an angle, expressed in radians.

ATAN2(x,y)   Returns the arctangent of the *x* and *y* coordinates as an angle, expressed in radians.

CEILING(numeric)   Returns the smallest integer greater than or equal to *numeric*.

COS(float)   Returns the cosine of *float*, where *float* is an angle expressed in radians.

COT(float)   Returns the cotangent of *float*, where *float* is an angle expressed in radians.

DEGREES(numeric)   Returns the number of degrees converted from *numeric* to radians.

EXP(float)   Returns the exponential value of *float*.

FLOOR(numeric)   Returns largest integer less than or equal to *numeric*.

LOG(float)   Returns the natural logarithm of *float*.

LOG10(float)   Returns the base 10 logarithm of *float*.

MOD(integer1,integer2) Returns the remainder (modulus) of *integer1* divided by *integer2*.

PI( ) Returns the constant value of PI as a float.

POWER(numeric, integer) Returns the value of *numeric* to the power of *integer*.

RADIANS(numeric) Returns the number of radians converted from *numeric* to degrees.

RAND([integer]) Returns a random floating-point value using *integer* as the optional seed value.

ROUND(numeric, integer) Returns *numeric* rounded to *integer* places right of the decimal point.

SIGN(numeric) Returns the sign of *numeric* as an integer. *numeric* < 0, -1 is returned. *numeric* = 0, 0 is returned. *numeric* > 0, 1 is returned.

SIN(float) Returns the sine of *float*, where *float* is an angle expressed in radians.

SQRT(float) Returns the square root of *float*.

TAN(float) Returns the tangent of *float*, where *float* is an angle expressed in radians.

TRUNCATE(numeric,integer) Returns *numeric* truncated to *integer* places right of the decimal point.

Time and Date Functions

This section describes the time and date functions included in the ODBC scalar function set.

CURDATE( ) Returns the current date as a date value.

CURTIME( )   Returns the current local time as a time value.

DAYNAME(date)   Returns a character string representing the day portion of date.

DAYOFMONTH(date)   Returns the day of the month in *date* as an integer.

DAYOFWEEK(date)   Returns the day of the week in *date* as an integer value. Sunday = 1.

DAYOFYEAR(date)   Returns the day of the year in *date* as an integer.

HOUR(time)   Returns the hour in *time* as an integer.

MINUTE(time)   Returns the minute in *time* as an integer (0-59).

MONTH(date)   Returns the month in *date* as an integer. (1-12).

MONTHNAME(date)   Returns a string representing the name of the month.

NOW( )   Returns current date and time as a timestamp value.

QUARTER(date)   Returns the quarter of *date* as an integer (1-4).

SECOND(time)   Returns the second in *time* as an integer (0-59).

TIMESTAMPADD(interval,integer, timestamp)   Returns the *timestamp* calculated by adding *integer* intervals of type *interval* to *timestamp*.

TIMESTAMPDIFF(interval,timestamp1, timestamp2)   Returns the integer number of *intervals* of type *interval* by which *timestamp2* is greater than *timestamp1*.

WEEK(date) Returns the week of the year in *date* as an integer (1-53).

YEAR(date) Returns the year in *date* as an integer value.

System Functions

This section describes the system functions included in the ODBC scalar function set.

DATABASE( ) Returns the name of the database corresponding to the connection handle (hdbc).

IFNULL(exp, value) If *exp* is null, *value* is returned. If *exp* is not null, *exp* is returned. The two data types must be compatible.

USER( ) Returns the name of the user.

Explicit Data Type Conversion

This section describes a single function found within the ODBC SQL data type definitions.

The ODBC syntax for the explicit data type conversion function does not restrict conversions. The validity of specific conversion of one data type to another data type will be determined by each driver-specific implementation. The driver will, as it translates the ODBC syntax into the native syntax, reject those conversions that, although legal in the ODBC syntax, are not supported by the data source.

CONVERT(value, data_type)

The function returns the value specified by *value* converted to the specified *data_type*, where *data_type* is one found in Table 6.3. Shown on the following page.

■■■■■ **Table 6.3** Valid Data Type Constants Understood by the **CONVERT** Function

SQL_BIGINT	SQL_LONGVARBINARY
SQL_BINARY	SQL_LONGVARCHAR
SQL_BIT	SQL_REAL
SQL_CHAR	SQL_SMALLINT
SQL_DATE	SQL_TIME
SQL_DECIMAL	SQL_TIMESTAMP
SQL_DOUBLE	SQL_TINYINT
SQL_FLOAT	SQL_VARBINARY
SQL_INTEGER	SQL_VARCHAR

■■■■

7

ACTIVEX

MULTIMEDIA

By now everyone realizes the wealth of information the Web can provide, but they also realize how static and boring the Web pages really are. Although the computer age is revolutionizing the multimedia world, exciting content has been despairingly missing on the Internet until now. ActiveX multimedia controls give Web developers the ability to easily incorporate streaming audio, animations, video, and slide presentations within their Web pages. Here are just some of the ActiveX controls that you can immediately incorporate into your Web sites.

- *RealAudio.* Used to include audio and streaming content
- *PowerPoint Animation Player.* Allows playback of slide and animation presentations created with Microsoft PowerPoint95

- *ActiveX Movie*. Play numerous animation and video formats as streaming content at a designated Internet connection rate, such as 14.4 kbs or 28.8 kbs
- *Shockwave*. Display exciting video and graphical animations produced with Macromedia Director
- *Surround Video*. Show video or static images that contain 360° of scenery content

The most important thing to remember is that these exciting new ActiveX multimedia controls not only revolutionize the Web, but they will revolutionize all desktop applications. In the very near future, you will not only be using these controls in your Web pages, but integrating streaming Internet audio and video content in a variety of desktop programs.

■■■■■■■ **TIP**

Should you have any problems running an ActiveX control, clean the cache directory of Internet Explorer and restart it.

■■■■■■■

Microsoft has successfully integrated Java with ActiveX controls. In your Web pages, you can include Java applets, which are recognized as ActiveX controls and can be integrated with other ActiveX controls using ActiveX scripting. The Web no longer sets limits on what you can do; that is determined by you.

Inline Audio and Video

Although there is a plethora of different ActiveX controls covering numerous multimedia types, there are times when you want to quickly deploy multimedia content. The Internet Explorer 3.0 supports two new HTML extensions for incorporating simple, nonstreamed audio and video content in your Web pages. Before exploring the potential of the multimedia ActiveX controls, you should consider using these two HTML extensions to revolutionize your Web site with audio and video in a matter of seconds.

BGSOUND Tag

Not many of the current box office smash movies would be entertaining without background music or sound. We are surrounded by sound and music in nearly everything that we do. On our way to work we listen to the radio, and at home at night we sit in front of the television. Now in a world so full of sound and music, there is no reason that your Web pages should be so silent.

In recognition of this fact, the Internet Explorer was developed to allow you to incorporate background audio files in your Web pages. This implementation currently doesn't use an ActiveX control, but rather a simple HTML tag. Using the <BGSOUND> tag, you can set up several different types of audio files as background sound for your Web pages. Here are the audio files currently supported:

- MIDI files
- .AU
- .WAV

The syntax used for including the <BGSOUND> tag in a Web page is simple, as shown in the sample code:

```
<BGSOUND  SRC="wldthing.wav"   LOOP=3>
```

The two main attributes associated with the <BGSOUND> tag are SRC and LOOP. Anyone who has placed images in Web pages should recognize the SRC attribute, which specifies the URL location of the file to play. The LOOP attribute specifies a numerical value ranging from 1 up to INFINITE, which indicates how many times you want the sound file to be played.

There are two things to remember when you are placing audio files in your Web page. First, because the audio files are not in the form of *streaming content*, the user will not be able to hear them until they are completely downloaded. Streaming content means that information is played as it is being downloaded rather than after the download is complete. You should use relatively small audio files such as MIDI. MIDI is an ideal audio file for background sound because long audio clips still maintain a small file size. Second, beware the desire to loop. Small audio files that constantly repeat can be extremely annoying.

When the <BGSOUND> tag is incorporated in a Web page, it runs invisibly. Users will hear the sound you have playing, whether they want to or not.

DYNSRC Attribute

Before long, people will forget that there was a time when you couldn't view video across the Internet. The Web pages that you create today can easily incorporate video information using a new attribute of the basic <IMG> tag. The DYNSRC attribute lets you specify the URL for a video file you want displayed on your Web pages. When you implement the DYNSRC attribute, there are several additional attributes, described in Table 7.1, that you can specify to customize the appearance of the video.

The other basic attributes associated with the <IMG> tag, such as WIDTH, HEIGHT, and ALIGN, are still applicable. Here is an example of the code used to display video on a Web page using the DYNSRC attribute along with the other attributes specified in Table 7.1.

For those browsers that don't recognize the DYNSRC attribute or don't support .AVI video content, the static image specified by the SRC attribute will be displayed instead. When no WIDTH or HEIGHT attributes are specified, the video appears with the proper dimensions. Figure 7.2 shows how the video content produced by the sample code above appears in a Web page.

■■■■■■ **Table 7.1** Attributes That Can Be Used with the DYNSRC
Attribute

Attribute	Description
CONTROLS	When specified, the playback controls for the video are displayed. This attribute does not accept any additional arguments (see code sample in Figure 7.1).
LOOP	Specify the number of times you want the video to be played, where n=1 to n=INFINITE.
START	Specify a user event to cause the video content to play such as OnMouseOver, or OnLoad.

■■■■■■

The DYNSRC attribute currently only supports .AVI video content, not
Quicktime or MPEG.

Streaming Audio

The current bandwidth limitations on the Internet have served as a
major limitation to the multimedia content you place in your Web page.

■■■■■■ **Figure 7.1** HTML source code for including an .AVI file in a
Web page using the DYNSRC attribute.

```
<HTML>
<TITLE>Video Content</TITLE>
<H1>Don's Multimedia Bazaar</H1>
<BODY>
<IMG DYNSRC="bubble2.avi" SRC="caracas.gif" LOOP=3 ALIGN=LEFT
START=mouseover  CONTROLS>
</BODY>
</HTML>
```

■■■■■■

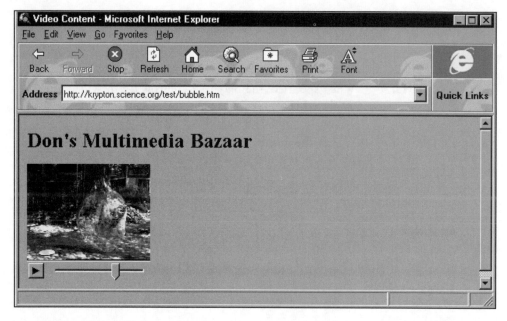

◼◼◼◼◼◼ **Figure 7.2** Use the controls to play or pause the video playback, or drag the pointer to see a particular frame.

A 20-second sound file could require several minutes to download, and most users visiting your Web site won't wait around to see it. The answer to this bandwidth problem has been streaming audio content. RealAudio was the streaming audio system developed by Progressive Networks for this type of Internet delivery system.

Recognizing RealAudio's almost immediate predominance on the Internet, Microsoft has incorporated the RealAudio system into the Internet Explorer 3.0 as the RealAudio control. Now when designing your Web site, you can insert RealAudio files and know that anyone using Internet Explorer will easily be able to listen to them. You can listen to some streaming RealAudio content by visiting the following URL:

```
http://www.realaudio.com/test/sites_snds.html
```

Internet Explorer actually launches a separate window for the RealAudio control when a RealAudio file is encountered. See Figure 7.3.

The user can choose to stop, pause, or play the audio file using buttons similar to what you would expect to find on a typical tape recorder. In addition, the user can also drag the pointer to any part of the audio file, and immediately begin listening to that particular audio selection without having to hear the entire file. When the RealAudio control first starts running, it downloads information to create a buffer and then begins playing the audio content as it is being downloaded.

Creating RealAudio Content

Before you can begin to provide streaming audio content, you must create the content. RealAudio content is provided as an audio file with a .RA file extension. To do this, RealAudio provides an encoder tool for converting conventional audio files into RealAudio files. These files can then be streamed to the RealAudio control on the user's system. You can download the RealAudio encoder at the following URL:

http://www.realaudio.com/products/encoder.html

The RealAudio encoder takes audio content, which can be present in three different file types, or live audio and converts it into streaming RealAudio

■■■■■ **Figure 7.3** The user plays or pauses the RealAudio file using the controls in the window.

files that can be compressed for either 14.4-kps or 28.8-kps delivery. Here are the types of audio content that can be converted into the RealAudio content:

- .AU
- .WAV
- .PCM
- Live audio feed from satellite, CD, or DAT tape, as long as the sampling rate of the stream can be specified

When you run the RealAudio encoder, it appears as shown in Figure 7.4.

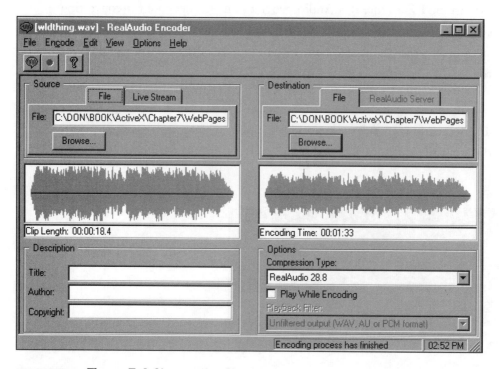

■■■■■■■ **Figure 7.4** Choose the file that you want to convert into a RealAudio file.

To convert your existing audio content into RealAudio content:

- Choose the file that you want to convert by clicking on the **Browse** button in the **Source** folder
- Choose the destination and filename of the .RA file you will create by clicking on the **Browse** button in the **Destination** folder
- Select the level of compression you want from the drop-down menu labeled Compression Type
- Click on the **Start Encoding** button or select the **Encode|Start Encoding** command

Now that you have created a RealAudio file, you are ready to provide this content to all the users that visit your Web site.

Providing RealAudio Content

You can provide your RealAudio content either in conventional fashion or stream the content to the user. Using the conventional method, you can quickly include RealAudio files on your Web site by making a link to the file.

When a user selects the link, the .RA file is downloaded to the user's system. Internet Explorer then prompts the user to open the file or have it saved to disk. If the user selects **Open it**, the RealAudio player is launched and the file that was downloaded begins to play.

```
<A HREF="audio/ondemand.ra">Click here to play.</A>
```

Providing a streaming RealAudio file on your Web site is a little more difficult than the conventional method. Because the audio content is provided as streaming content, a special RealAudio server is needed to provide it. These RealAudio servers must be purchased from RealAudio with the cost dependent on the number of streams you want to be able to provide simultaneously. RealAudio does provide a RealAudio Personal Server that you can experiment with for free. The RealAudio Personal Server lets you provide up to two external and one local connection with no appreciable loss of audio quality delivered. You can download the RealAudio Personal Server by going to the following URL:

```
http://www.realaudio.com/persserv/
```

Once you have downloaded the server, install it with these steps:

1. Run the Setup executable for the RealAudio Personal Server that you download.
2. Click on the **Setup** button on the RealAudio Personal Server Control Panel to designate the directory location in which the RealAudio files and log information will be stored.
3. Add the MIME file type for RealAudio to your HTTP server.

Once the RealAudio Personal Server is running, it should appear as shown in Figure 7.5.

After you have the RealAudio Personal Server installed and running, you must ensure that the HTTP server you are using is configured to provide the RealAudio MIME content. Most HTTP servers have a *MIME.TYPES* file in the CONFIG directory that indicates the content types it is capable of serving. Figure 7.6 illustrates the content of the *MIME.TYPES* file for the FrontPage Personal Web Server.

To configure the HTTP server to be able to provide the RealAudio content, the following information needs to be added to the *MIME.TYPES* file.

```
type: audio/x-pn-realaudio    exts: ra, ram
```

Now that both your HTTP server and RealAudio Personal Server are set up and configured, you can place streaming audio content into your Web

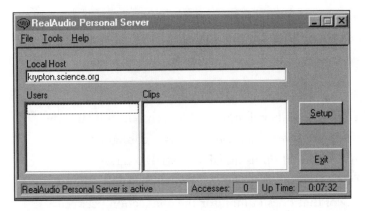

▬▬▬▬▬ **Figure 7.5** Click on the **Setup** button to modify the file directory for the audio files and log information.

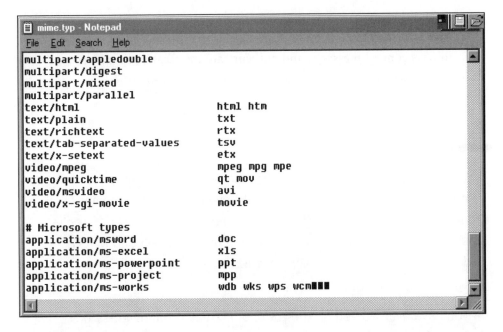

▬▬▬▬▬ **Figure 7.6** Add or delete the types of MIME content you want to provide on your HTTP server.

pages. You can place your RealAudio content on your Web page using the anchor HTML tag linked to the URL for the .RA file. The RealAudio server will be configured to serve the .RA file when the link is selected.

Firewalls

Many users who are behind firewalls will not be able to listen to RealAudio content, unless they have their server administer properly configure the firewall. RealAudio transmits information using UDP (User Datagram Protocol) rather than TCP (Transmission Control Protocol). UDP is known as a connectionless protocol that doesn't monitor the connection between the server and the client, unlike TCP. Users behind a firewall need the server administrator to configure a packet-filtering route to allow for transmission on the following ports:

- *TCP port 7070.*   Used to communicate with the RealAudio server to pass control messages and authenticate the RealAudio player
- *UDP ports 6970-7170.*   Used to receive audio content only

■■■■ **TIP**

As a developer, you may want to experiment with many of these multimedia ActiveX controls, but you don't have any multimedia clips readily available. Here is a URL that has an assortment of different multimedia files such as .WAV and .AU audio files, .AVI and MPEG video clips, and numerous .GIF images:

http://www.wintermute.net/pic.html

If you have ever wanted to see a video of a lizard eating grass or hear a bingo parody of the movie *Pulp Fiction* then this URL is for you.

At the Movies...

Providing streaming audio and video content is a very useful way to provide files that can be quite large across the Internet. Now a user can begin to view exciting multimedia presentations as soon as they click on a particular link. The problem in producing streaming multimedia content is ensuring that what you want to present meets the existing bandwidth limitations.

ActiveMovie is the control that Microsoft has created to allow you to stream a wide variety of multimedia content across the Internet. This content can be displayed in a Web browser, or you can even integrate the ActiveMovie control into your Visual Basic, C, or C++ applications. ActiveMovie is a step toward the integration of entertainment, computers, and telecommunications, in the form of the Internet or intranets.

The ActiveMovie Player is the control that allows .ASF files to be viewed. The ActiveMovie .ASF files that you create can encapsulate audio, image, and video files. Here are just some of the different multimedia file types that the ActiveMovie control can encapsulate:

- Video type files such as MPEG, .AVI, and .VCM (Video Compression Manager)
- Audio files such as .WAV or .ACM (Audio Compression Manager)
- Apple Quicktime
- Still-image files such as .GIF or JPEG
- URLs and HTML documents

The ActiveMovie doesn't replace any of these file formats, but in fact acts as a container in which these multiple files can be placed and then served to users across the Internet. There are three main components

of the ActiveMovie system that allow you to create, view, and edit
content:

- *ActiveMovie Stream Editor.* A tool for creating .ASF ActiveMovie
  files. You can choose an audio soundtrack for your presentation,
  and then insert images in the order that you want them to appear.
  The ActiveMovie Stream Editor ensures that the content that you
  want to provide can be effectively streamed across the Internet, taking into account the bit-rate bandwidth limitations.
- *ActiveMovie Player.* The control that allows .ASF files to be
  viewed.
- *ActiveMovie Stream Add-on.* A SDK for programmers who want
  to integrate ActiveMovie content into their Visual Basic, C, or C++
  applications.

You can download these three programs by choosing ActiveMovie
Streaming at the following URL:

```
http://www.microsoft.com/advtech/
```

ActiveMovie Stream Editor

Creating movies with static images and audio is now simple using the
ActiveMovie Stream Editor utility. Choose a particular audio soundtrack
for your presentation, and then combine it with static image files positioned
along a timeline for movie-like display. The advantages of creating streaming movie content is that users can immediately begin to listen to and see
the ActiveMovie content you place on the page. The problem with streaming is that there are varying rates that users are able to download information. For example, a user who has a 28.8-kbs modem can receive up to
3600 bytes per second. Should you want to show a new image every two
seconds along with an audio soundtrack, you have to make sure that this
amount of content doesn't exceed the user's bandwidth restriction.

The Stream Editor lets you design the content for the bit rate that you specify, while it also has conversion tools for compressing content. The Stream Editor handles the timing and encoding of files placed in a presentation. It also lets you optimize the content in a presentation so that it can be delivered to individuals using the low bit-rate Internet. Here is the procedure for creating an ActiveMovie presentation with the ActiveMovie Stream Editor:

1. Create a project file (.ASP) that will contain the images and sound files constituting the ActiveMovie file.

2. Add the desired image and sound files.

3. Lay out the image and audio presentation of the ActiveMovie presentation you want to create.

4. Set the bit-rate properties of the network across which you will be providing the ActiveMovie content.

5. Compile the .ASF file by clicking the **Build** button on the toolbar, or selecting the **Stream|Build** command.

The first step in creating an .ASF ActiveMovie file is to create the .ASP project file. This file should have its own directory, because any image and sound file you place in your presentation will be copied to this directory. The ActiveMovie Stream Editor also allows only one .ASP project file per directory.

The next stage in creating an ActiveMovie Presentation is to add audio and image files. You can add files by selecting the **File|Add Files** command. You can add only those type of files that the ActiveMovie Stream Editor supports. The currently supported audio and image files are as follows:

- .GIF
- .JPG

- .BMP
- .RLE
- .WAV

The ActiveMovie Stream Editor also checks your system to see if it supports any additional audio or image file formats. Any file formats that have the proper audio compression manager (ACM) or image compression manager (ICM) added to your system will also be supported by the editor. The ActiveMovie Stream Editor will identify any new CODECs installed on your system and add them to the list of supported file formats. In addition to the various audio and image files, you can also add URLs to your .ASF ActiveMovie presentation. The Internet Explorer browser will launch to the indicated URL location whenever the ActiveMovie control encounters a URL in a presentation.

After you have added files to your project, the ActiveMovie Stream Editor should appear as shown in Figure 7.7.

The ActiveMovie Stream Editor consists of three main windows. The bottom window, known as the Content window, displays all of the image and sound files that you add to the .ASP project file you are creating. For convenience, these files are shown with an icon next to them to indicate the type of file. The middle window, known as the Edit window, gives a graphical representation of the bandwidth consumed to display the presentation along with the timeline. The top window gives you a quick reference to the image files you have in your project. When you place the mouse pointer over a particular image file in the Content window, a thumbnail of the image appears in the top window along with vital information about the image, such as file source and type.

Once the desired audio and image files are in the Content window, you can create your presentation. In the current version of ActiveMovie Stream

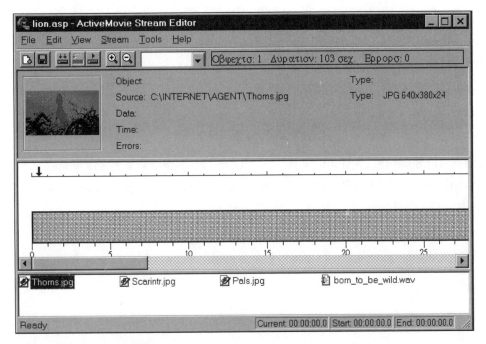

Figure 7.7 Add files to a presentation by dragging them from the Content window into the Edit window.

Editor, each .ASF file should contain at least one .WAV audio file. You can include more than one audio file, but all audio files should use the same CODEC. First add the audio soundtrack for your presentation by dragging the file from the Content window to the Edit window. In most cases the ActiveMovie Stream Editor will first have to compress the file before it can be added. To add images to the presentation, you can either drag them from the Content window into the Edit window, or you can use the Tap and Snap utility.

The Tap and Snap utility allows you to listen to the audio file in your presentation, and then choose at what point in the audio playback you want each image displayed. You can activate the Tap and Snap dialog box by first selecting the image you want to insert in the Edit window, and then selecting the **Tools|Tap and Snap** command to open the Tap and Snap window shown in Figure 7.8.

In the version of ActiveMovie Stream Editor tested during the writing of this book, you could not place .GIF images using the Tap and Snap utility. Instead you had to use the drag-and-drop procedure.

Before you build the .ASF file, you must set the bit-rate properties of your network. Select the **File|Properties** command to open the Project Properties window shown in Figure 7.9.

In the **Bit-Rate Properties** folder shown, you can specify the characteristics of the .ASF file that will be created. The available project bit rates include

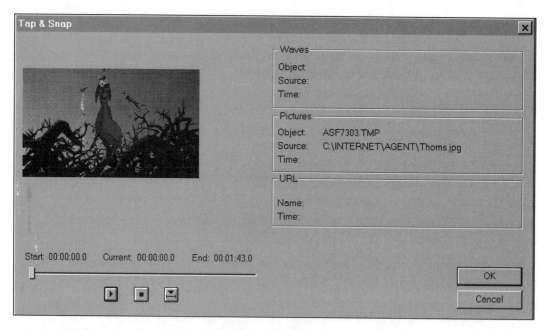

■■■■■■ **Figure 7.8** Click on the **Play** button to play the audio file, and then press the Spacebar at the point where you want the image inserted.

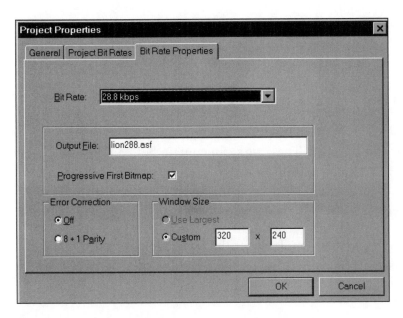

Figure 7.9 Select the bit-rate properties of the network on which the presentation will be provided.

the standard 14.4 kbs, 28.8 kbs, and 100 kbs for ISDN. If you have access to higher network speeds, you can create customized project bit rates in the **Project Bit Rates** folder. The bit rate that you specify for your .ASF file will greatly influence the size and number of the image and audio files that you assemble for your presentation.

Not only do you specify the desired bit-rate and output filename of the .ASF file in the Project Properties window, but you also specify the desired error correction. You should be concerned with this property only if you are providing the .ASF using the Microsoft Media server, in which case you should choose the 8+1 Parity selection. When you enable the 8+1 Parity error correction property, the quality of the .ASF playback will be improved when it is served by the Microsoft Media Server, and data loss is experienced in the transmission.

Once you have created the ActiveMovie content, you can provide the streaming content on current HTTP servers or on the new Microsoft Media Server.

ActiveMovie Control

The ActiveMovie Player is an ActiveX control that can view .ASF files (ActiveMovie Streaming Files). These files can contain both audio and image information. The key advantage is that you can produce streaming multimedia content that the user can immediately enjoy, rather than waiting for a .WAV or .AVI file to be downloaded first (see Table 7.2).

There are also several methods available for the ActiveMovie control, which should be self-explanatory to anyone who has a VCR:

- Play
- Stop
- Pause
- Rewind
- FastForward
- Seek

■■■■■■ **Table 7.2** Significant Properties of the ActiveMovie Control

Property	Description
Filename	Specifies the filename that will be loaded and displayed.
PlayCount	The number of times that the file should be played.
ShowControls	Indicates if the control panel is visible to the user.

■■■■■■

Some of these controls can be seen in Figure 7.10, which illustrates the appearance of the ActiveMovie control when displaying a file.

You will know if you installed the ActiveMovie control correctly, because any .ASF files will appear in your Windows Explorer with a movie camera icon. The sample shown in Figure 7.10 is the *bubble.asf* example that ships with the ActiveMovie Stream Add-on program.

TIP

The ActiveMovie control can't run in 16-color display mode. You must change the settings on your machine for 256 colors for this control to run.

PowerPoint Animation Control

Suppose you just gave a slide presentation to part of your company's sales force and you want to make it available to everyone on the Web. No, you

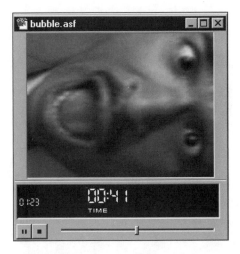

Figure 7.10 Use the control panel to select the content display.

don't have to convert every PowerPoint slide into that awful HTML language, but you can provide the slides on the Internet within seconds. If you use the ActiveX PowerPoint Animation viewer control with Internet Explorer, any user can now view your PowerPoint presentation on the Internet.

The PowerPoint ActiveX control is included in Internet Explorer 3.0, so most users will not have to do any additional download. For additional information or to download the PowerPoint Animation Player, you can go to the following URL:

http://www.microsoft.com/mspowerpoint/internet/player/

There are also several demos of the PowerPoint Animation control that will give you ideas on how to best use its capabilities on your own Web site.

Providing PowerPoint Content

Those developers who have PowerPoint95 can generate their own animation presentations, which can then be placed on Web pages. Before you can publish your PowerPoint content on the Internet, you need to install the PowerPoint Animation Publisher, which you can download from the previous URL.

■■■■■ **TIP**

The PowerPoint Animation Publisher currently only works with PowerPoint95 for Windows95 or Windows NT. Currently, those users who have PowerPoint 4.0 cannot use the PowerPoint Animation Publisher.

■■■■■

Once the PowerPoint Animation Publisher is installed, a command, **File|Export as PowerPoint Animation**, is added to the drop-down box, as shown in Figure 7.11.

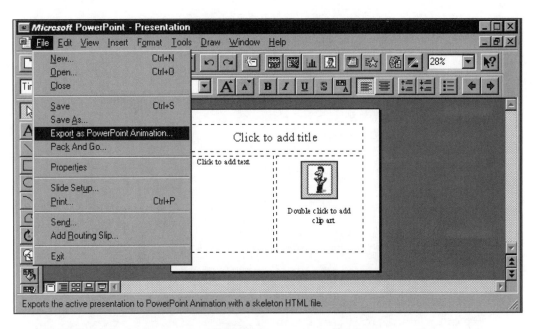

Figure 7.11 Select **File|Export** as the PowerPoint Animation menu selection to create PowerPoint content for the Web.

To create a PowerPoint animation for publishing on the Internet, you must first open the desired .PPT file in PowerPoint95. Then select **File|Export the PowerPoint animation,** and name the two files that will be generated with the .PPZ and .HTM extensions. The Animation Publisher also includes a link on the .HTM file that is generated so users who don't have the PowerPoint Animation Player control can download and install it. Figure 7.12 shows an example of the HTML code generated by the PowerPoint Animation Publisher that can immediately be used to provide multimedia content on your Web site.

In Figure 7.12 the <OBJECT> tag calls the PowerPoint Animation control, which is then activated in Internet Explorer. The <EMBED> tag has been included so that Netscape Navigator users will still be able to see the

■■■■■■■ **Figure 7.12** You can cut the <OBJECT> tag information generated and paste it into other HTML files.

```
<HTML>

<HEAD>

<TITLE>Untitled</TITLE>

<META NAME="GENERATOR" CONTENT="Microsoft PowerPoint Animation
Publisher 1.0">

</HEAD>

<BODY>

<CENTER>


<OBJECT CLASSID="clsid:EFBD14F0-6BFB-11CF-9177-00805F8813FF" WIDTH=280
HEIGHT=210>

<PARAM NAME="File" VALUE="dontest.ppz">

<EMBED WIDTH=280 HEIGHT=210 SRC="dontest.ppz"></EMBED>

<NOEMBED>This page contains a Microsoft PowerPoint Animation that your
browser was unable to view.<A HREF="dontest.ppz">Click here to open
dontest.ppz fullscreen</A></NOEMBED>

</OBJECT>


</CENTER>

<! Note: Both "PPZ" and "PPT" files are supported.>

<BR>

<A HREF="dontest.ppz">Click here to view dontest.ppz in a larger
size</A>

<BR>

<BR>

<HR>

This page contains a Microsoft PowerPoint Animation. If you can't see
it, <A HREF="http://www.microsoft.com/mspowerpoint/">download</A>
Microsoft PowerPoint Animation Player today and

learn how <B>YOU</B> can create multimedia for the Web!

</BODY>

</HTML>
```

PowerPoint presentation as a plug-in. The <NOEMBED> tag is also included to display text for those browsers that don't recognize either the <OBJECT> tag or <EMBED> tag. Figure 7.13 illustrates the appearance of this HTML example being played by the PowerPoint Animation control in the Internet Explorer 3.0.

The ActiveX Control Pad can also be used to insert the PowerPoint Animation control directly into a Web page. Using the Property window, you can designate the .PPZ file that you want the control to play as well as define other properties for the presentation.

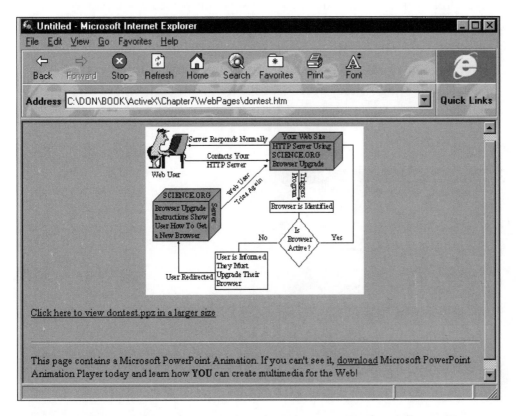

Figure 7.13 Click on the PowerPoint presentation to advance to the next slide.

Added Features

You can add advanced features, including hyperlinks and audio capability, to your presentation. You are no longer limited to providing silent PowerPoint presentations, because you can use the sound parameter to incorporate either ActiveMovie or RealAudio audio content.

```
<OBJECT CLASSID="clsid:EFBD14F0-6BFB-11CF-9177-00805F8813FF" WIDTH=340
HEIGHT=255>

<PARAM NAME="File" VALUE="dontest.ppz">

<PARAM NAME="Sound"  VALUE="http://krypton.science.org/try/test.ra">

</OBJECT>
```

Hyperlinks can be easily added to a PowerPoint presentation that you provide on the Internet. When developing a PowerPoint presentation, you select the object that you want to be a hyperlink to another location on the Internet. Then select the **Tools|Interactive Settings** command. In the window that opens (see Figure 7.14), click on the **Run** radiobutton and enter the desired URL for the hyperlink.

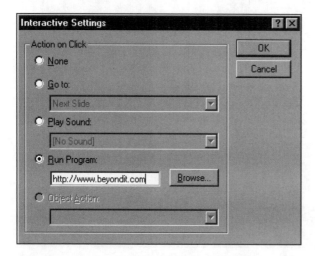

■■■■■■■ **Figure 7.14** Set the interactive settings of a PowerPoint presentation in this window.

Serving PowerPoint Presentations

Providing most types of content on the Web requires that you properly configure the MIME mapping of the server. Most servers have a *MIME.TYPES* file in which you can add information about the type of content and the recognized file extensions for the desired content. Here is an example of the code that needs to be added to the *MIME.TYPES* file for PowerPoint presentation content.

```
application/mspowerpoint        ppt ppz pps pot
```

The Microsoft Information Server doesn't have a typical *MIME.TYPES* file, but it has a content registry. Refer to Chapter 3 for information on how to add new content to the registry. Here is the information to add to this registry to enable it to provide PowerPoint presentation content:

```
"application/ms-powerpoint,ppt,,5"=""
"application/ms-powerpoint,ppz,,5"=""
"application/ms-powerpoint,pps,,5"=""
"application/ms-powerpoint,pot,,5"=""
```

Third-Party ActiveX Controls

The message is out: Microsoft has announced its Internet strategy, and it's called ActiveX. Now numerous companies are adapting their programs to conform to the ActiveX control specification. Because ActiveX controls are based on OLE controls, many of these companies can make this simple conversion in a short amount of time. This means that as a Web developer, you will have a wide assortment of third-party multimedia ActiveX controls that you can use on your Web site.

Shockwave

Macromedia Director is recognized as one of the premier multimedia development tools. There are already an estimated 250,000 users of Macromedia

Director. Director is used to create video and graphical animations for a wide assortment of products. Now it can be used for the Web. You can get information and download the Shockwave ActiveX control from the following URL:

```
http://www.macromedia.com
```

After the Shockwave ActiveX control is installed, you can appreciate how impressive it is by viewing several of the demos that are available.

Producing Shockwave Content

Details on generating the Director movies can be found in numerous books (check out the *Netscape LiveWire Sourcebook*) and materials. Once you have created a Director movie, you must still take several steps before you can provide this information on the Internet. The most important is that you must "burn" the movie using Macromedia's Afterburner software, which is basically a compressor utility. The limited bandwidth on the Internet encourages programs to have the smallest size possible so that they can be downloaded quickly. The Afterburner software compresses a .DIR file and creates a .DCR compressed file that can then be provided to users on the Internet. You can download this utility from Macromedia's Web site (see the previous URL) (see Table 7.3).

Figure 7.15 shows an example of the HTML code used to include the Shockwave ActiveX control in your Web pages.

Table 7.3 Properties of the Shockwave ActiveX Control

Property	Description
SRC	The URL location for the Director movie file you want to play.
AUTOPLAY	Indicates if the Shockwave movie should play automatically with the possible values True (default) or False.
SOUND	Indicates if sound should play with the possible values True (default) or False.

Figure 7.15 ActiveX scripting can be used.

```
<HTML>
<BODY>
<OBJECT CLASSID="clsid:166B1BCA-3F9C-11CF-8075-444553540000"
WIDTH="260"
HEIGHT="380"
HEIGHT="380"
ID="sw"
NAME="sw"
CODEBASE="../cabs/sw.cab#version=1,0,0,7">
<PARAM NAME="src" VALUE="movies/hypno.dcr"> </OBJECT> <br>
</p>
<CENTER>
<FORM NAME="SwForm">
<INPUT TYPE=Button size=40 NAME="btnSoundOn" VALUE="Sound
On"><br><br>
<INPUT TYPE=Button size=40 NAME="btnSoundOff" VALUE="Sound
Off"><br><br>
</FORM>
</CENTER>


<SCRIPT LANGUAGE="VBS">
Sub btnSoundOn_OnClick
        sw.Sound = True
End Sub
Sub btnSoundOff_OnClick
        sw.Sound = False
End Sub
</SCRIPT>


</BODY>
</HTML>
```

This example not only illustrates the HTML code used to insert the Shockwave ActiveX control in a Web page using the <OBJECT> tag, but it also demonstrates the integration of ActiveX scripting (see Figure 7.15). In this example, a simple form button is used to vary the SOUND property of the Shockwave ActiveX control so that the user can turn the sound on or off.

Net Lingo

Recognizing the value of including Shockwave content in Web pages, Macromedia has added several net-specific *lingo* commands to the Director software. Lingo is the scripting language used when creating .DIR animations to indicate the actions and events of different objects in a particular movie. Table 7.4 lists the lingo commands that are available, which you can use to modify your .DIR movie to take full advantage of the Web.

■■■■■■■ **Table 7.4** Net Lingo Commands

Lingo Command	Description
GoToNetPage	Creates a hyperlink to a URL.
NetOperationID	Returns an ID, allowing asynchronous operations to then execute.
NetAbort	Aborts a network operation.
NetDone()	Returns False until the asynchronous network operation is completed.
NetError()	Returns an empty string until the asynchronous network operation is completed.
NetMIME()	Returns a MIME file type.
PreLoadNetThing()	Loads a file into the disk cache.
NetLastModDate()	Returns the last date string from the HTTP header.
GoToNetMovie	Specifies another Director movie to play when a particular event is executed.

■■■■■■

Serving Shockwave

The Director files that are played by the Shockwave ActiveX control have a particular MIME-type that you must configure your server to provide, as shown:

```
application/x-director          DCR
```

Once this is done, you are ready to "shock" your Web site.

FutureSplash

The FutureSplash ActiveX control produces animations with a vector-based format to deliver exciting graphics and animations. Here are just some of the features:

- Streaming of graphic animations, allowing animation display while the file is still being downloaded
- Small file size of animations due to vector-based format
- Zooming in on graphics with no loss of image quality by a click of the right mouse button

The FutureSplash control developed by FutureWave will be downloaded to your computer when you go to the following URL:

http://www.futurewave.com/ie/fsindex.html

Using the FutureSplash control, you can place impressive animation graphics in your Web pages. The FutureSplash control is also very small, approximately 160K; therefore, you won't drive away potential viewers of your Web pages with long downloads of the software needed to appreciate your newest ActiveX content. You can view several FutureSplash samples at the previous URL.

The CelAnimator software, produced by FutureWave, allows you to produce the animations that will be viewed with the FutureSplash control. At the time this book was written, the beta version of the CelAnimator software was available for free download at FutureWave's site.

After you have created your animation, you can save it in several different formats by selecting the File|Export Movie command. The three formats of most interest are as an animated .GIF, .AVI, or a .SPL movie. The .SPL movie format requires the FutureSplash ActiveX control to view, while the Internet Explorer 3.0 is also capable of viewing animated GIFs.

Animated GIFs

Initially, .GIF files (see Figure 7.16) could only contain one image file. In 1987 the technical specification for .GIF files was expanded to allow one .GIF file to contain multiple images. In 1989 this specification was expanded to include timing and transparency capabilities. Of course, no one implemented this capability (known as the GIF89a standard) to any great extent, and it was forgotten as the advancements of the Web took place.

Now companies such as Netscape and Microsoft have ensured that their browsers are capable of displaying this kind of format. Using the animated .GIF format, you can put simple animations in your Web pages using the <IMG> tag. Here is an example of the HTML code used to display an animated .GIF in a Web page:

```
<IMG SRC="helo.gif" WIDTH=88 HEIGHT=31 ALIGN=RIGHT ALT="Best Viewed with
Microsoft Internet Explorer">
```

You can view one of these animated .GIF files at the following URL:

```
http://www.science.org/tedc/
```

Everything you ever wanted to know about animated GIFs can be found at the following URL:

```
http://members.aol.com/royalef/gifanim.htm
```

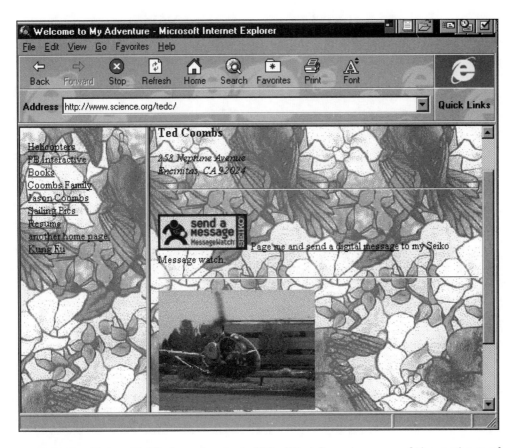

Figure 7.16 An animated .GIF of Ted Coombs, one of the authors of this book, flying a helicopter.

Display

When you want to display animations in your Web pages using the FutureSplash control, you must save the files with the .SPL extension. Inserting a FutureSplash animation in a Web page using the ActiveX control is simple. The main property you need to define is Movie, where the value you specify is the location and name of the animation file you want to display. Figure 7.17 shows an example of the HTML code generated by the ActiveX Control Pad for a FutureSplash animation.

■■■■■■■■ **Figure 7.17** Use the ActiveX Control Pad to define the properties of FutureSplash content.

```
<HTML>
<HEAD>
<TITLE>Future Splash Sample Run</TITLE>
</HEAD>
<BODY>
<OBJECT ID="FutureSplash1" WIDTH=401 HEIGHT=225
 CLASSID="CLSID:D27CDB6E-AE6D-11CF-96B8-444553540000">
    <PARAM NAME="_ExtentX" VALUE="10610">
    <PARAM NAME="_ExtentY" VALUE="5953">
    <PARAM NAME="Movie" VALUE="surfer.spl">
    <PARAM NAME="Loop" VALUE="-1">
    <PARAM NAME="Play" VALUE="0">
    <PARAM NAME="Quality" VALUE="AutoLow">
</OBJECT>
</BODY>
</HTML>
```

■■■■■■■

You can play with different values for the other properties, such as Play, Loop, and Quality. Although you can now easily insert the FutureSplash control content into your Web pages, you must make the control available to other people who want to view your site. Use the CODEBASE attribute to specify the URL location where the user's browser can download the FutureSplash control. You can simply take it off your system, or reference the FutureWave home page.

Too Cool Surround Video Control

Disneyland provides a 360° panoramic video theater, but why should Michael Eisner be the only one who can produce 360° panoramic video?

Using the Surround Video control, you can place impressive 360° video content on your Web pages. Navigate around by using your mouse keys like this:

- The ActiveX control that you download from this URL is named *SVIDEO.OCX*. Pan across the image by moving the mouse while holding down the left mouse button.
- The mouse pointer changes when over hotspots and hyperlinks that can be placed within the images and linked to other images or Web pages.
- A list of all the hyperlinks in an image appears when you right-click after the image has been loaded.

To produce this type of content requires either special 3D software rendering packages or a rotating camera. The power of the Surround Video technology is that it allows 360° images or videos to be presented on a flat screen. When video or images are captured with 360° cameras, the content typically must be displayed on a cylinder to show the proper perspective. If the content is displayed on a flat screen, the lines in the image have a curvature, which produces significant image distortion. The Surround Video technology uses a sophisticated mapping algorithm to allow 360° viewing on a flat display screen with no perspective alterations.

Black Diamond Consulting created this impressive control, which you can download from the following URL:

```
http://www.bdiamond.com/surround/svideo.htm
```

After you download the Surround Video ActiveX control, you can view several of the demos available at the above URL. When you view these pictures, you can pan up, down, left, or right by holding down the left mouse button and moving the mouse in the desired direction. The control even supports hotspots to other URLs or to other Surround Video content. When your mouse is over a particular hotspot, it will appear as a hand to indicate that the hotspot exists. Here is an example of the simple HTML code required to insert the Surround Video ActiveX control in a Web page.

```
<OBJECT CLASSID="clsid:7142BA01-8BDF-11cf-9E23-0000E8A37440"
        HEIGHT=150 WIDTH=500>
    <PARAM NAME="DataSourceName"
VALUE="http://www.bdiamond.com/surround/images/bridge.svh">
</OBJECT>
```

In this code, you can see that the DataSourceName property is the main parameter used to identify the URL location of the video content. To generate the .SVH video content, you can use the Surround Video SDK. The Surround Video SDK consists of several tools that allow you to modify and create the image content that you want displayed in the Web pages:

- Surround Video API
- Surround Video Link Editor
- Surround Video Editor
- Surround Video Internet Control

You can download the Surround Video SDK from the URL where you acquired the Surround Video ActiveX control. Before you know it, you too will be providing multimedia content on the Web that is truly next generation.

Java Applets

Microsoft now supports and embraces Java. Java is the exciting new computer language developed by Sun Microsystems that is sweeping the

Internet. Java has been described as object-oriented, simple, robust, and secure. The most important feature of Java is revealed by one of its catch phrases: "write once, run anywhere."

Java applets are a subset of the Java language that exemplify this capability. Java applets consist of code that is interpreted, rather than compiled. Because the language is interpreted as byte code, any machine running a Java Virtual Machine can interpret the code and convert it into machine code. This feature is the dream of programmers around the world.

Programmers have had to deal with the numerous operating systems that are in popular use. When they develop a particular application for one operating system, such as Windows, they then have to port that application to the other operating systems. With Java applets, this time-consuming ordeal is over. Now a programmer creates a single Java applet and does not need to make a Windows, Macintosh, and UNIX version. On the Internet, a user can download the Java applet and place it on a Web page, and the Java Virtual Machine present on the user's system converts it into the machine code for the relevant operating system.

■■■■■■ **TIP**

At the time this book was being written, the Java Virtual Machine was not yet a part of the Internet Explorer 3.0. To enable the Internet Explorer 3.0 so that it can view Java applets, you can download the Java Virtual Machine from the following URL:

http://www.microsoft.com/intdev/sdk/docs/javavm/overview.htm

When this program is run, the Java Virtual Machine is set up for the Internet Explorer 3.0, in addition to a byte code translator and a byte code verifier.

■■■■■■

The Java Virtual Machine recognizes Java applets as ActiveX controls. This not only allows Java applets to be placed in Web pages in the same fashion as ActiveX controls are, but it also allows Java applets to be placed as ActiveX controls in applications created with other programming languages, such as Visual Basic and PowerBuilder. Because Java applets are recognized as ActiveX controls, they can also interact with other ActiveX controls on a Web page, and they can be used in conjunction with simple ActiveX scripting.

In most cases, you must create the Java applet before you can place it in anything. Already, endless volumes of books have been written that detail how to create Java programs and applets. Suffice to say, Java is a computer language and typically requires programmer skill levels to develop applications with it. Sun created Java as an open language available to all developers for free, and you can download Sun's Java Development Kit (JDK) at their Web site:

```
http://www.java.sun.com
```

There are also numerous graphical Java development environments emerging that decrease the difficulty of creating new programs or applets. These programs include Microsoft's Jakarta and Symantec's Café.

For Web developers creating simple graphical Java applets, there are also tools such as Corel's *WEB.MOVE* that take an animation you create graphically and convert it into Java applet code. Of course the wonderful world of the Internet offers Web developers numerous Java applets that can be downloaded and used for free.

Java Applets in Web Pages

Java applets can be used to integrate a wide assortment of multimedia applications within your Web pages, ranging from scrolling graphical advertisements to IRC chat utilities. You can place Java applets in your Web pages using the <APPLET> tag. The <APPLET> tag has several

attributes associated with it, which make it appear similar to the
<OBJECT> tag (see Table 7.5).

The <APPLET> tag also has the familiar attributes WIDTH, HEIGHT, and
ALIGN that are commonly used with the <IMG> and other basic HTML
tags. Here is an example of the HTML code used to insert an applet in a
Web page:

```
<APPLET  CODEBASE="applets/NervousText"
CODE=NervousText.class
WIDTH=300
HEIGHT=50>
<PARAM NAME=text VALUE="Vote Republican!">
</APPLET>
```

As with ActiveX controls, Java applets can have parameters in the form of
NAME|VALUE pairs passed to them. In this case a text string is passed to
the Java applet, which will then display the text wiggling on the screen.

■■■■ **Table 7.5** Attributes of the <APPLET> Tag

Attribute	Description
CODEBASE	The URL of the location where the Java applet code can be downloaded.
CODE	The name of the applet class that will be downloaded.
NAME	The name of the applet that is created, where default is the applet class filename.
WIDTH	Width dimension of the applet that will be displayed.
HEIGHT	Height dimension of the applet that will be displayed.
ALT	Alternate text that should be displayed if the user's browser can't display applets.
ALIGN	Where the Java applet should be aligned: left, right, top, middle, texttop, absmiddle, baseline, bottom, or absbottom.

■■■■

The Java Virtual Machine is capable of recognizing and displaying applets specified with this HTML syntax for backward compatibility. In the near future, the <OBJECT> tag will replace the <APPLET> tag, and you will insert both ActiveX controls and Java applets with the same <OBJECT> tag. You can also use ActiveX scripting to link Java applets and ActiveX controls on a Web page the same way that you integrate multiple ActiveX controls together (see Chapter 5).

Sample Java Applets

The number of existing Java applets is already quite extensive. Some of the Java applets you find on the Internet provide the source code for free. These you can download, compile, and begin providing on your Web site. To compile the source code, you can use the tools that are available in the JDK.

JDK Demo

After you install the JDK, you will find several applets that you can begin to experiment with in the *java/demo* directory. When you open one of the sample directories, you will find that there is a sample HTML file that you can immediately load in Internet Explorer to see the applet.

Each directory also contains a file with a .JAVA and a .CLASS extension. When you create Java applets, you can write them in a program such as Notepad, but you must save them with the .JAVA extension. To create the applet, you must run the **JAVAC** command in DOS that creates the applet .CLASS file. The .CLASS file is the code that you reference with the <APPLET> tag in your Web page. Then it is just a matter of creating the HTML code with the <APPLET> tag, and the appropriate properties defined for the Java applet you want to display.

ButtonPlus

This particular Java applet allows you to define various text messages to appear on a button on a Web page that will change depending on the user-created events, such as an OnMouseOver or Click event. As with every ActiveX control, this applet has several properties associated with it (see Table 7.6).

Table 7.6 Properties of ButtonPlus Applet

Property	Description
URL	URL destination to go when the button is clicked.
IMAGE	The images that appear on the button when it is first loaded, MouseOver event, and when it is clicked. The value for this paramater is in the form of URL|URL|URL for the three images to appear for the three events.
TEXT	The text string that will appear on the button when it is first loaded, MouseOver event, and when it is clicked. The value for this parameter is in the form of string|string|string for the three text strings to appear for the three events.
SOUND	The sound that will play when the MouseOver event occurs, and when the button is clicked. The value for this parameter is in the form URL|URL for the two events.
BGCOLOR	The color of the button background, specified using RGB. Ex. 255,255,255 for white
TEXTCOLOR	The color of the text that will appear, specified using RGB. Ex. 192,192,192 for gray
HIGHLIGHT	When the value is greater than 0, the button will change color when clicked to make it appear to be depressed.
FONTSIZE	The size of the text that appears, the default is 12 point.

Other basic properties include TEXTALIGN, VTEXTALIGN, and FONT, which are self-explanatory. You can download the compiled class and see a demo for this particular applet at the following URL:

http://www.xm.com/café/ButtonPLUS/

Once you download the applet you are ready to provide this applet on your Web page. Here is a sample of the HTML code used to include this applet on a Web page.

```
<HTML>
<TITLE> A Little Button Test</TITLE>
<H1> Impressive Isn't It?</H1>
<APPLET CODE=ButtonPLUS2.class WIDTH=125 HEIGHT=40>
<PARAM NAME=HIGHLIGHT VALUE=4>
<PARAM NAME=URL VALUE=www.microsoft.com>
<PARAM NAME=FONTSIZE VALUE=14>
<PARAM NAME=TEXT VALUE="Click here!||Enjoy">
<PARAM NAME=BGCOLOR VALUE=200,100,50>
<PARAM NAME=TEXTCOLOR VALUE=0,200,0>
</APPLET>
</HTML>
```

You can see in this code example that when the TEXT property is used you don't have to enter a value for each of the different events, but you must include the proper number of delimiter (|) symbols. This also applies to the SOUND and IMAGE properties.

Mona Nixon Java Applet

One of the most interesting and funny multimedia Java applets can be found at the following URL:

http://www.rosebud.com/art/mona/nixon.html

Although you probably won't have any application for this particular applet, it does demonstrate how to incorporate simple animation with

audio and user events. You will never look at the Mona Lisa the same
again.

Valuable Java Resources

The resources available on the Internet for Java are already quite extensive.
A search in Yahoo on the word "Java" returns over 300 different Web sites,
and none of them are talking about coffee.

The first place to look for information about Java is at the site of the company that created it. Sun Microsystems's site offers the JDK for free download, in addition to having an extensive amount of documentation, and
up-to-date information on Java developments:

```
http://java.sun.com
```

One of the most complete sites of both Java programs and Java applets
is a site named Gamelan. Here you can choose topics such as multimedia
or business and see an index of numerous Java applications. Many of
these Java applications are available for free, and you can download the
program or source code to immediately begin using it on your own
Web site:

```
http://www.gamelan.com
```

Just-In-Time Compiler (JIT)

When you first run several of these Java applets, you may not be all that
impressed with their running speed. The speed of Java applets is slower
because they are interpreted rather than compiled. The solution to this
problem lies in the Just-In-Time (JIT) compiler. The JIT compiler reads the
byte code of the Java applet and converts it into machine code on the operating system. Once the Java applet is converted into machine code, it runs
as a compiled program. The JIT compiler can improve the run-time speed
of Java applets as much as 5–10 times.

Internet Explorer has a built-in JIT compiler. This produces much faster run-time of Java applets that it downloads and executes. The integration of the JIT in the Internet Explorer allows you to create exciting Java applet multimedia content knowing that your users will have no problem with a slow run-time.

8

ACTIVEX

CONFERENCING

Microsoft is making the office of tomorrow a reality today using the recently developed ActiveX Conferencing technology. Today's business environment is undergoing rapid change. The significant rise of travel costs has forced many companies to reconsider travel expenses. At the same time, companies are increasingly multinational, with divisions around the world simultaneously working on projects. The need to support collaboration between two or more individuals in video and audio conferences has become more important than ever before.

ActiveX Conferencing gives you access to these capabilities on your desktop. Some operating systems such as Windows 95 come with ActiveX Conferencing built in. ActiveX Conferencing technologies work in local intranets or across the Internet. Using ActiveX Conferencing, you can transmit data using these different transfer protocols:

- TCP/IP over the Internet or corporate LANs
- IPX networks

The ActiveX Conferencing technologies require at least a 14.4 kbs network connection, and the real-time voice communications are designed only for the TCP/IP protocol.

The discussion of the NetMeeting software in this chapter serves as an introduction to the potential of using the Internet for conferencing. Features of this tool include audio communication, application sharing, a whiteboard, and soon even video communication. The ActiveX Conferencing SDK gives you an understanding of the APIs used in the NetMeeting applications. These various APIs can also be integrated into new applications.

NetMeeting

Consider the following scenario. A user contacts your Web site, and after purchasing and downloading software you sold to them, they experience difficulties in its installation. By clicking a button on your Web page, the user can immediately speak real-time with one of your company's customer service representatives (CSR). Your CSR can even share with the user a desktop application to diagnose the user's problem.

This scenario is one of many that illustrates the potential of the new conferencing capability developed by Microsoft. The demonstration program that illustrates these different conferencing capabilities is called NetMeeting.

Microsoft has used the ActiveX Conferencing APIs to create a suite of conferencing tools. These tools are designed for developers to test the ActiveX Conferencing applications they create. These conferencing tools include the following capabilities:

- Whiteboard
- Program sharing
- File transfer
- Audio communications
- Chat

Before you design your own tools, you can explore the capabilities of the ActiveX Conferencing technology by downloading NetMeeting from the following URL:

http://www.microsoft.com/INTDEV/msconf/

You should have at least 16Mb RAM to run NetMeeting, but you can experiment with it using only 8 Mb. When you first run the application, it appears as shown in Figure 8.1.

Figure 8.1 Once you have established a connection, activate one of the many conferencing utilities.

Whenever you run NetMeeting, you are automatically logged onto Microsoft's User Location Service. This server lists the people who are currently connected and their Internet addresses. There are multiple servers running the User Location Service, and you can contact different ones to find a specific person. To change the server you contact for the User Location Service, edit the NetMeeting properties.

Before you can appreciate the capabilities of NetMeeting, you must first establish a conference with someone. There are several ways that you can contact a particular individual. On the main NetMeeting window, you will see two buttons, one for people and one for computers. You can click on the people icon or select the **Call|Directory** command. The Directory window opens, showing the users currently logged onto the same User Location Service (see Figure 8.2).

After you choose a person with whom to conference, the main window of NetMeeting reopens. Click on the phone button to contact the person with

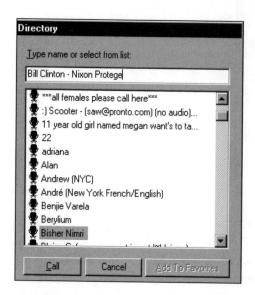

■■■■ **Figure 8.2** Enter the name of the individual you want to contact.

a request to set up a conference. If the person agrees, you then select the tools you want to use during the conference.

Conferencing Utilities

By setting NetMeeting properties, you can determine the performance and operating characteristics of various conferencing tools. To modify these settings, select the **Tools|Options** command to open the Microsoft NetMeeting Settings window (see Figure 8.3).

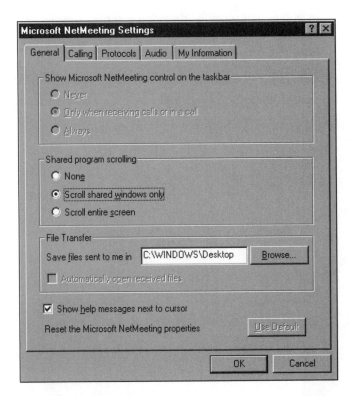

Figure 8.3 Choose a folder and modify properties of conferencing tools.

Real-Time Voice Communication

The Internet is no longer silent. NetMeeting has the same audio capability as the Internet phone. The only requirement for two people to communicate with each other is that they both need to have speakers and a microphone setup with the appropriate sound card. They can communicate with real-time voice communications, or choose to use the various collaborative tools of NetMeeting. To speak with someone, select the **Call|Place Advanced Call** command to open the window displayed in Figure 8.4.

Whiteboard

Using this utility, conference attendees can write or draw on a screen that is visible to everyone. Figure 8.5 shows how one particular conference session used a Whiteboard.

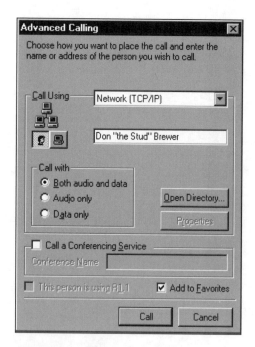

Figure 8.4 Choose to communicate either by audio only, or by both audio and data.

Figure 8.5 Use the Whiteboard only for information you want everyone to see.

Another way to use the whiteboard is to copy a window on your operating system and then copy it to the Whiteboard.

Chat

The NetMeeting chat utility is similar to other chat utilities, except that you do not have the option of selecting an avatar. Figure 8.6 shows the Chat window that conference attendees can use. Type a message and click the **Enter** button.

File Transfer

You are a few mouse clicks away from sending files to others in your conference. First click on the **Send File** command, and choose the file you want to send from your system. Once chosen, the file is transferred to all of the parties in a particular conference.

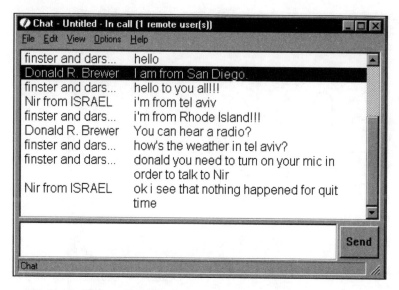

Figure 8.6 Remember, in contacting remote people around the world you become your country's ambassador.

Application Sharing

Before you can share an application during a conference, you must start that application and then click on the **Share Program** button on the NetMeeting toolbar. NetMeeting displays the programs open on your system that you can share. You have two options from this point, you can let people in the conference:

- See the program you are running but not have any control over it
- Have complete control of the application

For the first of these options, select the **Tools|Work Alone** command. For the second, select the **Tools|Take Control** command.

Sometimes difficulties arise in sharing an application if two parties in the conference have different screen resolutions. In the Microsoft NetMeeting Settings window shown in Figure 8.3, you can select the appropriate screen-sharing properties.

Your Own Conference

When you use NetMeeting, someone must begin by choosing to start the conference. Select the **Call|Conference Host** command, and then let people contact you.

To prevent unwelcome Internet visitors, you can set up the meeting so that you can screen users before they are allowed to join. You can modify these properties in the Microsoft NetMeeting Settings window. Should you need to remove someone from a conference that you are hosting, right-click on their name and select the **Disconnect** command.

ActiveX Conferencing SDK

ActiveX Conferencing technologies can be built into a variety of different applications. The SDK features eight APIs that you can integrate into your applications to enable them to work with the ActiveX Conferencing capability. You can download the ActiveX Conferencing SDK from the following URL:

```
http://www.microsoft.com/INTDEV/msconf/
```

The ActiveX Conferencing SDK also contains several sample programs. These programs include the ability to add conferencing capability to Word or to Excel.

Word Macro

In the sample directory of the ActiveX Conferencing SDK is a sample application for conferencing with Microsoft Word. To use it:

1. Copy the *ezonf.dll* file, found in the **ezconf** sample folder, into your *C:/windows/system* directory.

2. Place the *confmcr.dot* file, found in the **word sample** folder, into the template directory of Word.

3. Open a new file in Word using the *confmcr.dot* template, or add the template to an existing document using the **File|Templates** command.

After you open a document in Word, you can view the conferencing toolbar by selecting the **View|Toolbars** command. Figure 8.7 shows a document in Word with the conferencing toolbar activated.

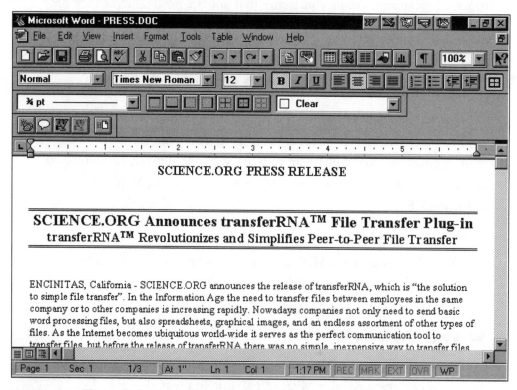

Figure 8.7 The bottom toolbar is the conferencing toolbar.

The conferencing toolbar features five different macros that use some of the ActiveX Conferencing APIs:

- *LaunchConferencing.* ConferenceConnect
- *ConnectUser.* Connect to a single user
- *ShareApp.* ConferenceShareWindow
- *UnShare.* ConferenceShareWindow
- *SendFile.* ConferenceSendFile

For you to implement this conferencing capability in Word, first click on the **LaunchConferencing** button to open NetMeeting and then specify the people with whom you are conferencing. At that point, you can transfer or share the document that you have loaded in Microsoft Word.

Overview of the ActiveX Conferencing API

ActiveX introduces a new API designed to enable the creation of simple network-based conferencing applications. The ActiveX Conferencing API makes it easier for developers to include basic conferencing features in their Windows software. This section gives an overview of the API functions, including functions that enable:

- Conference information management
- Application sharing
- Data transfer

The Multipoint Communication Services (MCS) and Generic Call Control (GCC) APIs are also available to enable more complex multiuser conferencing. The ActiveX Conferencing API is meant for simpler conferencing applications.

Managing Conference Information

All conferencing applications need to be able to start a new conferencing session, terminate an existing session, or find out if a conference is in progress. Many applications also need to be notified when a new conference begins or ends. There are five API functions that relate to managing conference information:

- **ConferenceConnect**

```
DWORD WINAPI ConferenceConnect(
    HCONF     * phConf,
    LPCONFADDR lpConfAddr,
    LPCONFINFO lpConfInfo);
```

- **ConferenceDisconnect**

```
DWORD WINAPI ConferenceDisconnect(
    HCONF hConf);
```

- **ConferenceGetInfo**

```
DWORD WINAPI ConferenceGetInfo(
    HCONF   hConf,
    DWORD   dwCode,
    LPVOID  lpv);
```

- **ConferenceSetInfo**

```
DWORD WINAPI ConferenceSetInfo(
    HCONF   hConf,
    DWORD   dwCode,
    LPVOID  lpv);
```

- **ConferenceLaunchRemote**

```
DWORD WINAPI ConferenceLaunchRemote(
    HCONF       hConf,
    LPCONFDEST  lpConfDest,
    DWORD       dwReserved);
```

- **ConfNotifyProc**

```
DWORD WINAPI ConfNotifyProc(
    HCONF   hConf,
    DWORD   dwCode,
    DWORD   dwParam,
    LPVOID  lpv1,
    LPVOID  lpv2);
```

ConferenceConnect and ConferenceDisconnect are used to connect or disconnect a conferencing session. ConferenceGetInfo is used to get information about a conference. ConferenceSetInfo is used to set conference information. Whenever conference information changes, a callback function can be triggered that informs the application of the change.

ConfNotifyProc is an application-defined callback function for conference events. An application that uses the ActiveX Conferencing API must implement this callback function in order to receive event notification concerning its conferences. Table 8.1 lists the possible notification codes that may be supplied through this callback function.

Sharing Applications

A common feature of conferencing applications is the ability to share windows. Two functions are provided in the Conferencing API for this purpose:

Table 8.1 Notification Codes Used with Callback Function

DwCode	dwParam	lpv1	lpv2
CONFN_CONFERENCE_INIT	—	LPCONFADDR	LPCONFINFO
CONFN_CONFERENCE_START	—	LPCONFADDR	LPCONFINFO
CONFN_CONFERENCE_STOP	—	LPCONFADDR	LPCONFINFO
CONFN_CONFERENCE_ERROR	—	—	—
CONFN_USER_ADDED	dwUserId	LPCONFADDR	LPCONFUSERINFO
CONFN_USER_REMOVED	dwUserId	LPCONFADDR	LPCONFUSERINFO
CONFN_PEER_ADDED	dwUserId	LPCONFDEST	—
CONFN_PEER_REMOVED	dwUserId	LPCONFDEST	—
CONFN_WINDOW_SHARED	HWND	—	—
CONFN_WINDOW_UNSHARED	HWND	—	—
CONFN_DATA_RECEIVED	the number of bytes pointed to by lpv2	LPCONFDEST	pointer to data received

DwCode	dwParam	lpv1	lpv2
CONFN_DATA_SENT	the number of bytes pointed to by lpv2	LPCONFDEST	pointer to data sent
CONFN_FILESEND_START	dwFileId	LPCONFDEST	LPCONFFILEINFO
CONFN_FILESEND_PROGRESS	dwFileId	LPCONFDEST	LPCONFFILEINFO
CONFN_FILESEND_COMPLETE	dwFileId	LPCONFDEST	LPCONFFILEINFO
CONFN_FILESEND_ERROR	dwFileId	LPCONFDEST	LPCONFFILEINFO
CONFN_FILERECEIVE_START	dwFileId	LPCONFDEST	LPCONFFILEINFO
CONFN_FILERECEIVE_PROGRESS	dwFileId	LPCONFDEST	LPCONFFILEINFO
CONFN_FILERECEIVE_COMPLETE	dwFileId	LPCONFDEST	LPCONFFILEINFO
CONFN_FILERECEIVE_ERROR	dwFileId	LPCONFDEST	LPCONFFILEINFO

- ## ConferenceShareWindow

```
DWORD WINAPI ConferenceShareWindow(
    HWND   hwnd,
    HCONF hConf,
    DWORD dwFlags);
```

- ## ConferenceIsWindowShared

```
BOOL WINAPI ConferenceIsWindowShared(
    HWND     hwnd,
    HCONF * phConf);
```

Each of these functions uses window handles (HWNDs) to identify the application. Changes in sharing status are indicated through callback functions.

Transferring Data

Most conferencing applications support data transfer between members of the conference. To make this feature easier to build into conferencing software, the API provides:

- ## ConferenceSendData

```
DWORD WINAPI ConferenceSendData(
    HCONF       hConf,
    LPCONFDEST lpConfDest,
    LPVOID      lpv,
    DWORD       cb,
    DWORD       dwFlags);
```

- ## ConferenceSendFile

```
DWORD WINAPI ConferenceSendFile(
    HCONF       hConf,
    LPCONFDEST lpConfDest,
```

```
LPCTSTR    szFileName,
DWORD      dwFlags);
```

ConferenceSendData is used to send data to a member of the conference. ConferenceSendFile is used to send an entire file. Incoming data is indicated on the recipient's computer through the ConfNotifyProc conference event callback function.

Handling Errors

Each of the ActiveX Conferencing API functions returns a DWORD that indicates any error condition. The DWORD error condition can have any of the values shown in Table 8.2.

▬▬▬ **Table 8.2** Error Codes Returned when Using API Functions

Error Code	Description
CONFERR_ACCESS_DENIED	Access to an object (file, user, and so forth) was denied.
CONFERR_BUFFER_TOO_SMALL	The buffer pointed to by a parameter is not large enough for the operation.
CONFERR_ENUM_COMPLETE	Enumeration complete.
CONFERR_FILE_NOT_FOUND	The file was not found.
CONFERR_FILE_RECEIVE_ABORT	The receiving of the file was canceled.
CONFERR_FILE_SEND_ABORT	The file send was canceled.
CONFERR_FILE_TRANSFER	There was a problem transferring the file.
CONFERR_INVALID_BUFFER	The buffer pointed to by a parameter is not valid for read/write.
CONFERR_INVALID_HCONF	The hConf parameter is not valid.
CONFERR_INVALID_PARAMETER	One of the calling parameters is incorrect.

■■■■■■■■ **Table 8.2** Continued

Error Code	Description
CONFERR_OUT_OF_MEMORY	A function could not allocate sufficient memory to complete the operation.
CONFERR_PATH_NOT_FOUND	The path was not found.
CONFERR_RECEIVE_DIR	There was a problem with the receive directory.
CONFERR_SUCCESS	The function completed the requested operation successfully.

■■■■■■

Building Windows programs that include conferencing abilities is greatly simplified with the introduction of the ActiveX Conferencing API. NetMeeting is but one example of the kind of functionality that can be built using the Conferencing API. Almost any application that includes a user interface could benefit from the addition of conferencing and data/window sharing ability.

Just think how much easier it would be for the end user to obtain technical support if they could click on a button that would connect them immediately to support staff over the network and initiate application and window sharing. With the Internet and ActiveX Conferencing, the power of network communications can be embedded in any Windows software.

9

EXTENDING

INFORMATION

SERVER

CGI is the zombie that's been dead for years but just isn't intelligent enough to lay down. There are now several ways of extending the capabilities of the HTTP/HTML environment without resorting to CGI. This book provides several Active strategies for developing Web-based applications, most of which rely on the client browser being Internet Explorer. This chapter describes a way to extend the capabilities of Internet Information Server (IIS) using ISAPI (Internet Server Application Programming Interface).

This server-based interface far exceeds Common Gateway Interface programs in functionality and efficiency. ISAPI uses system resources more effectively than the older CGI standard. One of the reasons for ISAPI's increased efficiency is that DLLs are loaded into memory and are executed immediately. In contrast, CGI programs are external applications that must be loaded and run.

ISAPI was developed by Process Software and Microsoft in conjunction with other software vendors to provide consistent standards for Web development and to ensure compatibility with a broad variety of applications. It currently runs with Microsoft's Internet Information Server, Process Software's Purveyor WebServer, and Nomad's WebDBC.

ISAPI lets you build dynamic linked libraries (DLLs) to handle requests and events confronted by IIS. The ISAPI filter sits between the Web server and the client Web browser. The ISAPI filter can view all data going to and from the Web server. The Internet Information Server makes use of functionality built into ISAPI filters, which are consulted each time the HTTP server is contacted by a Web browser. These capabilities include much more than simply responding to the browser. You can:

- Create thorough user-ID authentication programs that do more than check users' passwords. You can log which users access your applications and give them access to information based on their assigned security level.
- Redirect requests to other applications or other servers based on user information.
- Create programs that return dynamic Web pages or communicate directly with ActiveX objects.
- Provide data compression.
- Customize server logging procedures.
- Provide custom and increased server administration utilities such as Web statistics.

Each ISAPI-compliant Web server can have one or many ISAPI filters installed. Filters can be set up in a prioritized queue. ISAPI filters with the highest priority are called first, and so on down the line. If no priority is specified, the filter is called in the order it was loaded by the Web server.

Building ISAPI Filters

To begin building your own ISAPI filters, you must either know how to create a DLL in C or C++ or be willing to learn. This chapter assumes you have some working knowledge of building DLLs. You should use the latest version of Microsoft's Visual C++. There are two mandatory entry point functions you'll use when writing ISAPI filters: **GetFilterVersion**() and **HttpFilterProc**().

Getting Started with GetFilterVersion()

To get started, you need to build the startup function **GetFilterVersion**(). This function is one of the primary entry points for the ISAPI DLL and is required. As the name suggests, the **GetFilterVersion**() function is used to make sure that the ISAPI filter DLL was designed to meet the version supported by the server. This function is called only when Internet Information Server, or an ISAPI-compliant Web server, is started. Besides providing version information, this function plays a more important role: it sets the priority of the filter and registers the events to which a filter will respond:

```
BOOL WINAPI GetFilterVersion( PHTTP_FILTER_VERSION pVer );
```

This startup function takes a structure of type HTTP_FILTER_VERSION (Figure 9.1) as its only argument. In this structure, everything important is stored.

Your **GetFilterVersion**() function must fill in each of the HTTP_FILTER VERSION structure members:

▬▬▬▬▬ **Figure 9.1** Structure definition of HTTP_FILTER_VERSION.

```
typedef struct _HTTP_FILTER_VERSION {
  DWORD         dwServerFilterVersion;
  DWORD         dwFilterVersion;
  CHAR          lpszFilterDesc[SF_MAX_FILTER_DESC_LEN+1];
  DWORD         dwFlags;
} HTTP_FILTER_VERSION, *PHTTP_FILTER_VERSION;
```

▬▬▬▬▬

- *dwFilterVersion.* Fill in with the constant HTTP_FILTER_REVISION:

  ```
  filter->dwFilterVersion = HTTP_FILTER_REVISION
  ```

- *lpszFilterDesc.* Use the **strcpy()** function to save a string containing a textual description of your filter into this structure member like this:

  ```
  strcpy (filter->lpszFilterDesc,"A textual description of your ISAPI filter");
  ```

- *dwFlags.* This structure member keeps track of relevant flags such as what events the filter responds to or the priority of the filter using bit manipulation. See Tables 9.1 and 9.2 for lists of event flags and then set them like this:

  ```
      filter->dwFlags=( SF_NOTIFY_SECURE_PORT |
  SF_NOTIFY_NONSECURE_PORT |
  SF_NOTIFY_URL_MAP);
  ```

In the following tables, both the event flags and the priority flags are listed. As you add event flags, use the bit OR (|) symbol to separate them.

▬▬▬ **Table 9.1** ISAPI Event Flags

Event	Description
SF_NOTIFY_READ_RAW_DATA	Captures data headed for the server.
SF_NOTIFY_SEND_RAW_DATA	Captures the data headed from the Internet Information Server back to the Web browser.
SF_NOTIFY_AUTHENTICATION	Triggered when custom authentication is requested.
SF_NOTIFY_LOG	Captures information headed for a log. Used to implement custom logging.
SF_NOTIFY_URL_MAP	Triggered when the server is mapping logical paths to physical paths.
SF_NOTIFY_PREPROC_HEADERS	Triggered when the server receives preprocessed header information from a Web browser.
SF_NOTIFY_END_OF_NET_SESSION	Triggered when the user ends a session.
SF_NOTIFY_SECURE_PORT	Triggered whenever the server is communicating over a secure port.
SF_NOTIFY_NONSECURE_PORT	Triggered when the server is communicating over a normal HTTP connection.

▬▬▬

In this sample the events in the dwFlags member are set so that an event is triggered whenever data is either sent to or sent from the Internet

■■■■■■■■ **Table 9.2** Priority

Priority Flag	Description
SF_NOTIFY_ORDER_DEFAULT	Loads the filter at the default priority.
SF_NOTIFY_ORDER_LOW	Loads the filter at the LOW priority.
SF_NOTIFY_ORDER_MEDIUM	Loads the filter at the MEDIUM priority.
SF_NOTIFY_ORDER_HIGH	Loads the filter at the HIGH priority.

■■■■■■

Information Server using both the SF_NOTIFY_READ_RAW_DATA and SF_NOTIFY_SEND_RAW_DATA flags. Using these events, you can easily write programs that manipulate data either coming to the server or being sent from the server to the browser. For example, information going to a server might be redirected to a different server based on the information being sent from the browser. An example of information you can add being sent from the server to the browser is a custom button bar that appears at the bottom of every page. Rather than add that HTML to every page and maintain those pages for conformity, you can have the server add the HTML that will make your pages conform to company look-and-feel standards.

■■■■■■ **TIP**

Use only as many flags as you need for your application; using too many flags can greatly affect performance.

■■■■■

■■■■■■■ **Figure 9.2** Sample **GetFilterVersion()** function.

```
BOOL WINAPI GetFilterVersion (HTTP_FILTER_VERSION pMyFilter)

    {

    pMyFilter->dwFilterVersion = HTTP_FILTER_REVISION;

    strcpy (pMyFilter->lpszFilterDesc,"A textual description of your
ISAPI filter");

    pMyFilter->dwFlags=(SF_NOTIFY_ READ_RAW_DATA | SF_NOTIFY_
SEND_RAW_DATA    SF_NOTIFY_SECURE_PORT | SF_NOTIFY_NONSECURE_PORT |
SF_NOTIFY_URL_MAP);

    return TRUE;

    }
```

Also in Figure 9.2 are the SF_NOTIFY_SECURE_PORT and
SF_NOTIFY_-NONSECURE_PORT flags. One of these events will
always be triggered; a port is either secure or insecure. You should write
code to handle any special considerations you have for operating on
either a secure or insecure port. For example, if a port is secure and your
site accepts credit cards, you could request the card number securely. But
if the port is insecure, you might display your toll-free customer service
number instead.

The last flag in the dwFlags member of the sample is
SF_NOTIFY_URL_MAP. This can be the most useful of all the events. If
someone requests QUERY.HTML from a browser, and your ISAPI filter
intercepts this request and sees that QUERY.HTML was requested, the filter
could run a database query and return the results back to the browser. The
person at the browser thinks they've requested a static file. There are many
other things you can do, such as getting the requested file through FTP as
well as create a dynamic page. Figure 9.3 shows an example ISAPI filter.

■■■■■■ **Figure 9.3** Example from Microsoft's sample ISAPI authentication filter.

```
BOOL WINAPI GetFilterVersion( HTTP_FILTER_VERSION * pVer  )
{
    DbgWrite(( DEST,
                "[GetFilterVersion] Server filter version is %d.%d\n",
                HIWORD( pVer->dwServerFilterVersion ),
                LOWORD( pVer->dwServerFilterVersion ) ));

    pVer->dwFilterVersion = HTTP_FILTER_REVISION;

    //
    //  Specify the types and order of notification
    //

    pVer->dwFlags = (SF_NOTIFY_SECURE_PORT           |
                     SF_NOTIFY_NONSECURE_PORT        |
                     SF_NOTIFY_AUTHENTICATION        |
                            SF_NOTIFY_ORDER_DEFAULT);

    strcpy( pVer->lpszFilterDesc, "SQL Authentication Filter, version
1.0" );

    return TRUE;
}
```

If the **GetFilterVersion**() function returns false, the filter will be unloaded
and will not be able to receive any requests.

Using the Workhorse HttpFilterProc()

The **HttpFilterProc**() function is called every time an event is triggered. You can think of **HttpFilterProc** as the **Main**() function in an executable application. This workhorse function accepts three arguments:

- *filter context*. Which is an optional argument that contains information about the server session
- *notification type*. Which contains information about the triggered event and is particularly important because it indicates what code to process depending on the triggered event
- *pvNotification*. Which contains information stored about the event in a structure (see Table 9.3 for more information about the structures used with this argument)

```
DWORD WINAPI HttpFilterProc(PHTTP_FILTER_CONTEXT pfc, DWORD
NotificationType,
            LPVOID pvNotification);
```

The **HttpFilterProc**() function accepts two arguments: the filter context, a structure that can be used to associate context information with the HTTP request, and the pvNotification argument, which designates the event to which the filter is responding.

What your filter does in response to a particular event is up to you. The structure containing the data your filter will process is found in the filter context argument. The filter context argument is a structure whose type depends on the event that has occurred. See the notification types listed in Table 9.3.

Once your filter has either chosen to ignore the request or has processed the request, the **HttpFilterProc**() function should return one of the return codes listed in Table 9.4. These return codes let other ISAPI filters and the Web server know if they need to handle the request when this filter is finished with it.

Table 9.3 Structure Types Used with the **HttpFilterProc()** Function

Structure Type	Notification Type	Description
HTTP_FILTER_RAW_DATA	SF_NOTIFY_READ_RAW_DATA SF_NOTIFY_SEND_RAW_DATA	Data returned by a READ or SEND event.
HTTP_FILTER_PREPROC_HEADERS	SF_NOTIFY_PREPROC_HEADERS	Preprocessed header information.
HTTP_FILTER_AUTHENT	SF_NOTIFY_AUTHENTICATION	Client authentication information.
HTTP_FILTER_URL_MAP	SF_NOTIFY_URL_MAP	Physical path to a resource.
HTTP_FILTER_LOG	SF_NOTIFY_LOG	Log information.

■■■■■■■■ **Table 9.4** Filter Return Codes

Return Code	Description
SF_STATUS_REQ_FINISHED	The filter has handled the request and the server should disconnect the session.
SF_STATUS_REQ_FINISHED_KEEP_CONN	The filter handled the request and the server should keep the connection open for further communication.
SF_STATUS_REQ_NEXT_NOTIFICATION	Got it, handled it, and it's now fair game for the next filter in the queue or for the server to handle this request.
SF_STATUS_REQ_HANDLED_NOTIFICATION	
SF_STATUS_REQ_ERROR	An error occurred in the filter. Reserve this return for serious problems.
SF_STATUS_REQ_READ_NEXT	Request to see more of the data being passed back to the client or received by the server. Expects to be called again. This is only valid during RAW_READ events.

Installing an ISAPI Filter

For your ISAPI filter to operate, you need to make certain that it's registered on the machine where it will run. You should have either a setup program to register the filter DLL or send instructions with it. The setup program is probably the better option. Following is the procedure for creating one:

1. Run *REGEDIT32.EXE*.
2. Add the filter DLL name to the key:
   ```
   HKEY_LOCAL_MACHINE\System\CurrentControlSet\Services\W3Svc\Parameters\Filter
   DLLs
   ```

Debugging ISAPI DLLs with Visual C++

If you are using Microsoft's Developer Studio, you'll find this discussion of debugging ISAPI DLLs useful. The problem with trying to debug the DLLs with the debugger is that Internet Information Server runs as an NT service. As a result, you can't use the debugger to set breakpoints or watch statements in the ISAPI DLL. A tricky way around this problem is to run the Web server part of IIS as an application instead of as a service. For the full instructions on how to perform these tasks, access the following URL:

```
http://www.valley.net/~tpozzy/iisvcdb.html
```

INTERNET ACTIVEX

DEVELOPMENT

The first nine chapters of this book have explored World Wide Web site development using the ActiveX Web tools. The Internet is much more than the World Wide Web and creating Internet applications doesn't have to be done using HTML. Instead, building Internet applications will rely on components like ActiveX controls that have the ability to communicate with each other through means other than CGI, ISAPI, or other Web server technology.

Internet applications communicate with each other using one of the Internet protocols. The World Wide Web uses the HTTP (Hypertext Transport Protocol) to send messages between the Web browser and the Web server. You can build applications that use the standard Internet protocols to communicate, or build your own protocol with the WinSock controls using the Microsoft Internet ActiveX controls. The future holds an even more exciting promise: the ability to build your own ActiveX controls.

Imagine building an ActiveX control for your Web page that can communicate directly with other objects on your page, with objects running on someone else's page, with remote server applications, or with itself—all without using CGI or ISAPI.

The future of computer application development lies in building this type of component technology. For now, your applications can use WinSock to communicate with other applications; but, in the future, your applications will be distributed using DCOM (Distributed Component Object Model). No longer will you have to create complex communications protocols to communicate with remote objects or applications. Distributed computing will make writing network applications fast, simple, and powerful.

About the Controls

The Internet ActiveX controls are used to create applications that run over the Internet using many of the most popular communication protocols. These controls are time-saving components that allow you to build network applications without having to program the complexity of the communication protocols. Examples of these controls include:

- *FTP Client.* Sends files to, or downloads files from, an FTP server using the File Transfer Protocol object. FTP is widely used throughout the Internet to provide files freely to the public or to securely use a logon password.
- *HTTP.* The HyperText Transfer Protocol object allows you to communicate with HTTP servers from your program. This control isn't a Web browser. Instead, you can get textual information from an HTTP server and either display it in a text control or process the text in your program.

- *HTML.* This Web browser control can give users of your program access to the World Wide Web. You can let users browser freely or restrict access to certain Web pages.

- *POP.* The Post Office Protocol objects retrieve e-mail from a mail server.

- *SMTP.* The Simple Mail Transport Protocol objects enable your application to send e-mail.

- *NNTP.* The Network News Transfer Protocol object allows you to both send and receive Usenet News messages to and from an NNTP server. Using this object, you can build applications that query all the Usenet News groups, a specific group for information that can either be processed or displayed in your application. You can even create News robots that automatically post messages to news groups.

- *WinSock TCP.* Create both client and server network applications using the WinSock TCP object. All of the other major network protocols are built using TCP. Now, you can create your own simple socket applications or create your own network protocol.

- *WinSock UDP.* For those times when you need connectionless communications, the UDP socket object is what you'll need.

Use the ActiveX Internet controls in Visual Basic, Visual C++, Visual FoxPro, and Microsoft Access. The process of creating network-ready applications with these controls is very similar in each of these development environments. There are some minor installation issues that you should check before installing the controls for your development environment. This book discusses application development with the Internet controls using Visual Basic 4.0.

You can download the ActiveX Internet controls from Microsoft's Web site:

```
http://www.microsoft.com/icp/
```

Introduction to Network Applications

Writing a network application can be tricky if you've never written one before. The Microsoft documentation claims that "The Internet ActiveX Controls hide the complexity of creating Internet programs while exposing the versatility and power of ActiveX controls." This isn't exactly true. What *is* true is that these controls make it easier to implement these common protocols. You'll still need to understand all the steps these protocols follow to communicate between client and server applications. Before you can launch into writing network applications, you need to understand a few basic concepts.

A protocol is simply a way of communicating. (Remember that C3P0 of Star Wars fame was a protocol droid. He could communicate with many types of aliens.) A protocol is more than a language; it's the rules for communicating. If you write an application that returns a "goodbye" message whenever it receives a "hello" message, you've written your own custom protocol. A protocol can be as simple as this, or much more complex with hundreds of rules and keywords.

A Socket in Every Port and a Port in Every Storm

In a network application there is always both a server and a client side. An application that acts as a server creates a *listening socket*. A socket is a software device for setting up a virtual communication link between applications. These applications can be local (on the same computer) or remote (running on separate computers connected by a network). When a listening socket is created, the application can be said to be listening. Just as with radio, there can be many channels and your listening socket can only listen to one channel at a time. This communication channel is called a *port*.

■■■■■■ **TIP**

> In Visual Basic applications the port is set by setting the LocalPort property of the Internet control.

■■■■■■

Different network applications are assigned ports. For example, World Wide Web applications typically communicate using port 80. This isn't cast in stone; but if you expect to communicate with other Web applications, you can expect to communicate with them on port 80. Table 10.1 lists the ports associated with the ActiveX Internet controls that implement communications protocols. The WinSock TCP and WinSock UDP controls don't implement protocols. These are the controls you can use to develop your own protocols.

When you start writing network applications it's useful to know the port assigned to the *echo* port. Data sent from your application to port 7 is echoed back to your application. This is a good way to test your communications program. If you can successfully receive the data sent to port 7

■■■■■■ **Table 10.1** Ports Assigned to Network Applications

Protocol	Port
HTTP	80
HTML	HTML isn't really a communications protocol, although the HTML control communicates using the HTTP protocol; therefore, the port used by this control is 80.
SMTP	25
POP	109
NNTP	119
FTP	21 Command channel.
FTP-Data	20 FTP uses a separate channel for data transfer.

back again, the communications portion of your network application is working correctly.

The Client Side

A *client* is simply a network application that connects to a server. Client applications initiate communication sessions with server programs that sit around waiting for clients to contact them. A Web browser is a typical client application. A World Wide Web browser contacts an HTTP server and asks to be connected. Once a connection has been established, the distinction between a client and server application is not enough to mention. The two-way communications between the client and server are typically performed using a relatively small set of textual keywords, like *Quit* or *Help*.

Connect

Most clients *connect* to servers. This is a useful tidbit of information, as most of the ActiveX Internet controls are client controls. Therefore, the first thing you have to do with these controls is CONNECT to a server. With the exception of the WinSock UDP control, all of the other ActiveX Internet controls have a Connect method used to connect to a server.

```
object.Connect [RemoteHost], [RemotePort]
```

To connect to a server, you need to supply the host name of the computer running the server. Knowing the name of the host may not seem like enough information to connect to a specific application, but it is. The TCP/IP protocol running on the host knows to which applications to forward your connection attempt, based on the port it is trying to contact. In this way, the host "multiplexes" all of the traffic coming in over the network connection. (Remember that a PPP or SLIP connection over a phone line is an actual network connection.) The name of the host is supplied through using the RemoteHost property of the object, or you can override values stored in the property by supplying it as a parameter to the Connect method.

The bit of information required for the Connect method to work is the port number with which your application is going to connect. When creating custom applications, you should use port numbers greater than 1024. Ports below this number are assigned and reserved.

When a connection is successfully established with the server, a Connect event occurs. Place any code you want to process after a connection has been established in the Connect event. In case of a network error, an Error event is triggered. Of course, this is a good place to code error handling.

Authenticate

After you connect to a server application, the server typically requests information on who you are and whether you should be allowed to stay connected. This process occurs each time you log into a computer and enter your password. It is called authentication and is initiated by the client using the Authenticate method. The two Internet controls that require authentication as the second step in the communications process are POP and FTP. Sending e-mail via SMTP or connecting to an HTTP server do not require your application to log in or authenticate itself with the server.

The Server Side

Writing server applications is more complex than writing client applications. Still, following a few basic steps can simplify creating a server application. The WinSock TCP object can be used to write server applications. See the section on WinSock TCP for detailed information on creating server applications.

One of the factors that make server applications more complex than client applications is that clients normally carry on a single communication session with a server, whereas server applications can carry on multiple simultaneous communication sessions with multiple clients. For this reason, server applications typically use more than one socket to carry on communications.

The listening socket described earlier typically stays listening while handing off an incoming connection to a new socket. If this did not happen, a server application could carry on only one communication session at a time. Instead, the listening socket acts as a virtual switchboard operator. Once a connection request is received by the listening socket, it hands off the connection to a new socket that *accepts* the connection and continues the communication session with the client.

Note that an application can be both a server and a client. If your application is listening on a port and can connect to either itself or another server application at the same time, then it is also a client. Applications that are both servers and clients are becoming more common.

Installing Internet Controls Using Visual Basic

Before you can use the Internet controls to create network applications with Visual Basic, you must register them as custom controls. Registering the controls is as simple as selecting the controls you want installed from a dialog box opened by the Visual Basic **Custom Controls** command:

1. Select the **Tools|Custom Controls** command to open the Custom Control dialog box.
2. Choose the controls you want to install by clicking in the check box next to each control.
3. Click **OK**.

The custom controls you've installed appear in the controls toolbar. To place a control on a form, click on the control in the toolbar and then click and drag over an area on the form. If you click without dragging, your object probably will not appear on the form. You must drag, sizing the object, while placing it on the form.

Data Handling with DocInput and DocOutput Objects

Writing network applications requires that you send and receive data. Two objects make handling these communications easier by providing information on data transfer to and from an application. These objects are DocInput and DocOutput. They provide information about any type of data transfer initiated by an ActiveX Internet control.

When data transfer is initiated by an Internet control, such as the NNTP control or the HTTP control, an event is triggered. The names can be confusing because the event names are DocInput and DocOutput. If you write code that runs when one of these events is triggered, the corresponding object is passed as a parameter. For instance, when the DocInput event of an object is triggered, the DocInput object is passed as a parameter. The DocInput object will then contain valuable information about the data transfer that is occurring.

Here is an example: The GetArticleByArticleNumber of the NNTP object requests data from an NNTP (Usenet News) server. Specifically, it asks for a Usenet news article by number. This initiates data transfer and the DocOutput event is triggered. (The DocOutput event is triggered whenever data that is output by another application is received.) Figure 10.1 shows sample code from the Click event of a button. This code initiates a file transfer, which in turn triggers a DocInput event.

One of the states of both DocOutput and DocInput objects is an error state. When either the DocOutput or DocInput error state occurs, you can

■■■■■■ **Figure 10.1** The code necessary to initiate a file transfer.

```
Sub Button1_Click()

        NNTP1.GetArticleByArticleNumber UsenetArticle
End Sub


Private NNTP1_DocInput(DocInput As DocInput)
        'Use the DocInput properties to keep track of the file transfer
here.
End Sub
```

use the icError collection discussed in the next section to identify and handle the error.

icError Object and Collection

When data is transmitted over a network, errors can and often do occur. The icError and icErrors objects are used to store and access the resulting error information. When an Internet control uses methods such as GetDoc or SendDoc, the icErrors collection can be used to identify any errors. Either of these methods triggers the corresponding DocOutput or DocInput events. Using one of these objects to determine if an error has occurred is the first step. The second step is accessing and displaying the error information using the icError object. When bad things happen, the icError object is used to collect error information such as the error code and its description.

The Internet controls have a property called *error* that stores a reference to the icErrors collection. Once you've determined that an error has occurred, use this property to retrieve the error message or messages. The next example is taken from the Select Case statement of a DocOutput event. When the state of a DocOutput object is icDocError, then you can first store the collection of errors in a variable of type icErrors. Then, using the reference to the icErrors collection stored in the errors property of the control (in this case, the HTTP control), you store the errors in the *eCollection* variable. Using the Count property, which contains the number of objects in a collection, you can loop through the collection creating a text message with descriptions of the errors. (See Figure 10.2)

Here is a simpler bit of code that displays a single error message rather than looping through a collection:

```
Case icError
        MsgBox icErrors.Description
```

Figure 10.2 An error has occurred when DocOutput or DocInput icDocError states are set.

```
Case icDocError
        Dim eCollection As icErrors
        Dim iCnt As Integer
        Dim sErrors As String
        Dim iTotErrs As Integer

        Set eCollection = HTTP1.Errors
        iTotErrs = eCollection.Count
        For iCnt = 1 to iTotErrs
        sErrors = sErrors & eCollection.Item(iCnt) & vbCrLf
Next
eCollection.Clear
End Select
```

The amount of error handling you include in your application is a matter of taste. The more reliable you need your application to be, the more error handling you need to construct. The icErrors object makes handling error conditions hassle-free. As a result, you can concentrate on handling the errors and not building the entire error-handling infrastructure found in many network applications.

DocHeader Object and Collection

MIME, the Multipurpose Internet Mail Extensions, is a standard used in identifying data on the Internet. Historically, file extensions have been used to identify information types. With applications such as e-mail or information contained with a Web page, file extensions didn't apply, and a new standard was required for identifying this information. An e-mail message or Web page can contain many different types of data and MIME is used to describe the embedded data. The Internet controls make use of a special type of object used for creating MIME headers used to describe data. The DocHeader object contains the information on the kinds of data contained in an e-mail messages or Web pages.

DocHeader Objects

DocHeader objects aren't very complex. They contain two properties that together form a complete MIME description, also known as a MIME header. You've probably seen lists of these MIME headers in the helper applications section of your Web browser. Helper applications are started based on the information contained in the MIME headers that accompany a Web page.

Together, the name and value properties of a DocHeader object form a MIME header:

- *Name.* The MIME header label
- *Value.* The item value described by the MIME label

There are two ActiveX Internet controls that make use of DocHeader objects. The HTTP client control can access the MIME information from the <HEAD> section of Web pages and process that information as necessary. The SMTP object, used to send e-mail, requires the use of DocHeader objects when sending e-mail. Each e-mail message has a header attached to it with some required information used by mail servers to deliver the e-mail message. Not using a header would be like sending an envelope in the mail without an address.

DocHeaders Collection

DocHeaders are grouped together into a DocHeaders collection. You can refer to information in a DocHeaders collection similarly to how you would refer to individual items in an error collection. Unlike the icError collection, the SMTP object requires you to construct your own DocHeader collection. Think of this header as an address. Most addresses on a snail-mail envelope have multiple lines, such as a line for the recipient's name, one for the street address, and one for the city, state and zip code.

As with an address on an envelope, there are normally several MIME headers required to successfully send an e-mail message. These headers include the From, To, and Subject information. Each one of these pieces of information is stored as a DocHeader object with its respective Name and Value properties. Then the DocHeaders are grouped together in a DocHeader collection.

To create a DocHeader collection:

1. Create a *DocHeaders* variable.

2. Use the Set statement or instantiate a new instance of the DocHeader object.

3. Use the Add method of the DocHeader collection to add DocHeader objects.

You create the *DocHeader* variable and instantiate a new instance of the DocHeaders object using the Set statement, as shown here:

```
Dim dHeads As DocHeaders
Set dHeads = New DocHeaders
```

Add a single DocHeader to the collection using the Add method, which has two arguments: name and value. For example, the well-known From statement of an e-mail message is set using the word "From" as the name argument and the e-mail address of the sender as the value argument.

```
dHeads.Add("From", "tedc@science.org ")
```

You add multiple DocHeaders using the With statement. This Visual Basic statement allows you to perform multiple operations on an object. (See Figure 10.3.)

Figure 10.3 Add multiple DocHeader objects to the collection using the With statement.

```
With dHeads
        .Add("From", "tedc@science.org")
        .Add("To", "webmaster@internic.net")
        .Add("Subject", "Please add a link to my wonderful Web
resource.")
End With
```

As with the icErrors collection, the DocInput and DocOutput objects have a Headers property that contains a reference to the DocHeaders collection.

Using the FTP Client Object

FTP is one of the ways to transfer files on the Internet. The FTP protocol was created to do much more than simply transfer files; and because of its complexity, many people find using the FTP protocol difficult. Using FTP, you can handle many tasks, such as creating and removing directories, copying and deleting files, changing directories locally and remotely, and running local operating system commands.

This protocol was designed before IP connections were common and you had to use programs like FTP to manipulate file systems. FTP still has these capabilities, which you can choose to use when writing programs. When all you need to do is transfer files, however, you should consider an easier method. There are now other file transfer technologies, like transferRNA, that make file transfer simple. You can also build file transfer routines using the WinSock TCP object.

Building the FTP Client Application

To build an FTP client application, place an FTP control on a form, click on it, and set the properties using the Properties dialog box. Use the Custom option in this dialog box to set some of the important FTP control, client, and authentication properties (see Figures 10.4, 10.5, and 10.6).

When writing applications that need to connect with an FTP server, you begin by using two of the FTP object methods: Connect and Authenticate. The Connect method establishes the connection between the FTP client (your object) and an FTP server. Use the Connect method of the FTP client to

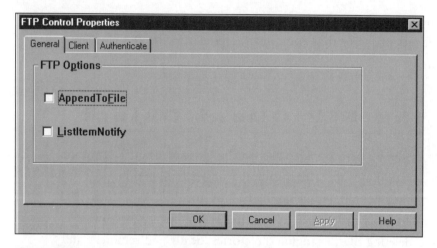

Figure 10.4 Configure the general FTP control properties.

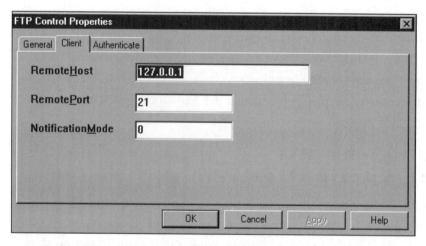

Figure 10.5 Configure the FTP client properties.

connect to a remote server. You can choose to supply the remote host and port as arguments. If you don't include this information, the RemoteHost and RemotePort properties of the FTP control are used:

```
object.Connect [RemoteHost], [RemotePort]
```

After a connection has been established, the Connect event of the FTP control is triggered. This is an excellent place to begin the authentication process required by all FTP servers. The Authenticate method negotiates the user ID and password:

```
object.Authenticate [userID] [Password]
```

FTP servers can accept two types of connections: anonymous and user account. Anonymous connections are publicly accessible connections to an FTP server for which the *userID* is normally **anonymous** and the *Password* is the **e-mail address** of the person connecting to the server.

Once authentication by the server has been completed, the Authenticate event is triggered. You can refer to the ReplyString property to see a message from the FTP server regarding your attempt to connect to it (Figure 10.7). You probably won't care about this message; if you receive it, you've successfully connected. If the server refuses your connection, your FTP.Error event is triggered.

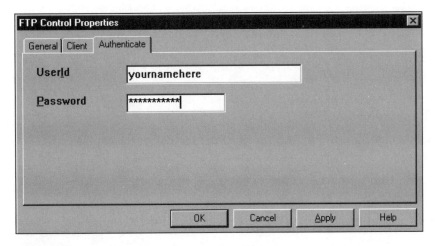

Figure 10.6 Set the authentication properties.

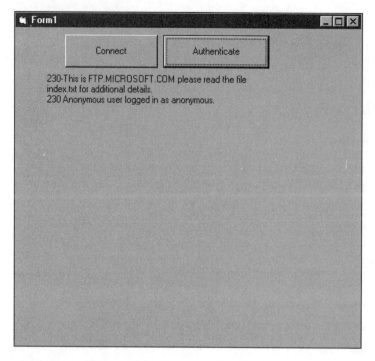

Figure 10.7 You can display the server response in a TextBox control.

To build your own FTP client, begin by placing the following controls on a blank form:

- FTP control named FTP1.
- A CommandButton for connecting to the server. Set the caption to **Connect**.
- A CommandButton for authentication. Set the caption to **Authenticate**.
- Label control named Status for keeping track of what's going on.

The sample establishes an anonymous (public and insecure) connection to a remote FTP server. Note that the FTP server to which you are going to connect must allow anonymous connections; otherwise, your connection will be refused. It's a good idea to use a traditional FTP client to test the connection before trying to figure out why your application isn't working.

Set the following properties for the FTP1 control by first clicking on the FTP control and then editing the properties in the Property dialog box. Here is an example of setting the RemoteHost property:

RemoteHost ftp.science.org

This value can also be set in a Visual Basic procedure, as shown here:

```
FTP1.RemoteHost = "ftp.science.org"
```

Because the example is using an anonymous connection, set the UserID property to Anonymous and the Password property to your e-mail address. FTP servers that allow anonymous connections require that your e-mail address be used as a password. By doing so, they can maintain accountability over who has accessed their server.

Place the code in Figure 10.8 in the Click event of the CommandButton labeled Connect.

■■■■■■ **Figure 10.8** Connect to a remote FTP server using an anonymous connection.

```
Private Sub Command1_Click()
        FTP1.UserID = "anonymous"
        FTP1.Password = "Harry@virtualcorp.com "
        FTP1.Connect
End Sub
```

■■■■■■■ **Figure 10.9** The Authenticate method can be called automatically or manually in the Click event of a button.

```
Private Sub Command2_Click()
        FTP1.Authenticate
End Sub
```

■■■■■■■

■■■■■■■ **Figure 10.10** Display the server's reply.

```
Private Sub FTP1_Authenticate()
        status.Caption = FTP1.ReplyString
End Sub
```

■■■■■■■

In the Connect event of the FTP object, you should update the status TextBox so that you know when the connection has been established. Typically, your application won't have an **Authenticate** button. This is where you would start the authentication process.

In the Click event of the **Authenticate** button, place the code shown in Figure 10.9.

In the Authenticate event of the FTP control, you can reference the ReplyString property to update the status TextBox. (See Figure 10.10.)

FTP is an involved and complicated protocol, and it's beyond the scope of this book to cover every one of its features. The code provided here is enough to connect to an FTP server and begin navigating through directories, receiving files, or sending files.

Here are some handy guidelines:

- Request directory information using the List method: *object*.List *directoryname*. Requesting directory information from the server triggers the ListItem event of the FTP client as long as the ListItemNotify property is set to True.

- You can navigate through the directories of the FTP server by using the ChangeDir method. This sends a request to the server to change the remote directory.

- Use the FTPDirItem object to retrieve file attributes.

- Retrieve the file from the FTP server using the GetFile method.

- Close your connection with the FTP server using the Quit method.

Using the HTTP Control

Long before there were graphical Web browsers, there were HTTP clients and servers. Textual information was transferred from an HTTP server and displayed in a text format. Graphics could be downloaded by clicking on a hyperlink embedded in the text. In just a few short years, we've advanced beyond the text-based Web browser with browsers such as Mosaic, Netscape, and Internet Explorer. But there are still uses for the old text browser (Lynx) and still reasons to transfer text using the HTTP protocol.

The HTTP control is a simple way to request data from an HTTP server. For more information on the HTTP control, see the sample application at the end of this chapter in the section "Building a Server."

Using the HTML Control

The HTML object is a Web browser control you can embed in your application. In fact, your entire application can consist of this single control.

One of the uses for this control is to access a particular Web site. Following is an example of a Visual Basic application that contacts the MovieLink Web site. If you haven't used this Web site, you'll find that it is an excellent source of information on movies playing almost anywhere in the United States.

1. Make certain that the HTML control has been added as a custom control.
2. Click on the HTML control icon (Figure 10.11).
3. Place the HTML control on the form.
4. Position and size the control. (Remember that displaying Web pages requires some space.)

Once you've placed the HTML control on the form, you need a way to have the control retrieve a Web page. The RequestDoc method of the HTML control is responsible for requesting documents from an HTTP server. It accepts the URL of the document you want retrieved as an argument. To create a simple application, you can have the HTML control retrieve the document as soon as the application loads. Place the RequestDoc method in the Form_Load() event of your form. (See Figure 10.12.)

■■■■■■ **Figure 10.11** Select the HTML control icon to place this control on the form.

■■■■■■■■ **Figure 10.12** Use the RequestDoc method to retrieve a Web page.

```
Private Sub Form_Load()
   HTML1.RequestDoc "http://www.movielink.com/"
End Sub
```

■■■■■■■

You may find it amazing that you can create an entire Web browser application by placing a single control on a form and writing one line of code. Run this application and see how well it works (Figure 10.13).

The MovieLink example contacts only a single site. By adding a ComboBox control to your application, you can add the ability to specify the URL of the Web page you'd like to load. Add a ComboBox and give it a name by specifying the name in the Properties dialog box. The example is named the ComboBox *cmbURL*. (See Figure 10.14).

```
If KeyCode = 13 Then
HTML1.RequestDoc cmbURL.Text
End If
```

In the KeyDown event of the ComboBox, you can enter the code shown in Figure 10.4. This event is triggered every time a key on the keyboard is pressed. In this case, the event is looking for the key that corresponds to 13, which is the **Enter** key. When the **Enter** key is pressed, the text value stored in the ComboBox is used as the parameter to the RequestDoc method of the HTML control. (See Figure 10.15.)

Using the SMTP Object

Use the Simple Mail Transport Protocol (SMTP) object to communicate with an SMTP server for sending e-mail. There are two protocols used in

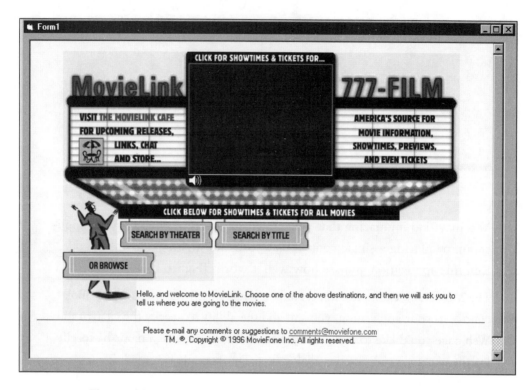

Figure 10.13 Create a Web browser with one control and a single line of code.

the processing and sending of Internet e-mail. The SMTP protocol sends the e-mail, and the POP protocol retrieves e-mail from a POP server. You can enable your application for Internet or intranet e-mail by including the SMTP object.

For example, a mission-critical application could send an e-mail message to a Seiko Message Watch, thereby paging a system administrator with a trouble message. Sending an alphanumeric message to an e-mail–enabled message watch is only one example of the unique things you can do with e-mail. Of course you can always have your application send traditional e-mail

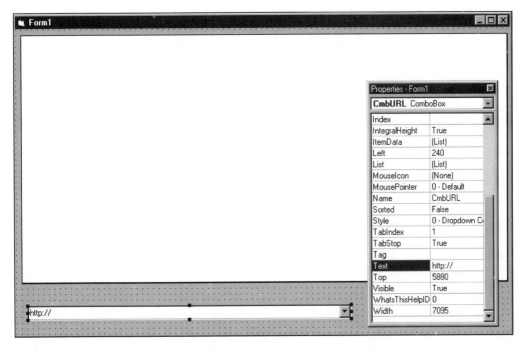

Figure 10.14 Set the properties for this ComboBox.

messages as well. By using Internet controls such as SMTP and POP, you can build a full e-mail information system. This type of application receives requests for information, processes those requests, and returns the information via e-mail. You can retrieve information to be sent to a requester using FTP, NNTP, or through socket communication interfaces to a database.

Connecting the Mail Server

To send an e-mail message using the SMTP control, you have to connect to a mail server. There are many types of mail servers and most of them support SMTP for sending e-mail. The Connect method of the SMTP object is used to connect to the mail server. In Figure 10.16 an SMTP control is placed on the form along with a CommandButton named ConnectButton.

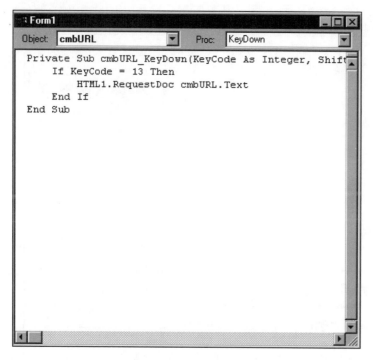

Figure 10.15 Use the KeyDown event to watch for the **Enter** key.

The SMTP control is named SMTP1. In the Click event of the CommandButton, the domain name of the host where the mail server is running is specified. This mail server can reside on either your local

Figure 10.16 Set the RemoteHost and connect to the mail server.

```
Private Sub ConnectButton_Click()
        SMTP1.RemoteHost = "mailserver.domain.com"
        SMTP1.Connect
End Sub
```

machine or on a machine connected to the network. Follow this with the Connect method.

Authentication

Once your application has successfully connected to the mail server application, the next step is to go through the authentication stage. You may remember this from the FTP control. Your application identifies itself, and the server decides if it should accept your e-mail to be sent out over the network. The SMTP control has a special Authenticate method for this purpose.

Once your application has successfully authenticated itself with the mail server, the Authenticate event is triggered. If for any reason your application can't connect, the Error event is triggered instead.

Creating a Collection of DocHeader Objects

The most complex step in developing an SMTP application is creating a collection of DocHeader objects. Each of these objects contains a significant piece of data that the mail server requires. The sample in this book first creates an object variable for the DocHeaders collection, and then creates an instance of the DocHeaders collection. The code uses the Add method of the DocHeaders collection to add several DocHeader objects to the collection (see Figure 10.17). The Add method requires two arguments, which are set to the Name and the Value property. (See the DocHeader and Collections section for more information on creating DocHeaders).

The minimum number of DocHeaders you'll need is two. Your e-mail header should always include a From line and a To line. A Subject line is nice, but not required.

Sending Your E-Mail

Your e-mail header is now ready to accept the message that will be sent. The sample provided here hardcodes the text of the message. You may

Figure 10.17 Create a DocHeader collection by adding DocHeaders to a DocHeader object.

```
Sub BuildDocHeaderCollection()
        Dim dHeads as DocHeaders
        Set dHeads = New DocHeaders

        With dHeads
                .Add "From", "Sue@Mydomain.com"
                .Add "To", "Ellen@Herdomain.com"
                .Add "CC", "Janet@Anotherdomain.com"
                .Add "Subject", "This is a sample subject line."
        End With
End Sub
```

want to read text from a file, or supply a TextBox for entering the message. You'll see how to use the SendDoc method of the SMTP control for configuring the source of your e-mail message.

TIP

All Internet e-mail messages must end with a period on a line by itself.

The SendDoc method has three arguments:

- Destination
- DocHeaders collection
- E-mail message

■■■■■■■■ **Figure 10.18** Send an e-mail message using the SendDoc
method.

```
Sub SendMessage(dHeads as DocHeaders)
      Dim sMessage as String


      SMTP1.RemoteHost = "mail.science.org"
      sMessage = "Hi, just wanted to keep in touch with you.
                  ."
      SMTP1.SendDoc , dHeads, sMessage
End Sub
```

Figure 10.18 takes a reference to the DocHeaders collection created in the
previous code and passes it as an argument to the SendDoc method.

Using the POP Object

The Post Office Protocol (POP) object is used to communicate with POP
servers for receiving e-mail. The Microsoft POP object implements version 3 of the POP protocol, often called POP3. Using the POP object is
simple, with only a few steps involved in communicating with a POP
server program.

First, as with all the client objects, you have to connect to a server. The
POP object has a Connect method for connecting to the server:

```
Pop1.RemoteHost = "your.internet.domain.com"
Pop1.Connect
```

The POP client authenticates in a manner similar to the other controls:

```
POP1.UserId = UserId
POP1.Password = Password
POP1.Authenticate
```

Once you've connected and authenticated, the primary goal of the POP client is to retrieve your e-mail messages. After authentication, the MessageCount property of the POP control indicates how many messages are waiting on the server to be retrieved. To retrieve them, you use the MessageRetrieve method to ask the server to begin sending the e-mail. This triggers the DocOutput event. For information on how to retrieve messages after they have been sent by the server, see the section on DocOutput objects and the sample application at the end of this chapter.

Using the NNTP Object

Imagine building an application that receives information by querying the World Wide Web, and then sends an e-mail request for authorization to post the information, waits for return e-mail, and posts the information to a Usenet newsgroup. By now, you can understand the power associated with using the ActiveX Internet controls together in an application. The NNTP (Network News Transport Protocol) control lets you retrieve and post messages in Usenet news groups.

The NNTP client connects to an NNTP (News) server using the Connect method of the NNTP client control. The NNTP server also requires that you authenticate yourself. Do this using the Authenticate method. There are still a few free NNTP servers, but most Usenet News providers charge a fee. Before you can test your NNTP client, you need to either install your own NNTP server (and there are some available for Windows) or pay a fee to connect to a Usenet service.

Once you've connected to a Usenet service, a typical first procedure is to download a copy of the list of newsgroups. Download this list using the

ListGroups method. There are close to 20,000 news groups at present, and this list is too long to fit in a Visual Basic TextBox. You can instead display it using the RichText control, which has no physical limit for the amount of text it can contain. A more clever idea is to create an HTML document of the list and display the list of groups as hyperlinks in an HTML control.

The NNTP control uses the DocOutput object to receive data from a News server. The NNTP control is a little different from other controls that use the DocOutput object. There is a special flag known as the event flag that can be used to determine the type of data being transferred from the News server. (See Figure 10.19.)

After you've downloaded the list of newsgroups carried by a particular News server, you then select a specific newsgroup. Use the SelectGroup method to select a group by passing the name of the newsgroup as an argument. Selecting a newsgroup triggers the SelectGroup event, which is where you add code to download the *article headers*. These are headers that identify either the author or the subject of the article. The

████████ **Figure 10.19** Check the EventFlag to see what type of data is being received.

```
Select Case EventFlag


Case LISTGROUPS
        'Process the list of groups here.
Case GETARTICLEHEADERS
        'Process Article Headers here.
Case GETARTICLEBYNUMBER
        'Process the text of articles here.
End Select
```

GetArticleHeaders method is used to download a list of all the article headers accompanied by an argument that specifies whether you want the author or subject headers.

Using the NNTP client control is a little more involved than some of the other controls because of the seemingly endless number of choices that have to be made before you get the text of a message. After you've downloaded the list of newsgroups, and then a list of the article headers, you have to select an article to download to retrieve the text. Use the GetArticleByArticleNumber method to download a specific article. After your article has been downloaded, process it in the same Select Case statement in which you processed the list of article headers and newsgroups.

The NNTP control is very rich with methods to control your interactions with an NNTP server. There are methods, for example, that allow you to download specific article headers, choose the method for selecting articles, view administration files, and view new newsgroups. Review the documentation that comes with this control for a full explanation of its many features.

WinSock TCP

WinSock is the implementation of UNIX *sockets* for Windows. The invention of WinSock made it possible for PCs to participate in the Internet revolution. TCP (Terminal Control Protocol) socket communications is a client/server–based communication strategy. A server socket listens until contacted by a client socket. Once connected, two-way communication exists between a server socket and a client socket.

Using the WinSock TCP control, you can build both client and server applications (see the sample application). Until distributed object computing becomes more widespread as a means of communication between applications, TCP will remain the primary means of communication. Currently, almost all Internet and intranet applications have been built using socket communications as their means of sending data between remote machines.

The server and client do not have to be on separate machines. Programs can carry on socket communications on the same machine. For example, the Internet Information Server listens on port 80 for a client to contact it. A Web browser, such as Internet Explorer, that is located on the same machine can connect to the Internet Information Server in the same way as Web browsers located on remote machines.

WinSock programming can seem overwhelming to people who've never tried it. This new control has taken some of the complexity out of socket programming. Follow the sample application for a brief introduction to socket programming using the WinSock TCP control. There are several excellent books on socket programming. A good Internet resource for information about WinSock is Stardust Technologies. For information, use this URL:

http://www.stardust.com/

WinSock UDP

UPD (User Datagram Protocol) sockets are connectionless. Unlike TCP sockets, which establish a connection between two applications, UDP sockets send information out without a pre-established connection. This method of transmitting data is a little like radio broadcasting. Use UDP sockets when you want to broadcast information without making a client/server connection.

UDP doesn't apply the concept of client/server because neither application—the one sending data or the one receiving data—is "listening."

A UDP application can both send data as well as receive it. Keeping the analogy of broadcasting, you can think of two applications using UDP as walkie-talkies. Where this analogy breaks down is that you do specify which computer the data is intended for by specifying the host name or host IP address as well as the port where the receiving application expects the data to arrive.

The WinSock UDP control has two methods:

- GetData
- SendData

To send data, make sure the RemoteHost and RemotePort properties of the UDP control are set correctly, and then initiate the SendData method. To receive data, use the GetData method in the DataArrival event. This form of communication is pretty dependable, even though it isn't absolutely guaranteed. Quite simply, sending data is "point and shoot" and receiving data is "oh, there's data on my doorstep, better get it."

Sample Application

Following is a sample application using some of the ActiveX Internet controls. The sample included builds both a client application as well as a server. The client application is currently a stand-alone desktop application. Using Visual Basic 5.0 or greater, you can compile this application into an ActiveX control and embed it within other ActiveX-enabled applications. In other words, while you are constructing Web pages out of ActiveX components, you can add your client application as one of those components. Your custom ActiveX control will communicate directly with your server application, bypassing server programs such as CGI or ISAPI.

The server sample uses the WinSock TCP control to communicate with the client application. When technology permits, you should consider using DCOM (Distributed Component Object Model) technology instead of WinSock to communicate between ActiveX objects in your client applications and ActiveX objects in your server applications.

The sample application has a client requesting information from a server. The server uses the HTTP object to retrieve information from a Web page and sends this information back to the client application, which displays it in a text control.

Building the Server

Begin building your server application by placing a WinSock TCP object on a blank form (Figure 10.20). Where you place the object on the form makes no difference; it is invisible when the application runs. Name the new TCP object TCP1 by filling in the Name property in the Properties dialog box (Figure 10.21). Add an HTTP control and a couple of label controls (Figure 10.22). One label control will be a fancy (and useless) title, and the other label will serve as a status indicator. Once your server is completed, you can remove the labels and code that sends data to the status indicator. Server programs generally don't have much of a user interface, if they have one at all. Most servers run invisibly. But, in order to provide pictures of the sample server in this book, the server program has been given a simple user interface. The interface also lets you watch what happens as people connect to the server.

Setting the Properties

Set the local port to some number, preferably greater than 1024. In the sample, the port number 1500 has been arbitrarily chosen. While you're setting properties, set the Index property for both the HTTP and the TCP objects to 0 (zero). This small change has a significant impact. Instead of having a single TCP or HTTP object in the application, you now have a potential array of TCP and HTTP objects. As a result, the server can accept

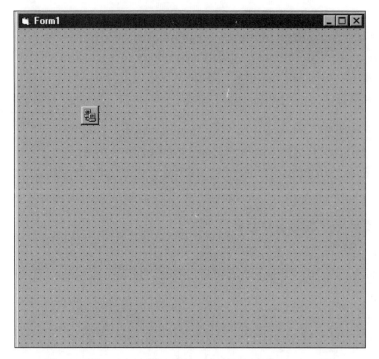

■■■■■■■ **Figure 10.20** Insert a TCP object on a blank form.

more than one connection at a time. Imagine a Web server that could only accept a single connection! You can build servers so that only a single connection can be established, but who would do so?

Setting the Global Variable

Double-click the TCP object to begin adding code. The first thing you add is a global variable to keep track of the current instance of the TCP object. Every time a connection request is received, a new TCP object is created, and it's important to keep track of each TCP object in an array of TCP objects. To add a global variable, select (General) from the Object drop-down list. Create the object using the *Public* keyword, and set the type to Integer. In the sample, the variable is called *gSockInstance*:

```
Public gSockInstance As Integer
```

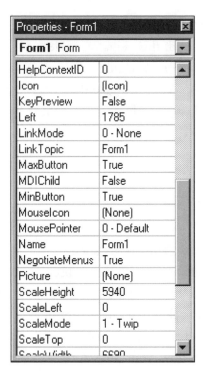

▰▰▰▰▰▰▰ **Figure 10.21** Set the properties of the form and objects in this dialog box.

▰▰▰▰▰▰ **Figure 10.22** The final product of the server form.

Creating the Listening Socket

Each time a new TCP object (socket object) is created, this global variable needs to be incremented, which takes you to the next step. Double-click on the form to edit the form's Load event. In this procedure, you take the first instance of the TCP object, index 0, and use the Listen method to cause this socket to begin listening on whatever port was specified in the LocalPort property.

```
Private Sub Form_Load()
TCP1(0).Listen
End Sub
```

The TCP1(0) object is known as the *listening socket*. This socket sticks around the entire time the server is running—which is why it is set to listen in the Load event of the form. The listening socket has one purpose: to hand off any connection requests it gets to a new socket that will accept the connection and continue communications. This new socket is called a *connected socket*. If you were to run your application now, your program would listen on port 1500. Nothing could connect at this point because you haven't built the ability to connect yet.

Creating Connected Sockets

Whenever the listening socket receives a request to connect, a ConnectionRequest event is triggered in the TCP object. So, by double-clicking on the TCP object, edit the ConnectionRequest event procedure (see Figure 10.23).

Because the ConnectionRequest event is triggered each time a client application attempts a connection, this is a logical place to create the new connected sockets. The first thing this procedure must do is increment the global variable that keeps track of the number of TCP object instances. Then, on the next line, the **Load** command is used to create a new instance of the TCP object (the new connected socket). Notice that it uses the global variable as the array index.

Figure 10.23 Create a new instance of the TCP object using the Load statement.

```
Private Sub TCP1_ConnectionRequest(Index As Integer, ByVal RequestID As
Long)
    gSockInstance = gSockInstance + 1
    Load TCP1(gSockInstance)
    TCP1(gSockInstance).Accept RequestID
    TCPStatus.Caption = "Socket " + Str(gSockInstance) + " started."
End Sub
```

The connected socket, TCP(n), can now accept the connection using the Accept method of the TCP object. The parameter, RequestID, is passed by value into the procedure. This is a special identifier for the socket connection received by the listening socket. By passing this parameter, the listening socket is handing off the new socket connection to the socket that accepts it.

The last line in the procedure is optional. This line simply updates the status label named TCPStatus. The sample includes the *gSockInstance* variable to keep track of how many connections exist.

Closing Sockets

After a socket is finished communicating, either the client or the server can terminate the communication session by closing the socket. When the client closes the socket, the server receives a Close event notification. And, when the server closes the socket, the client receives the notification. It's important to close and unload the TCP (socket) object when you are finished communicating. Otherwise, you will quickly run out of memory. In this example, the client closes the socket. So, in the Close event of the TCP object, use the Close method to close the socket and then the **Unload** command to remove it from memory. (See Figure 10.24.)

Please note: If you are following the Microsoft documentation, you'll see that in the Close event the global variable is decremented. *DON'T DO THIS!* This global variable becomes the "name" of the connected socket. Connected socket number one is TCP(1) and so forth. Let's say you have ten simultaneous socket connections. You'll have sockets named TCP(1) through TCP(10). Now, if TCP(2) and TCP(3) close, and you decrement the global variable, the *gSockInstance* now equals 8. When a new connection requests comes in, the code in the ConnectionRequest event will try and create TCP(9), even though there is already a socket named TCP(9).

Here are a couple of alternative approaches:

- Let the global variable continue to increment indefinitely. The downside to this approach is that you will eventually run out of integers and will have to switch to a Long data type. This is bit of a kluge; but for simple programs or while you're learning, this is OK.

Figure 10.24 Close the socket and remove the TCP object from memory.

```
Private Sub TCP1_Close(Index As Integer)
     TCP1(Index).Close
     Unload TCP1(Index)
End Sub
```

- Build a procedure that checks each index in the array of TCP objects to see if there are any index numbers available before incrementing the global variable. Eventually, your program will find free array positions, and gSockInstance will represent the greatest number of simultaneous connections. Scanning through the array is certainly more complex; but, for programs that are expected to run unattended for long periods of time, this level of complexity is necessary.

Communicating over Sockets

Up to this point, each step in building the server has been generic. Each of your server applications will have a listening socket, create connected sockets in the ConnectionRequest event, and close sockets in the Close event. The code you put in the DataArrival event is what makes your server program distinct. This is where you build your own protocol. Remember that protocols are rules for communicating.

Server applications typically don't initiate communications. They wait for the client to send them data, to which the server responds. Once a connected socket is established between the client and the server, the server could initiate communications, though this would be unusual. The role of most server programs is to do the bidding of the client.

To write the next portion of the application, you need to know what your client is going to request from the server. For this reason, writing the client and server programs in parallel is not unusual. In the sample application, the client can send only two kinds of messages. One type of message is a greeting to which the server either responds pleasantly with the word "greetings" or with the word "huh?" if the server doesn't recognize the client's request. The other type of message is a request to retrieve textual data from a Web page. For this type of request, the sample server program uses an HTTP control named HTTP1. Like the TCP control, it has an index of zero so that you can have multiple, simultaneous HTTP objects retrieving data. (See Figure 10.25.)

Note that the first parameter to the DataArrival procedure is the Index. This is the index of the TCP socket that caused this event to trigger. In

■■■■■■■ **Figure 10.25** When data arrives, it sits in a buffer waiting for the GetData method to retrieve it.

```
Private Sub TCP1_DataArrival(Index As Integer, ByVal bytesTotal As
Long)
        Dim iLoc As Variant
        Dim sURL As Variant
        Dim sData As String


        TCP1(Index).GetData sData, vbString
        TCPStatus.Caption = sData


        Select Case Mid(sData, 1, 3)
                Case "hel"
                        TCP1(Index).SendData "Greetings"
                Case "get"
                        iLoc = InStr(sData, " ")
                        iLoc = iLoc + 1
                        sURL = Mid(sData, iLoc)
                        TCPStatus.Caption = "Connect to: " & sURL
                        Load HTTP1(Index)
                        HTTP1(Index).URL = sURL
                        HTTP1(Index).GetDoc
                Case Else
                        TCP1(Index).SendData "Huh?"
                End Select
End Sub
```

other words, if TCP(3) caused this event to trigger because the client it's communicating with sent data, the Index parameter will equal 3.

```
Dim sData As String
```

```
TCP1(Index).GetData sData, vbString
```

Create a variable to hold the data that was sent by the client. The sample calls this variable *sData* and creates it as a String data type. Pass the *sData* variable as a parameter to the GetData method of the TCP control. The GetData method fills the variable with data sent from the client. Some programmers are not familiar with the idea of passing an empty variable to a variable, it's like sending in an empty box, to be filled by the method.

The second argument identifies the data type that the *sData* variable is expected to contain when it's filled by the GetData method. Table 10.2 contains a list of types you can identify in the **type** argument.

The next part of the procedure is a selection of choices that depends on the arriving data. You can exercise your creativity here, even though the sample is a little less than creative, taking the first three characters of the message and processing it accordingly. The sample has only three choices: "hel", "get", and everything else. If the client sends the word "hello", the server responds by sending the word "greetings" back.

▬▬▬▬ **Table 10.2** Types for the GetData Method

Data Type	Visual Basic Type
Byte	vbByte
Integer	vbInteger
Long	vbLong
Single	vbSingle
Double	vbDouble
Currency	vbCurrency

■■■■■■■ **Table 10.2** Continued

Data Type	Visual Basic Type
Date	vbDate
Boolean	vbBoolean
SCODE	vbError
String	vbString
Byte Array	vbArray + vbByte

■■■■■■■

```
TCP1(Index).SendData "Greetings"
```

Use the SendData method of the TCP control to return data to the client. The sample's less-than-intelligent server would respond with greetings if the client sent the word "helicopter".

The second Case statement in the example handles the word "get". The client is designed to send the word "get" followed by a URL. Here's how the sample parses the URL from the request:

```
ILoc = InStr(sData, " ")
iLoc = iLoc + 1
```

Look for the first blank space in the *sData* string and store its position in the integer variable *iLoc*. Then, increment the *iLoc* variable by 1, to identify the first letter of the URL.

```
sURL = Mid(sData, iLoc)
TCPStatus.Caption = "Connect to: " & sURL
```

The variable *sURL* is a string that now holds the URL. Update the status message on the form. The status message is optional, but useful while testing the application. Now, you're ready to create a new HTTP instance. Use the **Load** command to create the new object instance, and use the *Index* variable to identify the array index. Notice that the sample doesn't use a global variable to keep track of the HTTP object. Using the same index as the socket (TCP) object identifies the HTTP control with the TCP control. For example, you know that HTTP1(2) was created by TCP1(2).

```
Load HTTP1(Index)
HTTP1(Index).URL = sURL
HTTP1(Index).GetDoc
```

Finally, use the GetDoc method of the HTTP control to retrieve the document from a remote HTTP server. This is basically what you need to make the TCP control work. You can add error-handling code to the Error event (see the section on using the icError object).

Coding the HTTP Control

Once the TCP object creates a new instance of the HTTP control, and activates the GetDoc method, data handling is now up to the HTTP object. As soon as the remote HTTP server begins sending data back to the HTTP control the DocOutput event is triggered. Do not be confused by having the DocOutput event triggered when data is coming into the control.

The DocOutput event procedure has two arguments. The first is the index of the HTTP object that is receiving the data. The second argument is a DocOutput object. This special data-handling object informs you of what's going on with the data transfer, as well as retrieves the data from the input buffer using the GetData method. You don't need to be concerned with the input buffer. When data arrives, it sits in this buffer, triggers the DocOutput event, and waits to be retrieved by the GetData method. (See Figure 10.26.)

The example passes the variable *vtData* to the GetData method along with the data type (see Table 10.2). The GetData method of the HTTP control functions very similarly to the GetData method of the TCP control. You update the status label with the number of bytes transferred, and send the data on to the client using the TCP object again. Notice how nicely the

```
Private Sub HTTP1_DocOutput(Index As Integer, ByVal DocOutput As
DocOutput)
    Dim vtData As Variant
    Select Case DocOutput.State
    Case icDocBegin
        TCPStatus.Caption = "End Transfer"
    Case icDocData
        DocOutput.GetData vtData, vbString
        TCPStatus.Caption = "bytes:" & Str(DocOutput.BytesTransferred)
        TCP1(Index).SendData vtData
    Case icDocEnd
        TCPStatus.Caption = "End Transfer"
    End Select
End Sub
```

TCP and HTTP object are associated by the *Index* variable. Without this corresponding value, how would you keep track of which socket you need to use to send the right data to the correct client?

Information is transferred from the HTTP server in blocks. Each time a block of data is received, the DocOutput event is triggered and the next block of data is sent to the client, until all of the data has been transferred. At that point, the DocOutput object's State property is set to icDocEnd. There's nothing left to do except update the status label. With the HTTP client, you do not need to close the connection with the HTTP server.

This is a rudimentary server application that demonstrates how to communicate with a client application and use an additional Internet client control to communicate with a remote server. You could ask the question: "Why couldn't the client communicate directly with the HTTP server using the HTTP control we used on the server?" If you took that approach, you wouldn't be able to implement the greeting functionality, but otherwise it is a valid point. Server applications typically perform tasks that the client would not be able to perform locally. This server application also demonstrates how to create arrays of objects, which are not typically used in client applications. By starting with this basic template for a server application, you can let your imagination run wild creating all types of compelling server applications.

Building the Client

Unlike server applications, clients generally need a user interface. Visual Basic makes it easy to create good user interfaces. Note that the sample client doesn't have a good user interface; it's simply there to demonstrate how easy it is to build network client applications (see Figure 10.27).

To create a client, you need only a single Internet control: the WinSock TCP control. If you've already built the server application, you have a TCP object in your Visual Basic control toolbar. If you have not inserted any of the Microsoft ActiveX Internet controls, see the section on creating a server application for more information on adding custom controls. Here are the steps:

1. Place a TCP control on a blank form and leave its default name of TCP1.

2. Place a TextBox control on the form and name it txtData. At this point you can also add a label control to identify this TextBox. The label can have a caption such as **Enter text to send:**.

3. Add a CommandButton control and name it CommandConnect. Set the caption for this button to **Connect**.

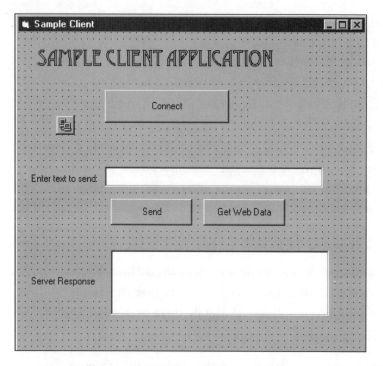

◼◼◼◼◼ **Figure 10.27** The client application needs a good user interface.

4. Enter the code shown in Figure 10.28 in the Click event of the
   CommandConnect button. This initiates the connection with the
   server specified in the RemoteHost and RemotePort properties. If
   you have not set these in the TCP object Properties dialog box, you
   can also set them in this button script using the **TCP1.RemoteHost**
   and **TCP1.RemotePort** properties.

```
Private Sub CommandConnect_Click()

     TCP1.Connect

End Sub
```

This initiates the connection with the server specified in the
RemoteHost and RemotePort properties. If you have not set these in
the TCP object properties dialog, you can also set these in this button
script using the TCP1.RemoteHost and TCP1.RemotePort properties.

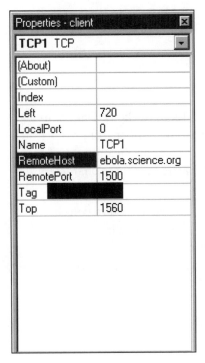

▬▬▬▬▬ **Figure 10.28** Set the RemoteHost and RemotePort properties.

5. Add another CommandButton and set its name to **cmdSend** and its caption to Send.

6. Add the following data to the Click event of the **cmdSend** button:

```
Private Sub cmdSend_Click()

    TCP1.SendData txtData.Text

End Sub
```

This code uses the SendData method of the TCP control to send any text found in the txtData control placed on the form in step 2. You can send data from a TextBox control to create simple chat applications.

7. Add another CommandButton and set its name to cmdWebGet and its caption to Get Web Data.

8. Enter the code to send a request for Web data in the Click event of the **cmdWebGet** button:

```
Private Sub cmdWebGet_Click()

    TCP1.SendData "get " & txtData.Text

End Sub
```

The SendData method expects a URL to be entered in the txtData control. The word "get" is prepended to the URL. Remember from the previous section on building a server that the server application takes a specific action when it finds the word "get" in the first three characters of the data it receives.

9. You now add code to the TCP control. The two events you're concerned with are Connect and DataArrival. In the Connect event you add code that can update a TextBox control named Status. If you choose to add this feature, you'll need to add an additional TextBox control and, of course, name it **Status**.

```
Private Sub TCP1_Connect()

    Status.Caption = "Connected"

    cmdSend.Enabled = True

End Sub
```

The code in the Connect event also enables the **Send** button, which has been disabled until the connection has been completed.

10. Lastly, you add the code to get the data from the buffer once it's been received and display it in the TextBox. Add a TextBox and name it ServerResponse. You can add a label for this TextBox (such as Server Response).

```
Private Sub TCP1_DataArrival(ByVal bytesTotal As Long)

    Dim sData As Variant

    TCP1.GetData sData, vbString

    ServerResponse.Text = ServerResponse.Text & sData

End Sub
```

Enter this code in the DataArrival event of the TCP control. It retrieves the data, setting the data type to vbString, and then displays the data in the ServerResponse TextBox.

Creating other types of WinSock applications is very similar to the process just completed because the dynamics of typical network applications are similar. The server application listens for a connection, accepts the connection, and then processes requests from a client. The client application connects to a server and then sends requests. It's that simple. This sample application is an example of the type of processing either a server application or a client might perform on data sent or received.

transferRNA

Sending a file from one person to another using the Internet is often not as easy as it should be. To use FTP, either the sender or recipient must be running an FTP server. To use e-mail, both users' e-mail clients must have the same encoding and decoding capability. Here is a list of some of the numerous difficulties encountered when trying to send files across the Internet using conventional file transfer methods.

- Whenever you run an FTP server, there is a security risk due to FTP user accounts.
- E-mail clients must have compatible encoding and decoding capability.
- Some e-mail servers have file size limits or are unreliable.
- There is no guaranteed delivery of files when using e-mail.

- E-mail is insecure because the message resides on numerous e-mail servers.

The researchers at SCIENCE.ORG recognized the numerous problems that exist in sending files across the Internet and developed the transferRNA software as a simple solution for immediate, person-to-person file transfer. Any two users who are running transferRNA and are connected to the Internet can transfer files directly to and from each other. They do not have to be concerned about encoding or decoding of the files, file size limits, or complicated FTP server software and security risks. The transferRNA software currently exists in several different forms:

- Netscape inline plug-in
- Stand-alone Windows software
- ActiveX control

Anyone can download the transferRNA software from the following URL:

`http://www.science.org/transferRNA/`

In the near future, transferRNA will also be available for Macintosh and Unix platforms, thus making it a truly ubiquitous method to transfer files on the Internet.

Using transferRNA

File transfer can't be any simpler than it is with transferRNA. Figure A.1 illustrates the user interface that appears when you run transferRNA.

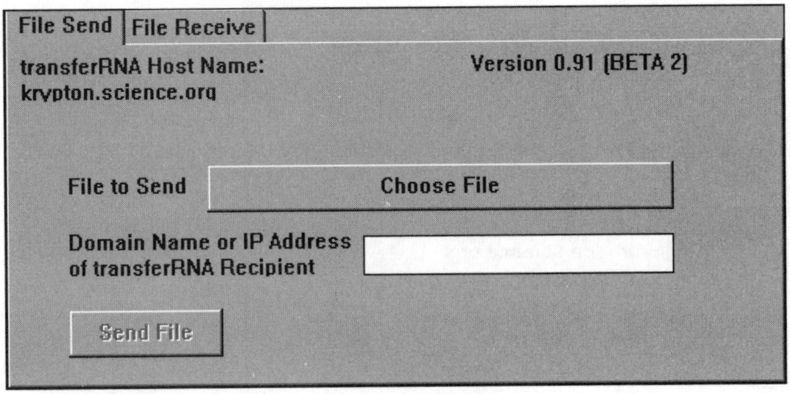

File Send | File Receive |

transferRNA Host Name: Version 0.91 (BETA 2)
krypton.science.org

File to Send | Choose File |

Domain Name or IP Address
of transferRNA Recipient

Send File

Figure A.1 Use transferRNA to send and receive files.

Sending Files

Here is the procedure to follow to send a file to someone on the Internet using transferRNA:

1. Both you and the recipient must be running transferRNA and be connected to the Internet.
2. The **File Send** folder is the default that appears when you run transferRNA. Click on the **Choose File** button, and select the file on your system that you want to send.
3. Enter the domain name or IP address of the recipient. The domain name of your computer appears in the top-left corner of the transferRNA program.
4. Click on the **Send** button.

Figure A.2 shows what the transferRNA client looks like when you follow this procedure.

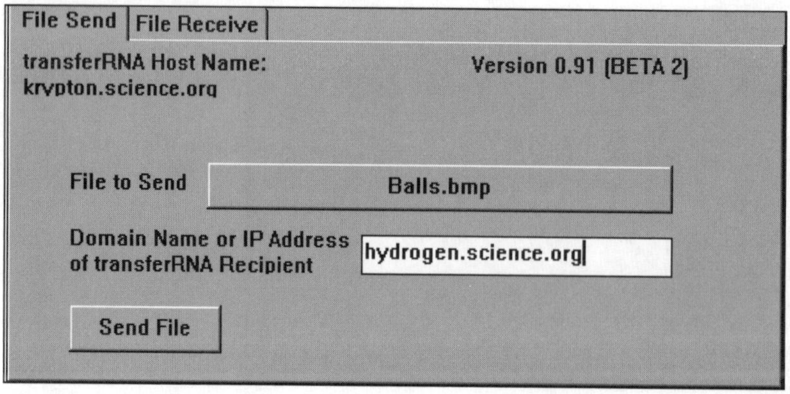

File Send	File Receive	
transferRNA Host Name:		Version 0.91 (BETA 2)
krypton.science.org		

File to Send　　　　　　　　Balls.bmp

Domain Name or IP Address　hydrogen.science.org
of transferRNA Recipient

Send File

■■■■■■ **Figure A.2** After you choose the file and enter the domain name, click on the **Send** button.

Receiving Files

Receiving files using transferRNA requires even less effort. You need to be running transferRNA and be connected to the Internet. The transferRNA client can be minimized on your desktop. When your transferRNA client receives a file, it automatically switches to the **File Receive** folder shown in Figure A.3.

Any files that are received are placed in a temporary directory and displayed in the **File Receive** folder. You can then copy these files to any location on your system by choosing the desired file, and then clicking on the **Copy File** button.

Programming with transferRNA

The transferRNA ActiveX control has a programming interface that allows programmers to drop this control directly into their applications and take advantage of its simple file transfer capabilities. The transferRNA ActiveX

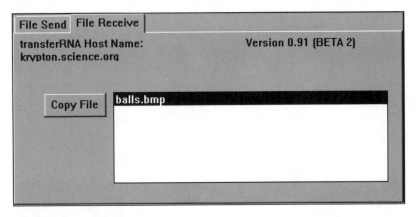

Figure A.3 Copy the files you receive to any location on your system.

control can be incorporated into other Windows software either as a visual component or invisibly so that transferRNA send and receive capability is implemented behind-the-scenes.

Check the ActiveX Source for more information on this and other ActiveX controls:

http://ebola.science.org/ActiveX/

The ActiveX Source page will direct you to further information and documentation about the programmable interfaces supported by transferRNA. The ActiveX Source page is an Internet information resource for developers and end users who are interested in using ActiveX technology to its full potential. Remember to visit the transferRNA home page at the following address in order to get a copy of the software and learn about recent developments:

http://www.science.org/transferRNA/

INDEX